Cities

For Lynda and Lynne

CITIES

REIMAGINING THE URBAN

Ash Amin and Nigel Thrift

Polity

First published in 2002 by Polity Press in association with Blackwell Publishing Ltd

Reprinted 2003, 2004, 2005

Polity Press
65 Bridge Street
Cambridge CB2 1UR, UK

Polity Press
350 Main Street
Malden, MA 02148, USA

ISBN 0-7456-2413-8
ISBN 0-7456-2414-6 (pbk)

A catalogue record for this book is available from the British Library and has been applied for from the Library of Congress.

Typeset in 10 on 12 pt Sabon
by Graphicraft Limited, Hong Kong

Printed and bound in Great Britain by Marston Book Services Limited, Oxford

This book is printed on acid-free paper.
For further information on Polity, please visit our website:
http://www.polity.co.uk

CONTENTS

ACKNOWLEDGEMENTS

This book would not have been written without the generous support of the Swedish Collegium for Advanced Study in the Social Sciences (SCASSS) in Uppsala, which provided both an intellectual forcing ground and social solidarity. For this we thank its directors and staff, as well as the Fellows in residence from January to June 1999. We also want to thank the two anonymous reviewers for their careful and attentive reading of the first draft. Their intervention pushed us a long way towards clarifying our project, and reminded us of the value of critical generosity. Then, we acknowledge the support of the UK's Economic and Social Research Council, which funded a study on Bristol co-directed by Nigel Thrift under its Cities Programme. Finally, we thank Trudy Graham for her patient correction of the final draft, Ann Bone for her diligent copy-editing, and Victoria Thrift for her knowledge of foxes.

INTRODUCTION

Cities have become extraordinarily intricate, and for this, difficult to generalize. We can no longer even agree on what counts as a city. We think of particular sites or moments when imagining a city: Paris as café life, New York as Manhattan, Calcutta as the noise of traffic. But most cities now sprawl across many miles, incorporating settlements of varying composition, derelict areas, parks and gardens, factories, shopping centres, parking areas, warehouses, dumps. Half of the world's population now lives in cities. Thirteen megacities have a population of more than 10 million: Tokyo, São Paolo, New York, Mexico City, Shanghai, Bombay, Los Angeles, Buenos Aires, Seoul, Beijing, Rio de Janeiro, Calcutta and Osaka.

The city is everywhere and in everything. If the urbanized world now is a chain of metropolitan areas connected by places/corridors of communication (airports and airways, stations and railways, parking lots and motorways, teleports and information highways) then what is not the urban? Is it the town, the village, the countryside? Maybe, but only to a limited degree. The footprints of the city are all over these places, in the form of city commuters, tourists, teleworking, the media, and the urbanization of lifestyles. The traditional divide between the city and the countryside has been perforated.

Yet we still name cities and think of them as distinctive places. A Londoner today might dispute which outer suburbs count as London, but swears that the city does not extend to adjacent urban centres such as Reading and Slough. Similarly, the Randstad region that incorporates Amsterdam, Utrecht, The Hague and Rotterdam is less than the sum of its parts for Deyan Sudjic, who insists that 'Amsterdam, Rotterdam and the Hague . . . are still distinct cities, even if they are only half an hour apart' (1992: 296). Then there are cities that are involved in the life of adjacent settlements. Sudjic, again, on Paris is certain that it is 'wrong to see the five Parisian new towns as distinct entities in their own right. Rather, they are essential parts of the city itself. They could not exist without the network of motorways, airports, and above all metro lines that constitutes Paris just as much as the picturesque crust of masonry buildings of Haussmann and his predecessors' (p. 296). We could say the same about the string of settlements radiating from, and sustaining, the megalopolis in the South, be it Seoul, Mumbai, Beijing or Rio de Janeiro.

Urban sprawl and the urbanization of social life thus do not negate the idea of cities as distinct spatial formations or imaginaries. The history of the naming of places plays a critical role here. The place called London, for example, has been fashioned and refashioned through commentaries, recollections, memories and erasures, and in a variety of media – monumental, official and vernacular, newspapers and magazines, guides and maps, photographs, films, newsreels and novels, street-level conversations and tales. The naming, of course, is highly selective, giving us London as the signature of empire, of crowded streets, art galleries, pubs, and people from around the world, of silent trains, well-trimmed suburban gardens, terraced houses. But somehow the fragments do come together into an enduring picture of London as a busy gateway to the world, a cosmopolis that is also homely.

What makes the city a spatial formation? Steve Pile (1999) identifies three aspects that distinguish cities as spaces: their density as concentrations of people, things, institutions and architectural forms; the heterogeneity of life they juxtapose in close proximity; and their siting of various networks of communication and flow across and beyond the city. Pile agrees with Doreen Massey that the 'spatiality' of the city – its density and juxtaposition of difference – has distinctive, generative effects. Massey explains that what makes 'spatial configurations generative' are the intense social effects resulting from 'dense networks of interaction' within them (1999: 160). Some of these effects are those emphasized by the great urbanists of the twentieth century, including social detachment as a way of coping with crowds (Simmel 1950), civic association beyond family and kinship (Mumford 1938), attachment to artefact, distancing from nature and tolerance of difference (Wirth 1938), and withdrawal from active citizenship into self-preservation (Sennett 1977). The 'citiness' of cities seems to matter, although it is debatable how far spatial propinquity remains a central feature of the sprawling and globally connected city.

The possibility of recognizing cities as spatial formations gives us a legitimate object of analysis. But how should we read them to make sense of their extraordinary variety and complexity? Cities are places of work, consumption, circulation, play, creativity, excitement, boredom. They gather, mix, separate, conceal, display. They support unimaginably diverse social practices. They juxtapose nature, people, things, and the built environment in any number of ways. Sudjic argues that we lack the means to grasp the new complexities:

> It is true that in its new incarnation, the diffuse, sprawling, and endlessly mobile world metropolis is fundamentally different from the city as we have known it.... This new species of city is not an accretion of streets and squares that can be comprehended by the pedestrian, but instead manifests its shape from the air, the car, or the mass transit railway.... But the equipment we have for making sense of what is happening to our cities has lagged far behind these changes. (1992: 297)

In recent years a momentum has been growing to understand cities in the way Sudjic would like. We see this book as a part of this new urbanism. What are the key features of this new work? To begin with, there is a strong emphasis on understanding cities as spatially open and cross-cut by many different kinds of mobilities, from flows of people to commodities and information (Appadurai 1996; M. P. Smith 2001; Urry 2000; Allen, Massey and Pryke 1999; Massey, Allen and Pile 1999). This is not just a simple statement of multiplicity, but a recognition that urban life is the irreducible product of mixture. Further, this mixture increasingly takes place at a distance, so challenging conventional notions of place. Even face-to-face contact increasingly involves a vast penumbra of distanciated interactions (for instance, via the internet, global travel or wire-less communication). These mixed spatialities necessitate a 'trans-national urbanism', an appreciation of cities as 'sites of transnational connections', moving on from a prevailing modernist urbanism in which ' "global" and "local" social processes have been framed in binary opposition, as mutually exclusive and inherently antagonistic explanations for urban development' (M. P. Smith 2001: 2).

Then, we call on the kinds of theoretical technologies at the back of much of such thinking on mobility. These are technologies of understanding which have all arisen from a dissatisfaction with the invocation of an abstract theoretical system which attempts to pull out certain elements of cities as primary forces, with the result that they freeze cities in place. In this book, we are not interested in systems, which so often imply that there is an immanent logic underlying urban life, but in the numerous systematizing networks (Latour 1988) which give a provisional ordering to urban life. These theoretical technologies are diverse and include actor network theory (Dosse 1998), some of the work on digitally inspired subjectivities (Hayles 1999), and approaches which emphasize the transhuman aspects of nature (Haraway 1997; Whatmore 2002).

In turn, this means that we want to conceive cities as virtualities (Rajchman 1999a, 2000; Deleuze 1994). That is, we understand the trajectory of cities not as being instanciated through replications of the present, but as a set of potentials which contain unpredictable elements as a result of the co-evolution of problems and solutions. Each urban moment can spark performative improvisations which are unforeseen and unforeseeable. This is not a naive vitalism, but it is a politics of hope. This does not mean an unbridled optimism for the future, but rather, a firm belief in the actualities of change that can arise from the unexpected reaction to the vagaries of urban life, the novel organizations that can arise, and, in general, the invention of new spaces of the political (Agamben 1999; Varela 1999).

For us, one of the crucial outcomes of this new thinking – some of which exists outside of the conventional urban literature – is that it is based around distinctive ways of showing up space and place. In particular, this has meant the struggle to name neglected spatialities and invent new ones, which, in turn, can help us to repopulate cities, only too often stripped bare by the rush to produce theoretical order. This new thinking attempts to do 'theory' in a different way, through, for example, the use of hybrid, in-between figures such as the actant or cyborg, designed to connect that which has been held apart, and thereby reveal the diverse urban worlds that have been edited out of contention. This work of naming has involved the invention of all manner of strange mappings – the network, the fluid, the blank figure – which pose a challenge to our conception of the conceptions of cities.

In short, the approach we pursue in this book is one which strives to be close to the phenomenality of practices, without relapsing into a romanticism of the everyday, and of action for itself. Necessarily then, we accept that urban practices are in many ways disciplined, but we also believe that these practices constantly exceed that disciplinary envelope. Each urban encounter is a theatre of promise in a play of power. Injecting this sense of the virtual and agonistic (Mouffe 2000) into urban theory allows us, at the very least, to move on from a politics based on nostalgia for a lost past of tightly knit and spatially compact urban communities – which still so often crops up in writings on the good city – to something different.

What we want most from the book is to make a contribution towards this new kind of urbanism. We see the book as a kind of staging post towards a different practice of urban theory based on the transhuman rather than the human, the distanciated rather than the proximate, the displaced rather than the placed, and the intransitive rather than the reflexive. What we also want is for the book to be read as a provisional diagram of how to understand the city. It is not a complete theory of the city that we offer, nor do we desire to offer one.

Our task has not been easy for three reasons. First, there is a problem of description. Often we do not seem to have the vocabulary to make the everyday life of the city legible; so much seems to pass us by. Second, there is a problem of epistemology. What counts as knowledge of the urban? Much of the new urbanism is based on symptomatic readings, but evocation cannot always be a substitute for systematic analysis. Third, in a short book of this kind, there is a problem of inclusion and exclusion of material and sites. So, for example, we have not had the space to cover issues of gender, race and the environment. Equally it is cities of the North which we have had in mind while writing the book. However, since we see the main aim of this book as opening up new perspectives that can be applied in a variety of ways, our hope is that these will be explored by others (and ourselves, for that matter) in the future.

The chapters of the book therefore provide sketches of different aspects of urban life. In chapter 1 we mark the territory of the book by considering some of the key metaphors deployed by the new urbanism, these being transitivity, porosity, rhythm and footprint. In chapter 2 we begin our critique and extension of the new urbanism by considering the notion of propinquity. By reworking this notion, we are able to demonstrate the multiple forms that community now takes in the city; forms which cannot be encompassed by old-style notions of community based on repeated face-to-face interaction. In chapter 3 we continue with the theme of propinquity. However, we move our focus of attention to the nature of the urban economy. We argue that the appropriate identification of what drives economic competition depends on the appropriate identification of the correct form of spatiality.

In chapters 4, 5 and 6, we redescribe the city as, at once, an ordering of uncertainty and as a political arena full of potentialities. In chapter 4 we build towards a transhuman approach to the city, based on the idea of the city as a machinic assemblage, which is both composed by, and institutionalizes, flow. At the same time we begin the task of repopulating the city with all those entities that have been erased by a conventional approach. In chapter 5 we continue the work of chapter 4 by considering how we might understand power and force within this new approach. In particular we examine the rise of new state practices and technologies, and how they fix and regulate urban life. Against the contemporary emphasis on proximity, we reinstate the role of the city as a resource rather than a cause. The final chapter continues with the theme of urban disempowerment and empowerment by focusing on the potentiality of democracy. In contrast to appeals for a return to a city built on negotiated consensus, we argue for the crucial role of disagreement and conflict, but within a framework of universal rights designed to build disciplines of empowerment.

1 THE LEGIBILITY OF THE EVERYDAY CITY

Introduction

In this chapter we begin our exploration of what counts as knowledge of the urban. We ask how we can theorize contemporary cities without losing sight of their extraordinary variety and vitality, and through intimations of the urban practices themselves. We deliberately avoid an essentialist reading, since we do not think that the multiple dynamics of the city allow it to be theorized in terms of driving structures. We turn to another urbanism that emphasizes the city as a place of mobility, flow and everyday practices, and which reads cities from their recurrent phenomenological patterns. Following Bruno Latour and Emily Hermant's remarkable photojournal of contemporary Paris (1998), this requires a view from the 'oligopticon' – vantage points above, below and in between the surfaces of cities.

This chapter draws out the central metaphors of this new urbanism of the everyday. We identify three metaphors which highlight the importance in the organization and vitality of urban life of transitivity, daily rhythms and footprint effects. These are situated, respectively, in the tradition of flânerie, rhythmanalysis and urban signature. While broadly sympathetic, we conclude that this urbanism overstates the city as a space of open flow, human interaction and proximate reflexivity. This prefaces our effort in the rest of the book to develop a different knowledge of cities, based on the instituted, transhuman and distanciated nature of urban life.

The New Urbanism in Context

Ambitiously, the great American urban theorists of the early twentieth century – Patrick Geddes, Lewis Mumford, Louis Wirth – sought to generalize
cities at different stages in history as holistic systems. They tended to see
the city as an organism. Underneath the clamour, clutter, confusion and
disorder of city life was felt to lie a certain organic integrity. The city was
considered a spatially bounded entity, embodying a particular way of life
(fast, civic, anonymous), with a distinct internal spatial and social division
of labour, a particular relation with the countryside, nation and the 'outside' world, and an evolutionary linearity (civilization and progress). They
wanted to theorize the city as a sociospatial system with its own internal
dynamic. Thus, for example, Mumford felt it right to develop a typology
of cities: 'Tyrannopolis', with its parasitism and gangster dictators;
'Megalopolis', with its greed, dissociation and barbarism; and 'Nekropolis',
with its looting and primitivism following war, famine and disease.
Mumford's treatment of each type as an organic system is striking.

Regardless of whether cities through the ages can be seen in this way,
contemporary cities are certainly not systems with their own internal
coherence. The city's boundaries have become far too permeable and
stretched, both geographically and socially, for it to be theorized as a
whole. The city has no completeness, no centre, no fixed parts. Instead,
it is an amalgam of often disjointed processes and social heterogeneity, a
place of near and far connections, a concatenation of rhythms; always
edging in new directions. This is the aspect of cities that needs to be
captured and explained, without any corresponding desire to reduce the
varied phenomena to any essence or systemic integrity.

In the last fifteen years, urban theory has moved a considerable way
towards recognizing the varied and plural nature of urban life. Most of
the major contemporary urbanists, including Manuel Castells, David
Harvey, Saskia Sassen, Edward Soja, Richard Sennett, Mike Davis and
Michael Dear, acknowledge the inadequacy of one positionality on the
city. They note the juxtaposition of high-value added activities with new
kinds of informed activity, the co-presence of different classes, social
groups, ethnies and cultures, the stark contrast between riches and creativity and abject poverty, and the multiple temporalities and spatialities
of different urban livelihoods. It is, however, fair to say that while they
get to the complex spirit of the urban, the tendency to generalize from
prevalent phenomena or driving processes remains strong.

There is, however, another tradition that has studiously avoided such
generalization, attempting to grasp the significant banality of everyday

life in the city. Everyday life has many dimensions. For Henri Lefebvre, for example, it incorporates 'daily life', defined as recurrent human and material practices, the 'everyday' as an existential or phenomenological condition, and 'everydayness', understood as a kind of immanent life force running through everything, 'a single and boundless space-time for "living"' (Seigworth 2000: 246) flowing through time and space. How cities manifest everyday life is a question that exercised, for example, the surrealists, and later, the situationists, who attempted to grasp this through non-conventional urban itineraries and mappings, manifestos and poetic musings (Sadler 1998). It also marked Walter Benjamin's wanderings as a meditative walker in the depths of different cities, and his study of urban sites of mass consumerism as an emerging way of life. We find the same impulse in Michel de Certeau's (1992) work on how banality as the 'overflowing of the common' (p. 5) 'introduces itself into our techniques' (p. 5) as the 'grammar of everyday practice' (Gardiner 2000: 174).

Underlying this urbanism of the everyday is a sense of the need to grasp a phenomenality that cannot be known through theory or cognition alone. In part, this arises from an understanding of everydayness as an immanent force, 'an excess that derives neither from a body or a world in isolation, but from the banal movements of pure process' (Seigworth 2000: 240). How is such an ontology of 'process in excess' to be grasped? For Seigworth, 'in order to "go beyond appearances", a philosophy of everyday life must have its attention toward "Life" – not merely its immediacy . . . but life in all of its sticky and slack human/ nonhuman, inorganic/incorporeal, phenomenal/epiphenomenal, and banal/intense everydayness' (2000: 246). An everyday urbanism has to get into the intermesh between flesh and stone, humans and non-humans, fixtures and flows, emotions and practices. But, what is to be kept in, and what out? Then, it needs to know the city beyond the powers of cognition, venturing into the realms of poetic invocation and sensory intimation. But, here too, the task is not unproblematic. How can we be sure that the latter take us into the city's virtuality? How do we avoid simply making empty gestures?

One possibility is the use of metaphors to capture recurring practices. In the rest of this chapter we discuss three strong metaphors in the tradition of everyday urbanism. The first is *transitivity*, which marks the spatial and temporal openness of the city. The second captures the city as a place of manifold *rhythms*, forged through daily encounters and multiple experiences of time and space. The third notes the city as *footprints*: imprints from the past, the daily tracks of movement across, and links beyond the city.

The Flâneur and Transitivity

Walter Benjamin's speculative philosophy, 'at its strongest moments does not seek truth in completeness, but in the neglected detail and the small nuance' (Caygill 1998: 152). This is most evident in his studies of the cities he roamed: Paris, Naples, Marseilles, Berlin and Moscow. Benjamin used the term transitivity to grasp the city as a place of intermingling and improvisation, resulting from its porosity to the past as well as varied spatial influences.

The term dances into play in the 1924 flâneur's tale of Naples, with Benjamin clearly overwhelmed by the city's theatricality, its passion for improvisation, its ironies. Naples visibly shows off its transitivity through the priest publicly harangued for indecent offences, but still able to stop to bless a wedding procession; the Baedeker guide that is of no help in finding architectural sites or the trails of the underworld; and the play of opportunity in a busy piazza, where a gentleman negotiates a fee with an overweight lady to pick up the fan she has dropped. 'Porosity is the inexhaustible law of the life of this city, reappearing everywhere', including how 'building and action inter-penetrate in the courtyards, arcades and stairways . . . to become a theatre of new, unforeseen constellations. The stamp of the definitive is avoided' (Benjamin 1997: 171, 169).

Transitivity/porosity is what allows the city to continually fashion and refashion itself. While it is particularly marked in Naples as a series of street-level improvisations, Benjamin is clear about its relevance for all cities. In the case of Moscow in the 1920s, he writes of the transitivity of a new socialism, based on the co-presence of the state bureaucratic machinery and the silent improvisations of individuals involved in informal trade and barter. The city's transitivity is manifest in the juxtaposition of a new monumental architecture against the mats and boxes laid out on pavements by the city's thousands of hawkers trying to sell whatever they can. Transitivity in both cities has radically different effects, but in both cases the concept encapsulates the city as everyday process, mobilized by flesh and stone in interaction.

What are the tools with which transitivity can be grasped? To begin, Michael Sheringham claims that the 'latent principle of mutability' that drives urban life requires a 'corresponding mobility on the part of the witness'. Traditional tools based on maps, description, emulation, distillation of essence are of little use. Enter the reflexive walker, the flâneur, who, through sensory, emotional and perceptual immersion in the passages of the city, engages in a 'two-way encounter between mind and the city', resulting in a 'knowledge that cannot be separated from this interactive process' (1996: 104, 111). Thus, Sheringham notes that, for André Breton, knowing the city depended on an attitude of lyrical expectancy and openness, expressed through a mixture of the poetic and the factual. For Benjamin, instead, the autobiographical walker aspired to an 'idleness' in which purposive activity gives way to phantasmagoric experience. Benjamin's journey through Marseilles was helped by the controlled use of hashish in order to slow down and see things differently. The tale of Naples, in contrast, draws on the ecstasy of the Berliner's reaction to a dazzlingly theatrical Mediterranean city, while in Paris he relies on measured reflections on the architecture of its arcades. Similarly, Jacques Réda saw Paris in the 1890s through allegory, as he charted a route based on strong associative connections prompted by wandering.

Contemporary urbanism has renewed the tradition of flânerie to read the city from its street-level intimations. Here too, we encounter the idea that the city as 'lived complexity' (Chambers 1994) requires alternative narratives and maps based on wandering. A wonderful example is the work of Rachel Lichtenstein and Iain Sinclair (1999) who have retraced the life and walks of a Jewish scholar and hermit, David Rodinsky, to produce, with other writings, an A–Z retraced on foot by Iain Sinclair (1999) of the significant sites for this Jewish East Londoner before the 1960s. This is a 'psychogeography' of strange spaces, selected monuments and boroughs and Jewish sites, a London signalled by biographical markings. We get a glimpse of this in the extract from Sinclair's introduction to the A–Z in box 1.1.

The 'theorist' is the gifted meditative walker, purposefully lost in the city's daily rhythms and material juxtapositions. The walker possesses both a poetic sensibility and a poetic science that is almost impossible to distil as a methodology for urban research. Benjamin, for example, was doing much more than opening himself to the transitivity of Naples, Moscow and Marseilles. He was not the naive and impressionable dilettante. He was armed instead with a transcendental speculative philosophy that allowed him to select, order and interpret his sensory experiences of the city. These were reflexive wanderings underpinned by a particular theorization of urban life, with the demand from theory to reveal the processes at work through the eye of a needle.

For some it is precisely the flâneur's sensibility linking space, language and subjectivity that is needed to read cities. Such intellectual wandering should not romanticize, but portray the multiple uses of the street, the unexpected subversions of the stereotype. Jerome Charyn's (1987) depiction of New York is illustrative:

Box 1.1   Rodinsky as psychogeographer

'Rodinsky was an artist in the tradition of Tom Phillips or the Surrealists, a re-maker of found objects. He bent the maps to fit his notion of how London *should* be – as if he was describing it for the first time. Maps were prompts rather than definitive statements. If a particular page [of the London A–Z] took his fancy, Rodinsky would attack its margins with a red biro. Other districts – Enfield, Stanmore, Willesden, Chingford, Hendon, Purley, Crystal Palace, Surbiton, Tooting Bec, Wimbledon, Richmond, Eltham, Peckham Rye – were of no interest to him and they were ignored. He was a taxonomist, breaking down the overwhelming mass of information into categories that excited his attention: prisons, asylums, burial grounds, children's homes, hospitals. These markings became a projected autobiography, a Dickensian fable of abandonment, destitution, and incarceration. This is how Rodinsky reads the world: a wilderness of unknowing, punctuated by dark places. Reservoirs of pain that solicit the heat of his red nib. His system of classification was shaped around privileged buildings that operated as colonies of the damned, institutions with strictly enforced rules of conduct, gulags of the disappeared. . . .

'What was his system? If buildings were singled out with no red track leading to them, did that mean they were significant but unvisited? Did the lines that tread strange routes represent journeys undertaken by bus or on foot? Arsenal football ground is ringed, but otherwise left alone. While Mare street is favoured with a red route that culminates in a triumphal circuit of Clapham Ponds. Has Thistlewaite Road been highlighted in honour of Harold Pinter (who lived there as a young man)? Was there a connection, some acquaintance or relative, shared by Pinter and Rodinsky? . . .

'In the suburbs, Rodinsky concentrates on "Jews' Hospitals" and "Jews' Burial Grounds", as if underwriting his own future; anticipating the routes that would finally carry him away from Princelet Street. . . . Here were the sites where the narrative of a lost life might be found: Heneage Street (the synagogue where Rodinsky was last seen, attending a Kiddush), Tower House in Fieldgate Street, Cheshire Street, Hawksmoor's Christ Church, the Brady Street burial ground. Islands where time was held within vessels of memory.

'I decided that the only way to make sense of Rodinsky's doctored maps was to walk his red lines . . .'

From Iain Sinclair, *Dark Lanthorns: Rodinsky's A–Z*, Goldmark, Uppingham, 1999, pp. 10–14.

If you want to 'discover' New York, go to the dunes: visit those caves in the South Bronx where breakdance began as ritualized warfare between rival gangs. Or stroll down Ninth Avenue, which hasn't been gentrified, and one can still feel the electric charm, a sense of neighborhood with some of the anarchy that a street ought to have. The old and the young mixing, mingling, with all kinds of quarrels and courtship rites. . . . Or go to Brighton Beach, where the Russian Jews have descended, drinking borscht and wearing 1950s' American clothes. Visit Mafia country in Bath Beach, where the young bloods stand in front of restaurants wearing their silkiest shirts. Travel to the Lower East Side, where the Chinese, the Latinos, and elderly Jews occupy the parks and the streets as if they'd all come out of a single crib. (cited in Marback, Bruch and Eicher 1998: 80)

There can be no doubt that such flânerie is able to reveal many inti-mate secrets of a city. But, the secrets revealed are particular secrets, and of particular parts of the city. They do not 'authenticate' a city, not least because the accounts are from distinctive subject positions. Flânerie has never been gender neutral, for example. The accounts have been mostly male, often loaded with sensual connotations (crowds, streets, salons, buildings, as sexually arousing or all-too-frequent analogies with the female body or femininity). Women are often stereotyped within a select-ive gaze, as Angela McRobbie notes:

it was partly through the various forced exclusions of women into the domestic sphere, into the household world of shopping and into the internalized world of the sexualized body and femininity and maternity that modernity allowed itself to emerge triumphant in the public sphere as a space of white, male, reason, rationality and bureaucracy. While some strata of young middle-class women could be drafted into carrying out the regulatory social work of the city, in the form of philanthropic visiting, their services were quickly dispensed of when it came to develop-ing the great infrastructures of state and government. . . . The power and privilege which allowed this minority of women such 'freedom' cannot in short be understood without taking account of the experience of those many women and girls who were the object of those concerned gazes and for whom the city was a place of work and livelihood, who lived in 'slum territory' and who travelled about the city not because they had gained some new found freedom, but as part of their everyday gainful activities. How else did working women through the centuries get to their work, run errands for their masters and mistresses, take some time for pleas-ure and enjoyment, and indeed escape the overcrowded conditions of their homes, but by walking about and by hanging about on the streets? (1999: 36–7)

Transitivity based on the experience of women going about their daily business does not feature. This said, we can find a current of 'flâneuse' writing. Deborah Parsons, for example, shows in her study of women writing about Paris and London between 1880 and 1940 that the flâneuse works in the details of particular sites with a 'gender-related city consciousness' (2000: 7). This includes an empirical knowledge of the city's grounded particularities, and through this, an exploration of being a woman in a city that is 'frequently enabling, sometimes difficult, always irresistible, providing spaces in which these women can explore their identities and their writerly voices' (p. 228). The 'city is always kept in interplay with a focus on the particular life that takes place within them' (p. 223). Gender matters in quite significant ways then, in accounts of urban transitivity, depending on who is observing or being observed.

Another problem with flânerie is whether the transitivity of the contemporary city based on endless spread and multiple connections is best grasped through wandering/wondering. How useful, for example, is the flâneur's knowledge in revealing the porosity of urban life associated with travel, such as the effects of large-scale daily population change? Consider this observation on London by Nick Barley:

> The 100 million airborne arrivals who descend on London each year are equal to almost twice the population of Britain. Travel on this scale now makes it impossible to characterise cities as stable entities. They're no longer simply geographical locations but urban contexts adapting themselves to constant flux. As much as it is a collection of buildings, a city is a shifting set of conceptual possibilities, robust enough to expand and contract on demand without losing its essential identity. . . . When one of London's airports is in fact in Cambridge, with kilometres of rolling countryside in between, the city has become more a territory for the imagination than one with a measurable physicality. (2000: 13)

The flâneur's poetic of knowing is not sufficient. The city's transitivity needs to be grasped through other means. Some of these can draw on now routine technologies of knowing, historical guides and photographs charting change over time, imaginaries which illustrate the city in motion (such as airborne video-shots), and books or films displaying the city's global connections (tales of diaspora cultures or a city's global food chain). We have gone a long way towards developing tools that are at one remove from the street and which no longer depend alone on the insight and tools of the knowledgeable flâneur (Featherstone 1998), as the two examples reveal in box 1.2.

Box 1.2   An alternative transitivity

Wanderers and everyday travellers too record the transitivity of cities, without the diagnostic theories and tools of the flâneur. Their travels, and the observations they make during the journey, can mark the city's spaces in quite distinctive ways, and with equally telling effect. Look how an alternative Los Angeles dances into play through Sikivu Hutchinson's description of the bus-rides of a largely poor, and female, motor-less public in this city of cars:

> Riding the bus in L.A. is a parallel city.... Riding enables another mode of looking, seeing, hearing, and smelling that 'eludes the discipline' of automobility even as it reproduces it. The street plans of this parallel city skirt the edge of automobility. They flow in quiet asynchrony to the virtual city beyond the car window, enclosing the women who wait with their packages in front of hospitals, grocery stores, check-cashing places, day care centers. From Los Angeles to New Haven, the bus is a city of women.... working class women of color form the backbone of bus riders in intensely exurban cities like L.A. The Lincoln Institute of Land Policy estimates that only 4 to 5 percent of trips in the United States utilize public transportation. Yet this figure does not adequately account for rates of use in communities of color, where women depend heavily on buses and subways throughout the day for trips to the workplace, public agencies, and the homes of friends and relatives. The elliptical nature of women's journeys through the city is the underside of exurban capital (2000: 108)....
>
> Driving past the MTA bus stops on an early weekday morning, 'they', the riding public, are invisible to the street traffic, testament to the otherworldly economy of L.A's sidewalks, to the now clichéd observation that 'nobody' walks in L.A. Despite sixty years of the streetcar, to be car-less in L.A. is to be faceless, possessed of an unenviably intimate knowledge of the rhythms and cadences of the city's streets, of the grinding commerce of each intersection and transfer point. (2000: 117)

Then, there are other vernacular insights which involve little knowledge of the city itself. The evocations of strangers from afar, often with a sense of place that draws rather more from a diaspora imaginary than from the locality itself, are a typical example. Consider the porosity of London via the West Indies that runs through

Tanty's excursions in Harrow Road in Samuel Selvon's novel *The Lonely Londoners* (1956):

Well Tanty used to shop in this grocer every Saturday morning. It does be like a jam-session there when all the . . . housewives does go to buy, and Tanty in the lead. They getting on just as if they in the market-place back home: 'Yes child, as I was telling you, she did lose the baby . . . half-pound saltfish please, the dry codfish . . . yes as I was telling you . . . and two pounds rice, please, and half-pound red beans, no, not that one, that one in the bag in the corner . . . (p. 78)

She used to get into big oldtalk with the attendants, paying no mind to people waiting in the queue. 'If I know Montego Bay!' she say. 'Why I was born there, when I was a little girl I used to bathe in the sea where all those filmstars does go. . . . Why I come to London? Is a long story, child, it would take up too much time, and people standing in the queue waiting. But I mind my nephew from when he a little boy, and he there here in London, he have a work in a factory . . .' (p. 80, cited in Akbur 2000: 70)

Riad Akbur (2000) comments that Selvon's protagonists fail to access the real London, but this is to miss the point that Tanty's London is as real as in any other account, grasping, as it does, the stretched and perforated sense of place of millions of immigrants, who identify a city, and their experiences in it, through their local–global geographies.

Rhythms and Rhythmanalysis

Like Benjamin, Henri Lefebvre observed that cities rely on relations of immediacy – on the 'music of the city' that needs to be 'discovered by reflection' (1996: 227, 101). Looking from a window above a crossroads in the centre of Paris, Lefebvre notes the multiple speeds and movements: people crossing the street, cars stopping and accelerating, crowds of people pursuing different aims, the mingling of noises and smells. He adds, 'to this inexorable rhythm which at night hardly abates, are superimposed other, less intense, slower rhythms: children going off to school, a few very noisy piercing calls, cries of morning recognition. Then, around 9.30, according to a schedule which hardly ever varies . . . the arrival of shoppers, closely followed by tourists' (p. 221). He notes that the rhythms are not simply those we can see, smell and feel, but also others which 'present themselves without being present' (p. 223), such as the rules of traffic control, the opening times of schools and shops, the itineraries recommended by foreign tour operators, and so on. The rhythms are of presence and absence.

The study of urban rhythms is becoming important in contemporary urbanism. But, what are urban 'rhythms'? John Allen clarifies:

> By city rhythms, we mean anything from the regular comings and goings of people about the city to the vast range of repetitive activities, sounds and even smells that punctuate life in the city and which give many of those who live and work there a sense of time and location. This sense has nothing to do with any overall orchestration of effort or any mass co-ordination of routines across a city. Rather it arises out of the teeming mix of city life as people move in and around the city at different times of the day or night, in what appears to be a constant renewal process week in, week out, season after season. (1999: 56)

The rhythms of the city are the coordinates through which inhabitants and visitors frame and order the urban experience. The city's multi-temporality, from bodily and clock rhythms to school patterns and the flows of traffic, need not be read as a loss of control, as some influential commentators claim (Godard 1997). Rather, the city is often known and negotiated through these rhythms and their accompanying ordering devices (traffic rules, telephone conventions, opening times, noise control codes). Even without these devices, order can be exerted through the overlayering of daily rhythms (Picon 1997). Indeed, in the city of manifold practices across its hundreds of spaces, there is a surprising absence of chaos and misunderstanding, partly owing to the repetitions and regularities that become the tracks to negotiate urban life (see chapter 4).

The metaphor of city rhythms can highlight neglected temporalities. Most readings focus on daytime rhythms, while studies of the city at night only too often focus on the unexpected and dark happenings. As darkness falls, the city becomes unidimensional, a place of pleasure and vice, or a place of terror masked in muffled noises and illicit activity. Joachim Schlör's *Nights in the Big City* (1998) is a rare exception. It is a wonderful study of night rhythms and their ordering technologies. The book focuses on the history of the night in the streets of Paris, Berlin and London between 1840 and 1930. It charts changing rhythms associated with historical shifts in public morality, state regulations (drink laws, curfews) and night technologies (street lighting, policing technologies).

Schlör shows, for example, how city curfew laws came to be lifted, with night security passed from civic watchmen into the hands of a nascent police authority helped by the arrival of street lighting. This opened up the night to the new rhythms of revellers, itinerants and tramps, as the once sole occupants of the street (criminals and prostitutes) were pushed into the shadows. Then, as life in the street at night became more complex, new opening and closing times emerged. As industrialization progressed, work-time extended into the night, with people busy in the utilities, factories, hospitals, presses, market halls, warehouses and police stations. Later, the night without curfew laws, replete with new forms of bourgeois and proletarian entertainment linked to industrialization, saw new efforts to regulate its rhythms (licensing laws, codes of public behaviour). As the comings and goings of the night came under increasing control and public moralizing, new demons of the night emerged: into the twentieth century, the night in Paris, London and Berlin became recast as the time of the underworld, spies and patrols, outcasts and vagabonds; the 'abnormal'.

Little of all this appears in 'big picture' urban theory, where much of urban life is left out. For example, strangely, the everyday rhythms of domestic life have rarely counted as part of the urban, as though the city stopped at the doorstep of the home. But domestic life is now woven routinely into the urban 'public realm'. How else are we to interpret the rise of home-working and teleshopping, and 'public' involvement through the consumption of goods, television, the internet and the growing exposure of domestic life in chat shows and fly-on-the wall television? The rhythms of the home are as much part of city life as, say, the movements of traffic, office life, or interaction in the open spaces of a city. Its rhythms, too, need incorporating into an everyday sociology of the city.

But, how to grasp the rhythms of the city? Lefebvre invoked 'rhythmanalysis', practised at a 'spectral' distance. If the reflexive wanderer reads the city from within and with a certain poetic sensibility, 'spectral analysis' contemplates the rhythms of a city from a more detached vantage point. According to Lefebvre, the elevated and closed window, for example:

> offers views that are more than spectacles. Perspectives which are mentally prolonged so that the implication of this spectacle carries its explanation. . . . Opacity and horizons, obstacles and perspectives are implicated, for they become complicated, imbricate themselves to the point of allowing the Unknown, the giant city, to be perceived or guessed at. (1996: 224)

The window allows the city to be read from a certain height and distance so that the comings and goings can be perceived in combination. The window is thus both a real site to view varied rhythms juxtaposed together, and a tool for speculation, presumably with the help of techno-logy such as maps, drawings, texts, photos and film.

But this is only the starting point of rhythmanalysis. Lefebvre is clear that for two reasons 'the city and the urban cannot be recomposed from the signs of the city' (1996: 143). First, phenomena alone do not reveal how the rhythms of the city combine, overlap, dissolve and recombine, to generate a certain urban synthesis. Second, recording the rhythms of daily life does not provide access to the immanence or excess of process noted earlier by Seigworth (2000). For Lefebvre, what is required is a certain 'praxis that can take charge of . . . the gathering together of what gives itself as dispersed, dissociated, separated, and this in the form of simultaneity and encounters' (1996: 143).

He is frustratingly elusive, however, about the tools of such a praxis. Like flânerie, there are no clear methods for rhythmanalysis, only other metaphors such as receptivity and exteriority. The rhythmanalyst has to be captured by the rhythm: 'One has to *let* go, give in and abandon oneself to its duration' (Lefebvre 1996: 219, original emphasis). For this, 'exteriority' is necessary, because to 'extricate and to listen to the rhythms requires attentiveness and a certain amount of time' (p. 223). In the end, the window in spectral analysis remains a stimulant for the gifted artist/analyst to mobilize a lot more than the powers of perception and reflex-ivity. But we can only guess at these other powers, which presumably include powers of abstraction to name and order the immanent forces behind the instanciated rhythms of the city. We get a glimpse of the power of such a combination of theory and receptivity in Sigmund Freud's psychoanalytic interpretation of the rhythms of Roman piazza life in a letter he wrote to his family from Rome on 22 September 1907 (box 1.3).

This is a subtle interpretation of the crowd, with no sense of nostalgia or loss. Freud weaves into his account of the happenings of the piazza the technologies that animate (lantern slides, cinematic projections, flashing signs, electric *tranvia*). We see 'an urban scene in which an individual and collective subjectivity takes shape in a multiplicity of images, sounds, crowds, vectors, pathways, and information', docu-mented through 'one particular attempt at cognitively managing and organizing that overloaded field' (Crary 1999: 365). Jonathan Crary is convinced that the insight is aided by techniques at the heart of Freud's new therapeutic enterprise:

In a paper first published in 1912, Freud put forward some essential 'tech-nical rules' for analysts to follow. The first of these techniques is what Freud called 'evenly suspended attention', which described a self-conscious

Box 1.3   Freud's letter from Rome

'My dear ones

On the Piazza Colonna behind which I am staying, as you know, several thousand people congregate every night. The evening air is really delicious; in Rome wind is hardly known. Behind the column is a stand for a military band which plays there every night, and on the roof of a house at the other end of the piazza there is a screen on which a *società Italiana* projects lantern slides. They are actually advertisements, but to beguile the public these are interspersed with pictures of landscapes, Negroes of the Congo, glacier ascents and so on. But since these wouldn't be enough, the boredom is interrupted by short cinematographic performances for the sake of which the old children (your father included) suffer quietly the advertisements and monotonous photographs. They are stingy with these tidbits, however, so I have had to look at the same thing over and over again. When I turn to go I detect a certain tension in the attentive crowd [*der Menge aufmerksam*], which makes me look again, and sure enough a new performance has begun, and so I stay on. Until 9 pm I usually remain spellbound [*so der Zauber zu wirken*]; then I begin to feel too lonely in the crowd, so I return to my room to write to you all after having ordered a fresh bottle of water. The others who promenade in couples or *undici, dodici* stay on as long as the music and lantern slides last.

'In one corner of the piazza another of those awful advertisements keeps flashing on and off. I think it is called Fermentine. When I was in Genoa two years ago with your aunt it was called Tot; it was some kind of stomach medicine and really unbearable. Fermentine, on the other hand, doesn't seem to disturb the people. In so far as their companions make it possible, they stand in such a way that they can listen to what is being said behind them while seeing what is going on in front, thus getting their full share. Of course there are lots of small children among them, of whom many a woman would say that they ought to have been in bed long ago. Foreigners and natives mix in the most natural way. The clients of the restaurant behind the column and of the confectioner's on one side of the piazza enjoy themselves too; there are wicker chairs to be had near the music, and the townspeople like sitting on the stone balustrade round the monument. I am not sure at the moment whether I haven't forgotten a fountain on the piazza, the latter is so big. Through the middle of it runs the Corso Umberto (of which it is in fact an enlargement) with its carriages and an electric *tranvia*, but they don't do any harm, for a Roman never moves out of a vehicle's way and the drivers don't seem to be aware of their right to run people over. When the music stops everyone claps loudly, even those who haven't listened. From time to time terrible yells are heard in the otherwise quiet and rather distinguished crowd; this noise is caused by a number of newspaper boys who, breathless like the herald of Marathon, hurl themselves onto the piazza with the evening editions, in the mistaken idea that with the news they are putting an end to an almost unbearable tension. When they have an accident to offer, with dead or wounded, they really feel masters of the situation. I know these newspapers and buy two of them every day for five *centesimi* apiece; they are cheap, but I must say that there is never anything in them that could possibly interest an intelligent foreigner. Occasionally there is something like a commotion, all the boys rush this way and that, but one doesn't have to be afraid that something has happened; they soon come back again. The women in this crowd are very beautiful (foreigners excepted); the women of Rome, strangely enough, are beautiful even when they are ugly, and not many of them are that.

'I can hear the music plainly from my room; but of course I cannot see the pictures. Just now the crowd is clapping again.

Fond greetings, Your Papa'

From Sigmund Freud, *The Letters of Sigmund Freud*, ed. E. L. Freud, Basic Books, New York, 1975, pp. 261–3.

strategy of 'not directing one's notice to anything in particular and maintaining the same evenly suspended attention . . . in the face of all that one hears'. . . . But the fundamental significance of his remarks is the attempt to define a state of receptivity in the analyst that will be commensurate with the spoken free association of the patient. . . . It presumes an ideal state in which one could redistribute one's attention so that *nothing* would be shut out, so that everything would be in a low-level focus but without the risk of schizophrenic overload. (Crary 1999: 367–8)

Freud's is, of course, only one possible technique for analysing the rhythms of the city, but the essential point is that receptivity does not come divorced from an analytic method.

Urban Footprints and Namings

Let us, however, continue our exploration of central urban metaphors. If rhythm, defined as 'localized time' and 'temporalized place' (Lefebvre 1996: 227), registers the daily tempo of the city, the metaphor of footprint overcomes an idea of the city as a contained space. Cities are, of course, demarcated, through planning and architectural rules and through transport and communications networks within and beyond the city. But the spatial and temporal porosity of the city also opens it to footprints from the past and contemporary links elsewhere. City spaces are always exposed, including the 'gated' communities that try everything possible to shut themselves off, but are still crossed by the fumes of the city, and the nightly escape of younger residents looking for entertainment in the city's more lively areas.

Similarly, the present is crossed by influences from the past. A vivid example is Doreen Massey's description of how in Mexico City the Square of the Three Cultures juxtaposes the ruins of an Aztec pyramid, a baroque Roman Catholic church, and contemporary buildings in the International Style, to reveal the 'elements of the three major cultures which have gone in to making this place' (1999: 100). Each stratum of the urban archaeology brings 'an intricate and active system of interconnections' across the globe, such that, 'when "the Spanish" met "the Aztecs" both were already complex products of hybrid histories' (p. 110). For Massey this 'multiplicity of histories that is the spatial' (2000: 231) permeates movement in space too. It is not confined to historical footprints in a situated place. The car journey, for example, involves a complex 'simultaneity of trajectories', composed of the practices and thoughts of those travelling, the histories of the places crossed, the trajectories of the places left, now getting by without you. The city is full of these footprints of simultaneity, loaded with spatiotemporal tramlines.

What difference does it make to acknowledge these urban footprints? First, it helps to discard the idea of the city as an ordered and segregated pattern of mobility, helping in turn to see myriad other trails of mobility in the city (commuters, shoppers, tourists, children, the homeless, but also sewers and foxes). This allows a vision of the city as spatially stretched patterns of communication, bringing distant sites into contact (maybe through visits to family and friends), but also separating adjacent spaces (as with neighbours with little in common with each other). These tracks allow the city to be known. We negotiate the city through used tracks and construct imaginaries around them of the known city. This is one way in which a city, with all its complexity, size and change, is named.

Second, an understanding of footprints reveals the 'mixity', as Massey describes it, of cities. One example is the presence of past footprints in popular and official symbols memorializing the city, which frame the city (for example, Mexico City as cultural gateway, as city of long-standing global connections). The markings define insiders and outsiders, territory and the city's irreducible mixity. Memorialization of this sort also works to erase sites, memories and histories which sit uncomfortably with a given imaginary (Klein 1997; Hayden 1997).

The city as palimpsest is known, according to Kevin Hetherington, through the way the urban bricolage is named:

> maps, photographs, paintings, televised images, textual descriptions, poems, and so on. . . . They arrange, order, include and exclude, they *make knowable* a space to everyone who might choose to look at these representations and also make it possible to compare it with another space. . . . Those representations contain truth claims (not necessarily scientific) about a space. They perform place myths as places. (1997: 189, original emphasis)

The last sentence is of crucial importance. A city named in certain ways also becomes that city through the practices of people in response to the labels. They perform the labels. As Marback, Bruch and Eicher suggest, 'When you hear or read about a particular city, almost automatically you draw upon what you previously heard or read about that city to judge what you are hearing or reading now' (1998: 3):

> Through this language, we gain images of places we have never been to. The bustling business world of Wall Street, the gleaming skyscrapers of Washington, D.C., the glitter of Las Vegas, the mosaic of separate ethnic areas in Los Angeles, and the ageing, abandoned factories of northern industrial cities like Detroit are all images that any of us can picture. Each of these images . . . represents the city as a certain kind of place. By representing specific cities as certain kinds of places, we are in a way determining our potential actions in those places. We would, for example, expect to have completely different experiences in Las Vegas and Detroit. So when we go to those places, we go expecting to do some things and not others. (1998: 6)

People and places script each other. Marback, Bruch and Eicher go further, to suggest, on the grounds that cities are now intensely visualized through images of one sort or another, that cities can be conceived as 'forms of writing, as conglomerations of communication between people through architecture and neighborhoods, through art and clothing and music, through daily activities and forms of entertainment, as well as through the mass media' (p. 12).

Cities take shape through a plethora of 'fixed namings'. The challenge of reading the city thus also lies in the study of the devices through which cities are named. The most obvious ones are tourist maps and city guides which select particular routes and historical reconstructions to frame cities as attractive places. A similar scripting is evident in the aestheticization of city centres through design, in shopping malls, marinas, recreation sites. But, as Jane Jacobs notes in her study of aboriginal expression in contemporary Australian cities, aestheticization also 'operates as the logic of many more modest urban transformations such as streetscaping, place making, and community arts projects. Some of these transformations assist in the selling of cities, but some may be addressing alternate agendas such as building identity or facilitating political formations among severely marginalized groups' (1998: 274).

Cities are named through a variety of means, and in ways which confirm or subvert stereotypes. Either way, the naming contributes to city identification. The history of the local media can be read in these terms. In chronicling local events, a narrative of the city is constructed, and over the years the city comes to be memorialized in detail. This street, that pub, that corner, that personality, become known, and through their collective naming we see others and other parts of the city. The city becomes accessible, and through the places named in the chronicles it becomes a spatial formation.

And when the media includes architectural critics commenting on the changing physical landscape – as Lewis Mumford did for the *New Yorker* on new developments in the 1930s – the city takes shape through these landmarks in the imaginary too. The cityscape is made known. Through Mumford's commentary New Yorkers came to see a city of skyscrapers and debated whether 'amid such a mass of new and almost new buildings, one has a fresh sense of shame over all this misapplied energy and wasted magnificence' (1998: 85). Now the city, through selective descriptions of the built environment, is given both history and memory, and a basis from which public opinion can praise or condemn.

The city, lastly, is scripted also in a literal sense, through its urban art forms. These include not only events in galleries and other closed spaces, but also open spaces used for artistic expression (concerts in parks, rap in the streets, ethnic festivals and parades) and the urban fabric itself used as canvass (murals, graffiti). The city is the medium itself shouting its stories directly. Take the example of urban graffiti marking particularly strong feelings of urban life in particular cities. In New York, for

Leonard Kriegel, 'the spread of graffiti is as accurate a barometer of the decline of urban civility as anything else one can think of', its politics 'pubescent sloganeering' (1993: 433–4). Others who are less condescending place graffiti with other vernacular art forms which manifest the cultural variety of the city, its diverse entrepreneurial energies, and the contested politics of the public realm (Kirshenblatt-Gimblett 1996). Either way, this form of naming also makes the city knowable, as Susan Smith (2000: 86) suggests:

Whose city is this?

Corporate identity shapes the skyline; commercial products line the streets.
Faceless thousands surge through nameless spaces.

Whose place is this, and how do we know?

Look to the 'twilight zone of communication'.
The signs in the streets, the measures, the markings, the meanings, the movement. . . .

Graffito: A drawing or writing scratched on a wall or other surface.

What's wrong with graffiti?

Graffito; . . . scribblings or drawings, often indecent, found on public buildings, in lavatories, etc.

What's wrong with graffiti?

Tricia Rose knows, she writes in *Black Noise*:
By the mid-1970s, graffiti emerged as a central example of the extent of urban decay and heightened already existing fears over a loss of control of the urban landscape . . .
And that's not all, as David Ley and Roman Cybriwski observe in 'Urban graffiti as territorial markers':
A zone of tension appeared, which is located exactly by the evidence of the walls. . . . Diagnostic indicators of an invisible environment of attitudes and social processes . . . far more than fears, threats and prejudices, they are the prelude and a directive to open behaviour. . . .
The walls are more than an attitudinal tabloid; they are a behavioural manifesto . . .

A Basic Ontology

In this chapter we have begun to look at the difference it makes to visualize the city as a process, without the pretence of total sight or generalization. We have reconstructed the tradition of everyday urbanism as one way of knowing the multiplex city. We have explored the potential of sensory metaphors which capture the transitivity and rhythm of urban life and also allow the city to be named in some way. We have suggested, however, that this urbanism balances on metaphors that lack methodological clarity.

In the rest of the book we want to open this tradition to other ways of knowing the everyday city by grounding it in an understanding of the structured and unstructured regularities of urban life. We consider the tradition as it stands to be flawed in three respects. First, the theoretical edifice rests on metaphors which imply an unlimited ebb and flow to urban life. This needs to be questioned. We have begun to see how urban life is placed by lines of mobility and travel and by namings and imaginaries. The city's rhythms are not free to roam where they will. Cities, as we suggest in chapter 4, also provide the machinery through which rhythms are directed, from traffic lights which regulate the temporality and pace of life, to rules of planning which 'instruct' the city in given directions (such as where and when shopping can take place). Similarly, we argue in chapter 5 that the city is heavily regulated by bureaucracy and other formal and informal institutions. Striating openness and flow are a whole series of rules, conventions and institutions of regulation and control. The city thus needs to be seen as an institutionalized practice, a systematized network, in an expanded everyday urbanism.

Second, the tradition of everyday urbanism is marked by a certain humanism, evident in the powers of reflexive wanderers and rhythmanalysts, the emphasis on human-centred aspects of urban life, and, as we show in the next chapter, the desire for face-to-face-contact and urban community. Yet much of city life (chapter 4) is about the machine-like circulation of bodies, talk and objects, as well as the presence and regulation of trans-human and inorganic life (from rats to sewers). The new urbanism needs to recognize the engineering of certainty through varied technologies of regulation (such as traffic signs, postal rules, waste management).

The third flaw is the strong sense of cities as places of proximate links, despite the references to spatial and temporal porosity. Time and again, the city is stressed as a site of localized flows and contact networks. Our argument, in chapters 2 and 3, is that so extensive have the city's connections become as a result of the growth of fast communications, global flows, and linkage into national and international institutional life that the city needs theorization as a site of local–global connectivity, not a place of meaningful proximate links. The new urbanism needs to note also the everydayness of spatially stretched and distant connections.

With these steps in mind, how might we understand the city? The ontology of the city we present below has an obvious philosophical bloodline which travels forward from writers like David Hume, John Locke and Baruch Spinoza, through those early twentieth-century geniuses like William James in psychology, Gabriel Tarde in sociology and Henri Bergson and Alfred Whitehead in philosophy, to a new later twentieth-century flowering found in the work of Michel Serres and Gilles Deleuze which has been so brilliantly expanded on and made practical by writers such as Bruno Latour. Its chief concern may be counted as an ontology of encounter or togetherness based on the principles of connection, extension and continuous novelty. The watchwords of this ontology may be counted as 'process' and 'potential', 'the actual world is a process, and . . . the process is the becoming of actual entities . . . the becoming of an actual entity in disjunctive diversity – actual and non-actual – acquires the real bite of the one actual entity' (Whitehead 1978: 22). In such a conception, the city is made up of potential and actual entities/associations/togethernesses which there is no going beyond to find anything 'more real'. The accumulation of these entities can produce *new* becomings – because they encounter each other in so many ways, because they can be apprehended in so many ways, and because they exhibit 'concrescence' (to use a Whiteheadian term), that is, when put together they produce something more than when apart, something which cannot be described by simple addition because it will exhibit what would now be called 'emergent' properties. Or as Whitehead puts it, 'the potentiality for being an element in a real concrescence of many entities into one actuality is the one general metaphysical character attached to all entities, actual and non-actual . . .' (1978: 22). In other words, it belongs to the nature of a 'being' that it is a potential for every 'becoming'.

All philosophies of becoming have a number of characteristics in common. One is an emphasis on instruments, on tools as a vital element of knowing, not as simply a passive means of representing the known. The second is their consideration of other modes of subjectivity than consciousness. The third is that 'feelings', howsoever defined, are regarded as crucial to apprehension. The fourth is that time is not a 'uniquely serial advance' (Whitehead 1978: 35) but rather exists as a series of different forms knotted together. Fifth, becoming is discontinuous, 'there is a becoming of continuity, but no continuity of becoming' (Whitehead 1978: 35). And finally, and most importantly, this means that new 'prehensions' (ideas about the world) can be constantly built. More and more can be put into the world (and this cannot be reliably forecast since so much of the activity of prehension is virtual). For example, consider the invention of the colour mauve by William Perkin in 1856. What mauve 'promised was a new way of looking at the world' (Garfield 2000: 69). The wide availability of the colour added a new visual register to the city streets as it was used in new fashions, quickly followed by colours like magenta (in 1859), and a host of colours which previously had had to be produced in arduous ways from natural products and which could now be produced artificially (such as madder and indigo). The new dyes quite literally coloured the urban world in new ways. What is clear, then, we hope, is that the ontology outlined below is an open one. It does not trade in notions of a fixed theoretical framework, or in definitive once-and-for-all results; there is no one account of a single urban thing but rather a generative multiplicity of divergent and discontinuous lines of flight with their own spaces and times.

So what exists in cities? How can we hold on to their potential and variety? At the most basic level, we can talk of *life*, teeming bare life, a being-together of existences. In taking this stance, we are trying to point in three directions. The first of these is to simply state that the city is an ecology made up of many species, not just the human, which live at faster or slower rates, gather in greater or lesser intensities, inhabit the city's earth, air and water multiply. Then, second, it is to signal that much of what goes on in cities is centred around the practice of biopolitics, the practice of engineering the body and the senses – and life more generally – so as to produce governable subjects. Power penetrates subjects' very bodies and forms of life. In other words, life is at the centre of all the calculations made about cities. And, third, it is to signal that the senses are a crucial element of urban life. Cities cast spells over the senses, spells which are increasingly engineered by the state and business. And mention of the senses in turn points to that whole realm of human life which is outside consciousness – consciousness is, after all, only one kind of mental process. These are all the reflexes and automatisms which make up the city's 'unconscious', and which account for the bulk of its activity. This is the constant push of habitual consciousness and the dance of gestural, somatic communication, which writers like Walter Benjamin and, later, Michael Taussig tried to show up, and which can be found in nearly every urban encounter:

> If, for instance, one comes upon two staunch friends unexpectedly meeting for the first time in many months, and one chances to hear their initial words of surprise, greeting and pleasure, one may readily notice, if one

pays close enough attention, a tonal, melodic layer of communication beneath the explicit denotative meaning of the words – a rippling rise and fall of the voices in a sort of musical duet, rather like two birds singing to each other. Each voice, each side of the duet, mimes a bit of the other's melody while adding its own inflection and style, and then is echoed by the other in turn – the two singing bodies thus tuning and attuning to one another, rediscovering a common register, remembering each other. It requires only a slight shift in focus to realise that this melodic singing is carrying the bulk of communication in this encounter, and that the explicit meanings of the actual words ride on the surface of this depth like waves on the surface of the sea. (Abram 1996: 80–1)

For now, it is a moot point whether new forms of life have joined the urban pack of late – such as informational entities which are no longer ghosts in the machine – or whether it even makes sense to write in these terms, because all life involves alliances of different forms of matter. What seems more important is to ask how life is enlivened, how it becomes a becoming.

We argue that this push comes out of distinctive cross-cutting ethologies, which are *networks* of enrolment, and the motion will produce particular spaces and times, as a consequence of the ways that the actors in these networks relate to one another. The consequences of taking such a stance in which multiple networks course through the city making their way as/in the world are – multiple. To begin with, there is a problem of description. The metaphor of the network is not necessarily the best one since it can conjure up a vision of a fixed set of nodes from which things circulate through fixed channels rather than a set of often tenuous fluid-like flows (Urry 2000; Latour 1999). Then there is a related problem. While these networks are clearly attempts to stabilize and pin down certain issues, ground the world by providing new worlds, they also contain within themselves – or through interaction with other networks, or both – the *potentiality* to become something else. Each network may diverge, or fold, on to others. Networks are, then, an attempt to depart from Cartesian space and Aristotelian place. As Deleuze (1992) puts it, 'I don't like points. *Faire le point* (to conclude) seems stupid to me. It is not the line that is between the two points, but the point that is at the intersection of two lines.' And, lastly, networks are always more or less interwoven with other networks. Thus, for example, human subjects which we conveniently describe as a unity of body and purpose are in fact aggregates of numerous subject positions which are parts of numerous networks. At any time, a 'subject' will therefore be the result of switching in and out of particular positions in particular networks, shuffling between particular spaces and times.

But this sense of a kaleidoscopic urban world, crammed full with hybrid networks going about their business, enables us to see, at the same time, the importance of *encounter*. Networks cannot be sealed off from the world, they are always in collision with other networks: touching, fighting, engaging, cooperating, parasitizing, ignoring – the variations are almost endless. In other words, encounter, and the reaction to it, is a formative element in the urban world. So places, for example, are best thought of not so much as enduring sites but as *moments of encounter*, not so much as 'presents', fixed in space and time, but as variable events; twists and fluxes of interrelation. Even when the intent is to hold places stiff and motionless, caught in a cat's cradle of networks that are out to quell unpredictability, success is rare, and then only for a while. Grand porticos and columns framing imperial triumphs become theme parks. Areas of wealth and influence become slums.

All this may seem abstract and diffuse, difficult to get a hold of because, like all ontologies, it only describes the bare bones of thereness. But, hopefully, we have given some sense of how rich we think such an ontology might prove. For in this ontology, cities cannot be reduced to one. They are truly multiple. They exceed, always exceed. Cities are machines of consumption? Yes, but never just that. Cities are artefacts of the state? Yes, but never just that. Cities are generators of patriarchy? Yes, but never just that. The next chapter continues this argument.

2 PROPINQUITY AND FLOW IN THE CITY

Introduction

The emphasis at the end of the last chapter on cities as sites of extension and extensive sites is something that we want to develop further in this chapter, by exploring in detail the meaning of propinquity. The argument is in four parts. The first part of the chapter outlines some of the ways of thinking the city which leading urban theorists have followed. Then we will focus in on one of the chief areas of confusion – propinquity. Our argument here is that what is taken for granted to be near and far in the city by urban theorists – and the accompanying moral economy – disables their explanations right from the start. Using the basic (and necessarily, therefore, very faint) ontology of the city outlined in chapter 1 which is founded on the centrality of encounter in the constitution of 'there', the third part of the chapter attends to the issue of community. In one way or another, much of the urban literature is concerned with community but works with a peculiarly static conception of community which interrupts some of the social and political goals that this literature sets itself. We outline a different set of 'coming urban communities', communities in process which cannot be entirely fixed in space. The conclusion to the chapter then considers how some of these issues might be concretely rethought through the example of modern architecture and performance art.

The Nostalgic City

A good many of the stories of modern urban life, and especially the most popular stories of writers like Georg Simmel or Walter Benjamin, tell a story of an authentic city held together by face-to-face interaction whose coherence is now gone. If the authentic city exists, it is as a mere shadow of itself, one that serves only to underline what has been lost. In the great accounts of history, the modern city is more loss than gain.

In the classic stories of Simmel and Benjamin, the blows to the city authentic come from four different directions, though all of them arise from the ever-increasing circulation and exchange of commodities. First, there is money. Confirming Marx's diagnosis, money is understood as a kind of cultural acid, a corrosive force that erodes sociability by spearheading commodification. More and more modern life is turned into a problem of 'mere' calculation. Simmel summed up this view in his observation that 'the complete heartlessness of money is reflected in our social culture, which is itself determined by money' (1990: 346). As everything becomes expressible in terms of 'mere money', so quality becomes quantity. Colour and difference is leached out of the world by this 'fraternisation of impossibilities' (Marx 1964: 169). And personal relationships are also subject to the 'growing indifference of money' (Simmel 1990: 444): increasingly they are only able to work through the limited expression allowed by the cash nexus. Thus, under the twisted ambitions of a money economy, the very quality of experience decays.

The second blow is a more general process of 'thingification'. The culture of things takes over from the culture of human beings. The increasingly autonomous movement of things threatens what it is to be human: 'the pessimism with which the majority of more profound thinkers seem to view the contemporary state of culture has its foundation in the ever-wider yawning abyss between the culture of things and that of human beings' (Simmel, cited in Frisby 1991: 89). Not all is negative, however. Neither Simmel nor Benjamin takes a simplistic anti-technological stance. They both regard technology as a new body for both humanity and nature, and the city is 'the technological site of human habitation, the place where the collision of technology and human tradition is most marked' (Caygill 1998: 131). But the new speculative possibilities of technology are continually reduced by the commodity to something much less than ought to be possible; the new home that the city might become is replaced by an alienated visual spectacle.

The third blow is the constant speed-up of life, leading to a dissolution of forms. The whirl of life in modernity uproots values, subverts fixed conclusions. In particular, there is a 'tendency to create a distance' in modern culture: social relations are characterized by a negation of truly intimate contact:

> the ease of transport to the furthest distant points strengthens this 'anxiety with regard to contact'; the 'historical spirit', the wealth of inner relationships to spatially and temporally more distant interests makes us all the more sensitive to the shocks and the discords that confront us from the immediate proximity and contact with human beings and things. (Simmel, cited in Frisby 1991: 77)

Then one more blow: the rise of the mass media which both typifies modernity and represents it. The mass media, typified by film, are part of a general 'shattering of tradition', a profound reorganization of experience. This reorganization can be interpreted in a pessimistic way as a liquidation of cultural heritage. The loss of aura, of originality and of uniqueness as properties of works of art is proof of a more general transformation of the structure of experience, towards an economy of drives, which can constitute a new barbarism. But equally, the reorganization can be interpreted more optimistically, as the institution of a new set of dreams and possibilities, as a folio of possible futures unleashed by art's speculative qualities. For example, Benjamin argues that film

> extends our comprehension of the necessities which rule our lives . . . [and] manages to assure us of an immense and unexpected field of action. Our taverns and our metropolitan streets, our offices and furnished rooms, our railroad stations and our factories appeared to have locked us up hopelessly. Then came film and burst this prison world asunder by the dynamite of the tenth of a second, so that now, in the midst of its far-flung ruins and designs, we calmly and adventurously go travelling. With the close-up, space expands, with slow-motion movement is extended. The encouragement of a snapshot doesn't simply render more precise what in any case was visible: it reveals entirely new structural formations of the subject. (Benjamin, cited in Caygill 1998: 112)

On a number of different levels, therefore, far becomes near, and distance is thereby redefined.

The upshot of these four blows is clear at least. This is a world that is or is in danger of going downhill fast and it is the character of modern urban experience that is at issue. If this is not a world that is running on social and cultural empty, then it is certainly getting close to it.

Let us just take one example of this prognosis at work: Simmel and Benjamin's notion of shock. For both these authors, modern life is a condition of overstimulation, a mass of stimuli so numerous that they can be neither meaningless nor meaningful. The reaction to this condition is essentially neurasthenic, consisting of overstimulated and tired nerves. And, in turn, this leads to a set of coping behaviours such as blasé attitudes. Benjamin's variant of this argument is a case in point. His understanding of modern experience was neurological. Thus he

> wanted to investigate the 'faithfulness' of Freud's hypothesis, that consciousness parries shock by preventing it from penetrating deep enough to leave a permanent trace on memory, by applying it to 'situations far removed from those which Freud had in mind'. Freud was concerned with war neurosis, the trauma of 'shell shock' and catastrophic accident that plagued soldiers in World War I. Benjamin claimed that this battlefield consequence of shock had become 'the norm' in modern life. Perceptions that once occurred as conscious reflections were now the source of shock impulses which consciousness must parry. (Buck-Morss 2000: 104)

Various means were available to the subject to organize this new experience. First among these was the creation of new means of tactile appropriation of the city, aided by the existence of new media like film which were both new sources of shock and new means of adjusting to such experience.

These kinds of accounts have become a constant refrain in the literature on the modern city, shored up by the kind of humanism that we outlined in the last chapter. Bolstered by constant cross-referencing, they have created a self-contained narrative of decline. It is not that we necessarily disagree with this narrative. How could we? On the whole, so little serious confirmatory empirical work has ever been done that we simply cannot know whether it holds. But we can certainly raise serious objections.

To start with, there is the little matter of money. A number of recent writers have disputed outright the depiction of money as a corrosive and culturally barren force (see Zelizer 1994; Dodd 1994; Leyshon and Thrift 1997; Thrift and Leyshon 1999; Furnham and Argyle 1998), an impersonal denominator which 'once it invades the realm of personal relations . . . inevitably bends these relations in the direction of instrumental rationality' (Zelizer 1994: 11). Instead they see a world of multiple monetary networks which depend on quite different monetary *practices*:

> different networks of social relations and systems of meaning mark modern money, introducing controls, restrictions and distinctions that are as influential as the rationing of primitive money. Multiple monies in the modern world may not be as visibly identifiable as the shells, coins, brass rods or stones of primitive communities, but their invisible boundaries

work just as well. How else, for instance, do we distinguish a bribe from a tribute or a donation, a wage from an honorarium, or an allowance from a salary? How do we identify ransom, bonuses, tips, damages or premiums? Then, there are quantitative differences between these various payments. But surely the special vocabulary conveys much more than different monies. Detached from its qualitative distinctions, the world of money becomes indecipherable. (Zelizer 1994: 25)

The practices which produce and are produced by these networks are highly variable over space and produce cities in which all kinds of monies are circulating under the guise of one tender.

Then there is the little matter of things. On a general theoretical level, things are now looked on much more favourably. They have assumed a place in the constitution of humanity that they never had in earlier social theoretical days. For example, actor-network theory mixes up humans and non-humans, subjects and objects. Instead of purified, homogeneous sets defined by similar types of action or rules, we have heterogeneous hybrid networks that involve 'flows of instruments, competencies, literature, money, which tie and connect laboratories, enterprises, or administrations' (Latour 1993). Thus pure face-to-face social acts no longer exist, they are always mediated by things. 'Face-to-face interaction exists among baboons, but not among humans' (Latour, cited in Dosse 1998: 97). And things have assumed a heretofore unknown importance on an empirical level too. For example, the explosion of ethnographic work on consumption has shown that things are central to human life, but, more than this, they are actively consumed in all kinds of networks of use: 'certain objects have social lives that are quantitatively different from others as well as correspondingly distinct potentials for constructing the lives of persons who control (or are controlled by) them' (Weiss 1996: 14). Some things are clearly commodities – and that has serious consequences (Stallybrass 1998) – but it is a mistake to think that the process of commodification is a be-all and end-all. 'Commodification never fixes all objects in the commodity form – that is, the trajectory of any object can be diverted over time' (Weiss 1996: 15). What all this suggests is that we need to think of things in much more heterogeneous ways and, at the limit, we can grant them their own kind of agency, either as part of wider human/non-human networks, as a result of the demands they make on their users (for example, various skills of use), or even as subjects in their own right (Pickering 1992; Collins and Kusch 1998).

Then there is the little matter of speed-up. At first sight, the idea that this is a world of ever-accelerating change seems an attractive proposition. But it does not bear up to close examination. Numerous critiques

have shown that the case is too often exaggerated to the point of carica-
ture (see, for instance, Thrift 1995, 1996b; May and Thrift 2001). To
begin with, it proceeds from gestural historical accounts which rarely
concede that alternative readings are possible and therefore never attempt to establish any countervailing evidence. Then, it usually depends
on a pervasive technological determinism which reads the characteristics
of objects off on to cultures, as though all that was happening was the
cultural mirroring of the fast getting faster. Other cultural practices which
do not fit the model are elided. And, finally, it proceeds out of a fundamentally linear view of change which takes the fastest examples as typical of the future, cannot take in the construction of new pockets of
slowness, cannot understand that spatial variation does not take place
around a mean but is itself constitutive, and does not therefore detect
that whereas certain networks may be fast, such networks are usually
very narrow and pass the majority by. As Benjamin recognized, great
care therefore needs to be taken, since the adoption of this perspective
can lead to either a nostalgic anti-technological perspective or a pro-
technological affirmation, or even celebration (Caygill 1998). In fact, the
effects of technological speed-up can be baleful (see Shenk 1998), but
they can also be positive (see, for example, Thrift 2000c).

One more little matter needs to be addressed. And that is the rise of
mass media. Since Simmel and Benjamin's day the mass media have
become general on a scale that even they might not have foreseen: they
now provide a comprehensive ambient ecology. So, for example, both
DeNora (2000) and McCarthy (2001), point to the large number of
ways in which recorded music and television, respectively, now variously
inhabit urban spaces and times, often marking them only very faintly
with their presence – but still there, even so. Un-remarkable. Every-day.
As the media have become more general, so their effects have become
more differentiated and more complex, as well as more powerful. It is no
longer possible to think of the mass media as one superordinate thing.
There are many different kinds of site-specific media being produced for
and by many different kinds of audience. The mass media both link and
fragment and their influence on cities cannot be reduced to either a
capitalist phantasmagoria of images, or a speculative extension of experience (Burgin 1998; Donald 1999). They represent a very broad range
of engagements, a statement which is underlined by the fact that 'place-
based media must always interact with the unpredictability of user trajectories and local systems' (McCarthy 2001: 113). In other words,
everyday localities in which the media are sited do not constitute simply
variations on a global theme (for example, network ideologies). They
cross and complicate in ways which are themselves constructive.

Near and Far

These little matters should at least give us pause as we fashion overarching theories of, for example, a capitalist imperium (Negri and Hardt 2000). In particular, they suggest we need to unpick some of the ways in which the global and the local show up in cities. In this section we will attempt this task through the notion of propinquity. Much work concerning the city has been concerned with either privileging or dismissing nearness and it is therefore propinquity that we will use as the motif which supports the rest of this chapter. We want to think propinquity through the city and the city through propinquity.

Commentators on the city very often reduce its problems to the re-placement of thick 'local' face-to-face interaction taking place in 'small' communities by thinner interaction taking place 'at-a-distance' in 'large' communities (see box 2.1). The switch from one form of sociospatial relation to another produces alienation, dysfunction, anomie. This kind of narrative was particularly popular in the nineteenth century as told through distinctions such as *gemeinschaft* and *gesellschaft* but has been reproduced into the twentieth-first century in concerns over, for example, the loss of the local in informated cities, which, at the same time, convey a profound threat to what it is to be human (Virilio, 1991). Another way of telling this story is as the progressive detachment of social organization from space – to be found in ideas like 'disembedding' and 'time-space compression'. This kind of narrative dates from Marx but has enjoyed a recent revival in the work of Anthony Giddens and David Harvey. Simmel put it best, perhaps, in his analysis of 'a progressive historical development towards forms of social organisation increasingly detached from space'. More specifically, for Simmel, 'space as the basis of social organisation (principle of locality) signifies a stage of development that emerges between particularistic (principle of affairs) and modern (money economy) techniques of organisation and domination' (cited in Frisby 1991: 107). The development of the full money economy results, therefore, in a progressive detachment from space, helped by communication techniques that enable space to be overcome by time.

For us, these kinds of narrative suffer from three failures. First, they are simply too simple. For example, by reducing technology to a kind of Promethean force rather than a *crystallized* social relation they produce tales of linear progress which are at odds with the historical evidence. Second, they are rooted in a humanism which mourns the death of the local as a pulling apart of all that is truly human, leaving only a simulated humanity shorn of the most important values. Third, they allow

Box 2.1   The geography of the face

For Simmel the 'mask of rationality' in cities defaced instincts and emotions, and restricted communications interaction to the informational equivalent of exchange value (Taussig 2000). That this thesis is, to put it but mildly, overwrought can be demonstrated by asking the question 'what is "face-to-face" communication?' Such a simple question turns out to be much more complex than might be thought, but that very complexity makes it difficult to accept Simmel's point of view.

For us, in large part, the city is made up of faces coming into and out of view. The face is clearly the most important element of the body's communicative apparatuses, containing, as it does, the eyes (and especially the cues provided by eye movement and blinking), the nose (smell is a potent social indicator), the mouth (which is both a visual cue and of course the means of vocalization), the forty-two muscles of the face, and the skin (with its capacity to blush and otherwise indicate bodily states). The face is clearly a rich communicative environment which, along with gesture – with which it is closely implicated (McNeil 1992) – is the chief indicator of affect and spontaneous expression (Ekman 1992). It is clearly foolish to argue that the range of signals and information provided by face-to-face communication can ever be fully substituted.

But we need to be careful to differentiate between the importance of face-to-face communication and the necessity of close contact. To begin with, we have the ability to read the face, and the body more generally, from surprisingly long distances. For example, a smile can be seen from up to eighty feet, a finger raised in anger from the same distance, and a shout can be heard from a hundred feet. As importantly, the face is increasingly mobile. A face can be seen on a television screen, on a video or film, on an advertising hoarding, and so on. As videophones appear, so the distanced face will sink into mundane practice.

But there are, even so, clear limits – according to the task in hand. Thus:

> all the technology in the world does not – at least yet and maybe never – replace face-to-face contact when it comes to brainstorming, inspiring passion, or enabling many kinds of serendipitous discovery. A study of geographically dispersed new product development

teams found that team members conducting complex tasks always would have preferred to have a 'richer' medium (that is, one supporting more channels and more interactive) than they actually had to use. Fax is fine for one-way communication, e-mail for two way, asynchronous, and relatively emotionless communication (where capital letters are 'shocking' and therefore taboo); telephone for communications that require no visual aids; and videoconferencing if no subtlety in body language is necessary. But face-to-face communication is the richest, multi-channel medium because it enables all the senses, is interactive and immediate. (Leonard and Swap 1999: 160)

Even so, the face has never been just embodied experience. There is, for example, evidence to suggest that the very existence of the face relies on the invention of tools. The disappearance of the muzzle in humans, essential equipment for most vertebrates, seems to be a result of the evolution of hands and tool-using: 'A muzzle thrusts teeth outward so they can close like a trap, killing and wounding . . . But our teeth lie within the skull and they make awkward weapons. We manufacture better ones instead, and our hands have evolved original grip positions to handle them and other tools' (McNeil 1992: 20).

So Simmel was wrong – but perhaps not for so much longer. For, increasingly, bodies can now be read by machine. We are reaching a point where voice recognition systems are able to read speech. And we are reaching a point where facial recognition systems are becoming surprisingly accurate, as a result of the evolution of systems like the Facial Action Coding System (FACS) (Ekman and Rosenberg 1997), and the various other 'advanced recognition systems' which are already 75 per cent accurate. More ominously, these systems are able to infer 'internal' body states like emotions and various kinds of psychopathology. Before long machines will be able to simulate certain aspects of the face's communicative functions. The city will therefore become, through these systems, something that is beginning to read us. Perhaps, here, there is a new incarnation of the flâneur?

the effectivity of space no room; it is shoehorned into a narrative which leaves it no latitude; its history is predetermined. The sheer richness of the spaces that are possible in the city is reduced to a supine contingency. Space becomes a dependent variable of social process, never able to take any serious role in the flourishing of the urban social imaginary.

In other words, we have to be careful – and that care takes three forms. First of all, as we argued in chapter 1, the need to theorize without generalizing. Too often, writings about the city have taken hold of one process and presumed that it will become general, thus blotting out other forms of life. For example, commodification is assumed to be a remorseless process, a process which must end in a cultural meltdown. So shopping malls become the battleships of capitalism, bludgeoning consumers into unconsciousness. Or take the example of information technology, which, again, is very often assumed to be a linear process ending in cultural apocalypse. So the internet becomes the haunt of no-brainers, leaking their consciousness into the digital aether. Yet recent ethnographies of shopping malls and information technology not only show that such depictions are exaggerations which chronically under-estimate the skilled response of consumers, but, more importantly, show just how variegated the response to such processes can be, to the point where the whole notion of process needs to be retheorized as something more open.

Then we need to be careful about space. There are many different kinds of space, not just one, and the smallest spatialities can also have the largest social consequences. The different kinds of spaces are legion: there are, to name but a few, continuous, planar regions that emphasize exclusive-ness and borders; there-and-back again networks; fluid spaces that em-phasize interaction and proliferate; more than one place at once spaces that mix up proximity and distance, and so on (Thrift and Olds 1996). And these spaces make a difference. For example, recent work in anthro-pology has been able to show the way in which these spaces are con-structed and interfere with each other. Such spaces can express the chief tenets of a culture in the merest strip of interaction (Linde-Larsson 1998). Thus Weiss catalogues the minutest spatial traceries of Haya culture: the placement of a meal and the position of cooked food and of those who eat it all have a clear and coherent spatial and temporal integrity. 'A Haya household can define itself as a *place* only through its ability to control the relation of what is inside with what lies outside, and the passage that must take place between these positions' (Weiss 1996: 110). This work of definition takes place in all sorts of registers, from sight (being able to be seen, or not) to all kinds of other forms of tactility.

Then there is one more reason to be careful. And that is the matter of novelty. The city, through its complexity and certainty, allows for unex-pected juxtapositions at all kinds of levels – the meeting in the street, the rich and poor areas cheek by jowl, the lack of control of public spaces, and so on. All kinds of forces may conspire to nullify these juxtaposi-tions – greater and greater surveillance, the growth of programmed slips of interaction of the 'have a nice day' variety, and so on. But the fact remains that the city, through these juxtapositions, is also a potent generator of novelty. We should not overdo this – few unexpected juxtapositions set off jolts to the established order, but they can still grate and harry. The fact remains that it is much easier to depict the city as a generator of order than of disorder, as predictable than unpredictable, as striated rather than smooth. Somehow, however, we need to remember how open the city can be to possibility. As we argue in chapter 6, it consists of openings as well as closures.

Distanciated Communities

In order to provide some substance to the above discussion on propinquity and flow, let us move to the topic of the urban community. Why? Because it has proved perhaps one of the most consistently engaging topics in the urban literature, a topic that is continually returned to, both because it has never been satisfactorily addressed and because it is able to stand for so much.

Why has community held such a power to fascinate in the urban literature? There are, we think, five main reasons. To begin with, the history of community has been bedevilled by the idea of a collective, whose members move together and think as one, in a naturalized co-dependency (Buck-Morss 2000). Then, the community is usually seen as able to exist precisely because of the intimacy of face-to-face communication. The community is therefore present to itself, in a world where meaning is unmediated. Then again, the community extends into the past. As tradition, memory plays a crucial role: the present lies heavy under the weight of its legacy. It follows, then, that community is invariably 'local'. Messages pass from hand to hand. Protest takes the form of gatherings. And there is one more reason. Community is able to exist precisely because these kinds of characterizations have allowed it to be visualized, mapped, surveyed, pinned in place. A whole set of knowledges of community has come into existence – in part because of the devotion to an idea of community. Communities' attitudes and values are continually surveyed through various technologies that ensure that communities exist and can be measured (Rose 1999).

This, then, is a community of being rather than becoming, one spot in space, one slot in time. And it is a community of be-longing – for it is hard not to see in this literature a certain nostalgia for a way of life which has bypassed the actual history of the past in order to critique the symptoms of the present.

Whatever the case, we can say that community cannot and does not exist as a problem now in a way it did for former writers. The most obvious reason is that contemporary life has posed the question of community against a backdrop rather different from before. In particular, note must be taken of the very high levels of mobility that now typify western urban civilization. Modern cities are extraordinary agglomerations of flows. There is, to begin with, the movement of people. For example, each weekday morning in London, between 7 a.m. and 10 a.m., the number of people in the central city increases by 1.3 million: 85 per cent of these people arrive on public transport (41 per cent on trains, 35 per cent on the underground and 8 per cent by bus), 12 per cent travel by car and 2 per cent by bicycle. Of course, this movement of people in London doesn't stop at 10 a.m.:

> The 'rush hour' is only the beginning of a steady increase in commercial activity that peaks in the mid-afternoon, much of it involving short journeys which ensure pressure on the city's transport network is fairly constant. The statistics are breath-taking: during an average day, from 120,000 bus-stops around the city, travellers make four million journeys on 5,000 buses; while below street level with its 274 stations, 392 miles of track, 500 trains and a staff of 16,000, London Underground facilitates some 2.5 million journeys. (Barley 2000: 9)

Figures like these ignore other aspects of a city's footprint (see chapter 1), and in particular, air travel. For example, over 100 million passengers fly into the airports of Heathrow, Gatwick, Stansted, City and Luton each year, and these airports have themselves become major employers. Heathrow employs 55,000 people. And these figures ignore the vast movements of actual materials into and out of cities. Take the case of food. A city like London will need to import at least 5,000 tonnes of food a day, food which is coming from greater and greater distances. Between 1979 and 1994 the amount of food transported around the UK hardly changed, but the average distance travelled increased by 50 per cent. Food also comes from increasingly diverse and exotic locations. New Covent Garden Market in London forms the centre of the UK's wholesale trade in fruit and vegetables. On average, each day, some 45,000 vehicles visit the site to take away produce from all around the world. In the course of the year, traders source over 160 varieties of fruit and 180 vegetables, 70 per cent of which are imported (Barley 2000; Meier 1999).

Other forms of mobility are also important. Of these, the most salient is clearly information. Cities are, as Castells (1996) has pointed out, informational kaleidoscopes constantly producing new patterns of under-standing. A world city like London, for example, is an extraordinary conglomeration of fibre-optic cables, radio spectra, digital lines and good old-fashioned copper cable.

Thus, though there is currently a lot of hyperbole, it seems difficult to deny that the modern city is unprecedently based on mobility, and, more-over, a mobility that seems to increase year on year: passenger miles travelled in the United Kingdom in 1998 were 30 per cent higher than in 1990, while the average distance travelled per person in 1998 was 14,500 miles, up from 12,440 in 1990 (and 5,640 in 1960) (Imrie 2000). More importantly, what we experience as 'city' is premised on this mobility:

> London looks like it does, and is organised in the way that it is, precisely because people have always moved around it. It may be the landmark buildings which characterise individual cities in our minds, but while Big Ben and Nelson's Column let us know we are in London, the way we move around these immobile monuments has been especially important in the delineation of the city. London is London because of this. (Barley 2000: 12)

So, against the background of constant shuttle in which mobility has come to be taken for granted, how can we understand urban commun-ity? We argue that all kinds of communal bonds still exist in cities. Some of these are still *localized*. What few studies there are, for example (see Hoggett 1991; Finnegan 1989), suggest that in quite unlikely urban settings, all kinds of localized associations still continue to thrive (see box 2.2). But many other communal bonds are no longer localized: they successfully persist at a distance, posing new tests of reciprocal resolu-tion and commitment, constructing new forms of intentionality, building new types of presence. Once we move away from notions of face-to-face or heavily localized interactions as the only kind of authority, these communal bonds are not difficult to see. We will point to just five.

The first of these is the *planned community*. Although many comment-ators write about the jumble of urban life, in a number of very significant ways urban life has actually become more planned through the existence of various technologies of government, and especially the tyranny of the address that now prevails in modern societies. Based on the imperatives of the nation-state and, increasingly, commerce, the city is being fixed, positioned, guided as never before. The map, the census, postcodes, area codes, licence plates and other means of producing location have been joined to technologies like geographical information systems, global positioning systems and so on, and to the paraphernalia of choice and

Box 2.2   Urban anglers

Just how many 'little communities' exist in cities we do not know, but we can be sure that many have been overlooked because they do not fit the bill. Take the case of city anglers. Britain's major cities support 'an unexpected, passionate and buoyant community of fishermen who are out every day of the year throwing lines into the wide, fast-flowing, tidal rivers . . . park lakes, canals and heavily stocked commercial fisheries known as "holes in the ground"' (Spicer 2000: 45).

Take the case of London. In 1999 the Environment Agency sold just under 200,000 rod licences in London (a fifth of the total issued annually in England and Wales). 'Nearly all these London urban anglers are still . . . men: engineers, carpenters, first generation stockbrokers, kids, old boys and a few crooks. In a month, I met as many male strippers as women anglers, meaning one. None of them was posh' (Spicer 2000: 44). They go after barbel, rudd, tench, bream and roach: after three decades of clean-up, 116 species of fish can be found in London's waters. The most ambitious go for big fish like carp. 'The "carpers" are rough nutters. [They] will just go and sit with beers, a few spliffs, off their head sometimes. I enjoy bivvying as much as the next bloke, but I got into fishing cos I like nature and having a laugh. If these boys caught a f****** great pike, they'd just sling it on the side. Bream? They'd sling it. It's all competition for the carp's feed, innit?' (Spicer 2000: 44).

The city anglers mainly fish for recreation but there are competitive leagues: London has some of the best match anglers in the world. But the competition for the fish is undoubtedly growing. There are the cormorants, now breeding inland. There are the newly introduced species like Turkish crayfish, terrapins, goldfish and catfish which spread disease. And there are Eastern and Central European refugees who have started to take and *eat* (often quite legally) fish.

The waters themselves act as a kind of urban microcosm. The occasional body. The ubiquitous shopping trolley (a great lure for some fishes). The remnants of Hindu funerals. The menace of bike-riders who snap rods. The endless crisps packets and drinks cans. And in the middle, the angler: 'It's like meditation, firstly, the water is a mirror on your mind. When you are staring at the water you can't see any advertising hoardings, the city is there, but it is

not crowding into your head. It's a way to escape the nine-to-five'
(Spicer 2000: 46).

And communities like this work not only locally but also at a
distance. There are magazines, newsletters, websites, chat rooms –
all the paraphernalia of enthusiasm.

opinion like surveys, polls and focus groups, to produce a means of
continuous recognition which has two registers. To begin with, this new
set of fixes enables tracking of motion, allowing continuous adjustment
of system to circumstance. This is the modulated *society* (Deleuze 1992).
Then, the set of fixes also makes it much easier to produce spatial cat-
egorizations, so that the portion of human subjects dwelling in databases
becomes increasingly determinate: you become where you live.

The second form of community is a *post-social* and post-human one. As
software and other technological entities become more prominent in cities,
so the notion of the relationship, and of sociality, needs to be disassociated
from its fixation on human groups (Knorr-Cetina 1999, 2001). This is to
say more than that all relations are modified by technological objects.
Rather it is to say that non-human objects now act with humans in ways
which are not subordinate and which challenge accepted notions of reciprocity and solidarity. They build sites on which a whole world is erected.
For example, think of the predominance of computer screens in cities.
These are not just passive intermediaries. They assemble and implement
on one platform the previously dispersed activities of a whole series of
diverse human agents, taking those activities to themselves.

The third form of community is more familiar: the growth of *new
forms of human sociality*, new modes of reciprocity, which extend social
relations in new ways. A series of those forms come to mind. To begin
with, there are new means of *'light' sociality*; groups that come together
briefly around a particular purpose and then disperse again. A good illus-
tration of such groups consists of young people involved in consumption,
at malls and other such sites, who are able to produce certain dimensions
of their identity through this kind of social contact (cf. Shields 1994;
Miller et al. 1998).

A second group consists of 'enthusiasts', 'little platoons' of those with
like interests. These *bunds* (Schmalenbach 1977; Hetherington 1998) are
forms of mobile sociation which involve 'community building that is consciously and freely chosen on the basis of mutual sentiment and *emotional
feeling*' (Urry 2000: 143). Such groups tend to be relatively informal,

overlapping networks defined culturally (rather than politically or socially in terms of a national civil society), and are joined out of choice. Urry (2000) lists a series of contemporary examples, all of which thrive in modern cities: food, gender, animals, vegetarianism, DIY, pets, alternative medicine, local places, the countryside, festivities, road protests, dance culture and the array of specialized leisure practices based on heritage, conservation and preservation. Bunds depend heavily on technologies that overcome distance – cheap travel, the internet, and so on – to survive. A third group consists of *friends*. Negative factors like the decline of the extended nuclear family have combined with positive factors like the large numbers of pubs and clubs and other institutions of sociality in large cities, the rise of same-sex cultures, the increasing ease of travel and the increase in shared homes. Friendship has become a motivating force in cities (cf. Thrift 1996b). These are the families we choose.

Then there are *diasporic communities*, where the belonging and identification is anything but local. The close-knit family, clan, kin and ethnic connections within a diaspora enable it to set up circuits of migration *and* subsequent mobility (in contrast to old-style migration) which are clearly dependent on a few very particular cities. Thus as bell hooks writes, 'home is no longer one place, it is locations' (1991: 148). Some of these locations are sites around the world, but others are relationships and imaginaries of a different kind, which also contribute to community. With the intensive growth of global migration and travel, many cities have seen a remarkable flowering of these new forms of mobile sociality whose chief characteristic is that they can and do thrive over long distances. 'The concept of space is itself transformed when it is seen in terms of the ex-centric communicative circuitry that has enabled dispersed populations to converse, interact, and more recently even to synchronise significant elements of their social and cultural lives' (Gilroy 2000: 129). None of this is to say that there is no yearning for community. Indeed, given conditions of displacement, local hostility and the highly self-conscious nature of many of these cultural constructions, this yearning may well be greater than that felt by non-diasporic communities. Rather than a 'pre-given sameness', there has to be 'will, inclination, mood, and affinity' (Gilroy 2000: 133).

There is a further form of community. This is *everyday life* itself. We do not have to take on the romanticism of de Certeau's notion of tactics to validate everyday life because large parts of what goes on in the city are still uncontrolled, a part of the city's processual excess. This excess consists of both the 'whatever', 'the white space of conjunctions, meetings and discussions, the part of the event which is non reducible to the state of things, the mystery of the begun-again present' (Deleuze 1986:

108), and the 'meanwhile', that moment between that which 'neither takes place or follows, but is present in the immensity of the empty time where the event can be seen that is still to come and yet has already passed' (Deleuze 1997: 5). In other words, everyday life always has an 'extra' term, that goes 'beyond', as found, for example, in Lefebvre's conception of 'everydayness' as a lived force (Lefebvre 1991; Seigworth 2000) which is also a kind of virtual commonality, one in which terms like 'far', 'deep' and 'distant' are replaced by rhythms which fold time and space in all kinds of untoward localizations and intricate mixtures. In a sense, everyday life is 'what is left over' when all the systems of the city have been factored out – but that is, we would argue, a lot.

Everyday life, in a residual sense, defined by 'what is left over' after all superior, specialized, structured activities have been singled out by analysis, must be defined as a totality. Condensed in their specialization and this technicality, superior activities leave a 'technical vacuum' between one another which is filled up by everyday life. Everyday life is profoundly related to all activities, and encompasses them with all their differences and their conflicts; it is their meeting ground, their bond, their common ground. And it is in everyday life that the sum total of relations which make the human – and every human being – a whole takes its shape and form. In it are expressed and fulfilled those relations which bring into play the totality of the real, albeit in a certain manner which is always partial and incomplete: friendship, comradeship, love, the need to communicate, play, etc. (Lefebvre 1991: 97).

Thus, the community of the banal and the mundane, but also the community of improvisation, intuition, play. The community of taking place, not place. The community that cannot be classified. The community without an identity in which 'humans co-belong without any representable conditions of belonging' (Agamben 1993: 86). The community we have in common. The coming community. We shall explore some of the implications of this position in the last chapter of the book.

Finally there is one more community we need to consider, the community at-a-distance of modern forms of *sympathy* for others. This is the mediatized version of Adam Smith's *Theory of Moral Sentiments* (see Thrift 1997). For it is clear that an extension of sympathy for others is going on, as a result of the capacity of modern media to construct and dramatize terrible events occurring at a distance, and to mobilize support for ameliorative actions. One does not have to fall into either 'a sunny celebration of the notion of kindness or an easy denunciation of the perverse spectator' (Boltanski 1999: xiv) to see that this is an important phenomenon. In particular, we can see the gradual joining together of the descriptions and depictions of people suffering and the concern of those informed of that suffering through effects on speech ('did you see . . . ?', 'what can we do?' and so on), emotion, and the self (Taylor 1991), leading to a politics of pity which undoubtedly contains all kinds of ambiguity (distress as entertainment, emotional wallowing, passive suffering, etc.) but also contains capacity for action. But it is not easy, uncomplicated action:

> the multiplication of victims, their distance in time and space, the difficulty of counting them and above all of bringing them together under the same rubric (as victims of imperialism for example) and ranking them tends to exhaust the reserves of indignation and give way to 'indifference and apathy'. [The] emphasis on the need to reach victims in order to give a political meaning to pity is not solely due to the scarcity of the technical means which can be deployed to come to their aid but also, or perhaps especially, to the scarcity of media space which cannot be filled by the representation of every case of suffering all at the same time and finally, as [Amato] explicitly suggests, to the relative scarcity of emotional resources which can be mobilised to cope with it. (Boltanski 1999: 169)

The wonderful thing is that the contemporary city can be understood in all these ways, and yet is not reducible to any one of them. Though we are still the heirs of *gemeinschaft* and *gesellschaft*, we are moving towards a different, more restless and more dispersed, vocabulary through a constant struggle over the three Rs of urban life: new social relationships, new means of representation and new means of resistance. Together, the experiments with these three Rs may add up to new, more 'distanciated' modes of belonging, which we can now at least glimpse.

The Restless Site

Perhaps the most exacting, exciting and enticing attempts to produce these new modes of belonging have been taking place in contemporary architecture and performance art as they have tried to redefine – in practice – what is meant by place as liv*ing* rather than liv*ed* space. In these disciplines, there is both a growing sense of the importance of tacit, embodied spatial stories (like the layout of childhood houses) which inhabit our dreams and produce a kind of spatial unconscious, and, at the same time, a continuing sense of social critique. In other words, the language of built form can never be severed from either dwelling or critique, and so the sign is never allowed to lord it over significance (Harries 1996). This kind of 'place theory' (Dovey 1999), though often written off as nostalgic or uncommitted, is actually crucial to how we are able to understand belonging, which must always take place as specific phenomenalities.

The grand scheme is always shot through by an enfilade of spatial practices, which have their own rhythms of appearance and disappearance, anticipations and memories (Lees 2001). The new performance art and architecture therefore have four characteristics. First, they are dynamic, they are 'characterised precisely in their acting out of a process' (Oldenburg 1967: 51), which, like its object, is continually 'on the way between one point and another' (Kaye 2000: 123). Second, they attempt to produce this dynamic by understanding the city as a gradual unfolding of spaces and times, working at different speeds and in different measures. Buildings are seen as mobile and as in movement, as in Zaha Hadid's operations on space, which are intended to open out the potentiality of a particular space through general techical means. Third, they rest on a particular understanding of architecture, somewhat in line with Benjamin's notions of architecture as 'tactile appropriation', as constantly being transformed by use, its boundaries renegotiated by habits. Thus Benjamin regarded architecture as

> the perennial art, the one which is in many respects the most porous and sensitive to change from outside, whether in technology or in its 'relationship to the masses'. [Benjamin] reads a litany of art forms (which) have developed and persisted – 'tragedy', 'epic', 'panel painting' while architecture adapted and survived. The key to its survival lies not only in its porosity, but also (and relatedly) in the 'canonical value' of its 'mode of appropriation'. This is both 'tactile' and 'optical' based in 'use' and 'perception'. Against the attentive, conscious contemplation of the viewer of paintings Benjamin poses the distracted, habitual use of architecture. By 'distracted' he does not mean lack of attention, but rather a different, more flexible mode of perception. This form of perception is a response to the effects of the technological transformation of the space and time of experience. 'For the tasks which face the human apparatus of perception at the turning points of history cannot be solved by optical means, that is, by contemplation, alone. They are mustered gradually by habit, under the guidance of tactile appropriation.' (Benjamin, cited in Caygill 1998: 115)

Furthermore, these habits are developed and practised collectively; tactile appropriation proceeds by collective testing and communication of results (Caygill 1998: 115). In other words, rather like Cézanne's paintings, this is a kind of questioning of the material by pushing it to 'the point where it encounters paradox, and begins to follow a contrary logic' (Clark 2001: 94). It is a kind of ethic of performance and improvisation which is both consoling and encouraging. Then, last, both performance art and architecture are therefore engaged with trying to redefine be-longing. But not naively. For example, they are well aware of the import of Benjamin's technological unconscious, and most particularly of late the way in which digital technology redefines both possibilities and palette. Hence, the work in architecture of say Bernard Tschumi or Greg Lynn or Steven Holl or Lebbeus Woods contrives a thickening of space and time made possible by new technological quotations which themselves question presenced belonging, in which horizons are 'spinning points in space-time' (Holl 2000: 18) and modes of expanding thought, not just optical conditions.

To summarize, what both architecture and performance art offer is an expansion of potential, 'a widening of the ways that space might be in-habited in . . . cities' (Vidler 2000: 202). This is a kind of studied optimism about the virtualities of space. 'The essence of the claim is this: space exists not by fiat, but only by virtue of action, and choice is action's highest form' (Vidler 2000: 208). Easy enough to communicate, no doubt. And yet this *art of the question* can – perhaps – itself form a kind of restless politics of ellipses, drifts and leaks of meaning which keeps defamiliarization alive by juxtaposing events rather than just facades (Tschumi 1996).

Conclusion

It is something of an irony that at a point where there is considerable questioning of the notion of community in the urban literature it is being imported into work on urban economies, as a key explanation of differ-ential economic success. For example, writers such as Michael Storper, Allen Scott, and many others, whom we discuss in the following chapter, have used a notion of locally based untraded interdependencies (such as reflexivity and learning deriving from local business ties) in their explana-tion of why some cities are more competitive than others. Yet a similar argument concerning the importance of social ties in the economic life of cities (such as trust, reciprocity) could be made without reducing these ties to a local field of interaction. Trust, for example, in transnational corporations is increasingly constructed around communities of dispersed employees and plants, supported by varied technologies of travel and communication, which are neither global nor local. In the next chapter we further develop our theorization of proximity by reinterpreting some of the recent writings on the urban economy, in an attempt to shift the analytical register away from the urban economy as a bounded space towards the urban economy as a dispersed space of circulation.

3 CITIES IN A DISTANCIATED ECONOMY

Introduction

The new vocabulary of distanciation that we have developed in chapter 2 has crucial consequences for how we think of the spatiality of the city. Nowhere is this clearer than in questions concerning the foundations of urban economic life. For a long time now, work on urban economies has been framed in terms of points, lines and boundaries. Thus cities have been seen as entities that can be cut up into centres and peripheries, positioned against other cities in an urban hierarchy, sites of production or consumption, but rarely both. The latest manifestations of this kind of thinking can be seen in work on global cities and on industrial districts and knowledge-based agglomerations. Though much of this work acknowledges the role of cities as relay stations in a world of flows, still, it falls back on a language of clustering, agglomeration and localization. This language, almost inevitably, replicates a number of exclusionary dualisms which are not helpful in considering the nature of modern cities: the world as a space of flows versus the urban as a space of fixity, the global as remote versus the local as proximate, face-to-face as small versus distanciated as large, and so on.

Yet what seems clear about modern economies is that they can no longer be contained by these kinds of habits of thought because they are always both local and global, here and there, in between. They are increasingly structured around flows of people, images, information and money moving within and across national borders. This, in turn, as Urry puts it, 'generates within any existing "society" a complex, overlapping, disjunctive order of off-centredness, as these multiple flows are chronically combined and recombined across times and spaces often unrelated to the regions of existing societies, often following a kind of hypertextual patterning' (2000: 36).

Following this cue for an alternative topology (see also Amin 2001), we propose a different kind of reading of the economy of cities. Instead of conceiving cities as either bounded or punctured economic entities, we see them as assemblages of more or less distanciated economic relations which will have different intensities at different locations. Economic organization now is irremediably distributed. Even when economic activity seems to be spatially clustered, a close examination will reveal that the clusters rely on a multiplicity of sites, institutions and connections, which do not just stretch beyond these clusters, but actually constitute them. For example, Silicon Valley is instanciated by the policies of the Indian and Irish governments to produce a steady flow of highly qualified software engineers through select universities. Economic life has travelled far along the road of industrial organization, and it is no longer obvious that cities remain a central institution. Markets are no longer proximate or locally regulated; production is globally organized and globally sourced; economic resources – from capital and labour to information and know-how – have become extraordinarily mobile; everyday contact is now possible at a distance through the availability of digital and fibre-optic technology; economic regulation occurs through rules and standards set by national and international institutions; and economic power is exerted through the activities of large corporations, cartels and business organizations.

With an understanding of economic organization as distanciated, we advance three readings of the urban economy in this chapter. First, we see cities as institutional settings and as sites of economic circulation, not forcing houses of competitiveness, nor the ground on which economic inputs and outputs combine. We suggest that cities could be seen as sources of institutionalized knowledge, or sites of sociability which help to cement economic transactions. This is a role of the lubrication and translation of economic flows, not that of securing economic returns to place.

Second, given the growth of industrial organization, we suggest that it makes sense to interpret the economic significance of cities in institutional terms. If there is any 'grounding' of the economy in cities, it is through the routinization of 'site practices'. This might be through the density of informal institutions such as meeting places, or formal institutions offering business services and know-how. Such an emphasis on institutional assets allows us to retain a sense of the centrality of cities in economic life, but without the assumption often made in economic geography that the spatiality of cities (the powers of agglomeration, density, proximity) generates special economic effects.

Third, we wish to take the discussion on the economics of cities beyond local supply considerations. We wish to recover the role of demand, while recognizing that urban consumption is less and less met through local provision, as we have already pointed out through the example of Covent Garden in chapter 2. The urban economy gathers a variety of services (producer, personal, public and welfare), activities associated with retail, leisure, recreation and tourism, and initiatives in the informal and non-profit sectors. These too need recognition in any theorization of the economics of cities. However, such theorization has to acknowledge that the definition of the local is historically specific. Today, with labour markets constantly expanding, commuter belts constantly extending, and distribution networks feeding ever-growing market areas, the urban – or whatever counts as a city – is constantly being redefined, even though administrative boundaries constantly lag behind this process. In other words, in nearly every economic register, cities are becoming increasingly unbound as discrete spaces. Hence, even in our account of consumption, we stress the economics of circulation.

We begin with a history of the prevailing literature and the recent tendency to reduce cities as territorial sources of economic competitiveness. We then develop an alternative account that situates cities in the context of distanciated economic flows and networks. We shift the emphasis away from the localized practices of firms towards the light support provided by varied urban institutions and towards the economics of everyday consumption.

The Urbanized Economy

In the 1950s and 1960s the link between industrialization and urbanization encouraged researchers to explain industrial agglomeration and its effects on economic performance. Critics of equilibrium economics such as Albert Hirschman, Nicholar Kaldor, François Perroux and Gunnar Myrdal asserted that agglomeration in cities offered firms increasing returns to scale linked to market size, as well as new business opportunities associated with growing urban density and specialization. In turn, agglomeration was said to help firms to enhance economic performance by reducing transport and transaction costs and making available varied specialized skills, inputs, services and know-how. The city was seen to offer rich market opportunities, the advantages of proximity and the benefits of product specialization. Here is a typical example of this kind of bounded account of the urban economy:

> To an economist, a city is a dynamic system of interrelated and inter-
> dependent markets characterized by great density and specialization of
> economic actors as well as certain institutional conditions that influence
> decision making by many different governments, each of which has limited
> authority and competence. These markets serve and are served by large
> numbers of persons and firms located in relatively close proximity. Cities
> specialize in efficiently providing households and firms with contacts and
> flows of information at lower cost than do other spatial forms of spatial
> organization. (Hirsch 1973: 2–3)

It became common to describe the organizational space of the national
and international economy in terms of a hierarchy of urban economic
systems, with firms seen to derive initial market opportunities and sources
of competitive advantage from within each system.

Such an interpretation of the urban economy was challenged in the
late 1970s, when, with the onset of metropolitan deindustrialization,
urban density came to be treated as an economic cost (traffic congestion,
housing shortage, high rents, the militancy of the mass worker). The
dispersal of industry to remote regions and non-metropolitan areas was
now seen by some as economically desirable, as it offered, for example,
cheap labour, compliant workforces, new markets. The link between
localization and economic performance was no longer seen as necessarily
virtuous.

A further push came from the rise of Marxist and Weberian thinking
keen to replace the earlier spatial fetishism with an analysis of cities in
the context of the varied and uneven geography of the capitalist economy.
Thus, famously, Manuel Castells (1977) and David Harvey (1985)
explored the link between urbanization and capital accumulation, by
emphasizing, for example, the role of capital sunk in the built environment, while Doreen Massey (1984) highlighted patterns of urban change
associated with developments in the capitalist division of labour (for
instance, the internationalization of production in the hands of large
corporations). Capital, rather than space, became the prime unit of
explanation.

With this kind of displacement, urban economic theory no longer
assumed local linkage and local systemic integrity. Instead, the city
became a site linked to and constituted by a wider capitalist spatiality.
The economic power of major cities was explained in terms of their role
as centres of global command and control, based on the presence of
global corporations, the transnational capitalist class, and labour power
from around the world (Sassen 1994). Similarly, Castells (1989, 1996)
developed his thesis on the rise of a new phase of capitalism, to describe
cities as the hubs and spokes of knowledge production and transmission

in a new global 'space of flows' of information, people and commodities. Where evidence was found of industrial clustering (financial centres, high-tech clusters, industrial districts, media clusters), these sites were seen, at least by some, as the forcing houses of international networks (Amin and Thrift 1992).

The parochial gave way to the cosmopolitan, and the local was seen as part of the global. In this new setting, a question that concerned urban practitioners was whether global integration implied local economic disintegration. City leaders worried about whether localized linkage would lose out to international linkage through the activities of transnational corporations or the rise of global sourcing and subcontracting patterns. What, they asked, would it take to reconcile international integration with self-sustaining local economic development? While policy-makers puzzled over this question, a new line of interpretation of the urban economy emerged in the 1990s. It was an account that rediscovered the territorial foundations of the economy. Economists such as Paul Krugman (1991) insisted that international trade advantage continued to draw on economies of scale offered to firms through local market opportunities in agglomerations. The home base, and local market linkage, thus still mattered. Michael Porter (1995) similarly stressed the urban base as a source of international competitiveness, through advantages enjoyed by firms in clusters of interrelated industries. Then, sociologists and geographers working on the spaces of the post-mass production economy argued that the new competition would be between region/city-based economic systems. Michael Piore and Charles Sabel (1984) famously claimed that a growth in demand for design-intensive goods favoured a return to local networks of specialized and interdependent firms, able to respond through such organization to the new market circumstances. Similarly, Allen Scott (1988) argued that a new organizational tendency towards vertical disintegration favoured the return of industrial production to cities, with agglomeration helping to reduce transaction costs. Later, Michael Storper (1997) went on to highlight the role of local 'untraded interdependencies', constituted around tacit conventions and informal agreements deemed crucial for economic learning and economic adaptation.

The result is a new localism that is full of policy promise. It allows practitioners to reassure local and national communities that prosperity and economic security remains possible in a borderless world: globalization can be an opportunity. There are new powers to be had from building local community. Through this kind of thinking, places, rather than particular actors within them, are gaining economic subjectivity, a new agency (Rimke 2000). The new localism is producing a new 'urban governmentality' (Osborne and Rose 1999: 755) centred around the powers of spatial proximity (intensity of face-to-face transactions, local knowledge transfers, agglomeration economies). It rests on two major territorial assumptions: first, that urban agglomeration sustains international competitiveness; and second, that cities are the resource base for a new knowledge capitalism. We review these in turn below.

Competitive cities

In May 1999 the entire issue of the journal *Urban Studies* was devoted to the theme of 'competitive cities'. Article after article invoked Alfred Marshall, the classics of the 1950s mentioned earlier, and contemporary lights such as Michael Porter and Paul Krugman, to propose cities as sources of (international) economic competitiveness. The argument made was a familiar one: proximity contributes to productivity by reducing transport and transaction costs for goods, people and ideas (Glaeser 1998); urban density allows labour pooling, product specialization, technological spillovers and further growth through cumulative causation (Krugman 1991, 1995); agglomeration stimulates the clustering of inter-related industries with upstream and downstream linkages (Porter 1995); proximity allows easy travel of ideas due to labour mobility and interfirm contact (Glaeser 1998), while further knowledge spillover (Audretsch 1998) is encouraged by the local industrial atmosphere (Marshall 1890) produced by product specialization and the associated division of labour between firms. In short, the competitiveness of firms is enhanced by cost savings, and knowledge gains and complementarities associated with industrial agglomeration.

The circle can be squared. The prosperity of firms can be tied to the prosperity of cities. The domain of corporate power can be read as the domain of urban power. But can it? What evidence is there to show that firms locate in cities for export orientation or enhanced competitiveness? Do firms depend primarily on local linkage for competitive advantage? The evidence skates on thin ice. Krugman himself is careful to note the limits of how far international competitiveness can be claimed from co-location in cities. He observes, for example, that even in a global powerhouse such as Los Angeles, the bulk of employment is unexceptional, concentrated in 'non-base' activities such as goods and services provided for local consumption, with the export base confined to just a few industries. He comments, 'when you look at the economies of modern cities what you see is . . . a steadily rising share of the work force produces services that are sold only within the same metropolitan area' (Krugman, 1997: 211). Similarly, a study of firms of different sizes and sectors in London found that for 35 per cent of the 4,000 firms surveyed, London was the main market, while only 16 per cent exported overseas (Jones 2000; see also Gordon 1999 for similar findings for business service firms in London). Rightly, as Ian Gordon notes:

> a place's success depends on the productivity, innovativeness and market-orientation of all sectors of the local economy, and not simply on those which are most extensively traded. There is a general temptation to over-look this point by characterising places in terms of the highest-order, most cosmopolitan activities in which they are engaged. (1999: 1009)

What of the role of ties of proximity – the benefits of interfirm coop-eration, face-to-face contact, local transactions, shared knowledge? One study has approached this question by measuring the influence on export performance within 10,000 Swedish manufacturing firms of (a) proxim-ity to similar or related firms ('localization effect'); (b) access to the public goods offered by cities ('urbanization effect'); and (c) internal economies of scale (Malmberg, Malmberg and Lundequist 2000). The study shows the 'localization effect' to be 40–80 times smaller than the 'urbanization effect', and 50–100 times smaller than the effect of scale economies on export performance. It concludes that 'it is the old-fashioned type of economic geography, which is almost extinct today, in which economies of scale and sectoral composition are emphasised, that has given the most accurate identification of the important factors facing firm performance' (2000: 317).

There is no reason to believe that the results are peculiar to the Swed-ish space economy. For example, a study of London-based businesses has found that 'the views of businesses about the key location factors for their type of activity tend to emphasise basic issues of accessibility and the cost/availability of relevant kinds of labour and premises, rather than more sophisticated aspects of the business milieux, which tend to be significant only for small minorities of business' (Gordon and McCann 2000: 522). The study also shows, from evidence gathered for the 1996 London Employer Survey, that only 25 per cent of private sector employment in London is in 'businesses perceiving some advantage in proximity to related activities' (p. 523). These businesses tend to be in specific industries (such as financial and professional services or retailing and leisure) and in particular inner London areas (such as Soho, Covent Garden, City of London, City of Westminster), with clustering offering 'classic' benefits such as shared intelligence, customer attraction and interaction potential. But for the majority of firms – in other sectors and other locations – agglomeration is shown to be of no significance for business performance, and indeed, in some instances, a threat in the form of labour poaching and raised competition.

Other studies have questioned the effects of local networking on business innovation. For example, Jones's study of London cited earlier (Jones 2000) has found very little evidence of learning and innovation based on trust and cooperation with other local firms (for instance, suppliers), or the existence of informal local social ties (though 40 per cent of the firms declared membership of a London-based association or club). Instead, what firms identified as stimuli for business innovation and performance were internal know-how and technological capacity, access to external codified knowledge such as R&D and trade journals, competitor imitation and client-based suggestions. Thus Jones observes that 'propinquity between businesses need not imply close contact, and that factors other than the need to maintain close contact with peers, rivals, suppliers, or customers must be used to explain the apparent geographical "clustering" of certain types of business in London' (2000: 1). Similarly, another study of 1,800 firms located in ten different European regions has shown that product innovations are shaped by intrafirm variables, not regional variables. This applies even in a high-tech region such as Munich, where, if the city matters, it is for the supply of R&D centres and highly qualified technical labour rather than the offer of informal sources of learning and innovation (Sternberg and Arndt 2000).

In summary, much more evidence is required before we can confirm that it is cities rather than firms that compete (Krugman 1997; Begg 1999), that the city has 'a kind of quasi-organic life of its own' (Osborne and Rose 1999: 756). It is on a shaky premise that we seem to have returned to the old idea of the economy as a chain of city systems.

Knowledge cities

The second strand of the new localism places cities at the centre of the knowledge economy. It stresses the cultural resources of the city needed to sustain knowledge entrepreneurs and workers, and it sees cities as a rich source of tacit or formal knowledge. It offers a seductive vision of urban prosperity, one increasingly embraced by city leaders.

The concept of knowledge capitalism has become a mantra. Its gurus predict the weightless economy based on intangible goods and informatics (Coyle 1997; Quah 1997); the incorporation of education, learning and knowledgeability into the everyday decisions of a reflexive society (Giddens 1994); new 'sources of competitive advantage – innovation, design, branding, know-how' (Leadbeater 1999: 10); and risky markets or rapidly changing standards which require a culture of continual learning (Burton-Jones

1999). The new protagonists are the knowledge entrepreneur, adapting specialized know-how for different media (for instance, cooking skills adapted for books, magazines, TV), the fast-paced knowledge worker with no fixed job and no lifelong employment (Leadbeater 1999; Sennett 1998), and the 'wired' subject who, 'animated by virtues of boldness and risk-taking', flits from project to project in the new age of work without careers (Flores and Gray 2000: 21). In the new economy, trust and complementarity will drive success, since 'ideas for new products usually emerge from teams of people drawing together different expertise' (Leadbeater 1999: 13).

As our interest here is in the spatiality of the economy, we do not wish to comment on this broader vision in any detail. Against the hyperbole, however, we would highlight the enduring demand for standardized and tangible goods; the danger of confusing the digitization of communications with the dematerialization of economic transactions (at the end of the wire lie tangible people and tangible goods and services); the persistence in many occupations (such as teaching, public services) of careers and work-based ideologies; the continuation of values of public service, admittedly with an extra dose of entrepreneurialism and increased job mobility; and the continuing value of an older grounded know-how – for instance, in retail and distribution, the care sectors, production and personal services, and in servicing the knowledge economy itself (see Amin, Massey and Thrift 2000).

Let us return to the role of cities in the knowledge economy. They are meant to be a place of orientation and vitality for the *déraciné* knowledge entrepreneur/worker. Leadbeater, himself a freelance journalist, intellectual and consultant, considers himself lucky to live in London because it is 'where ideas and people circulate at great velocity' (1999: 13). The city is a place for knowing, through its density of knowledgeable and creative people and its offer of meeting places for such people. Similarly, another commentator, rather breathtakingly, claims that the 'tyranny of proximity' has become the key asset of the postindustrial city, as trade becomes increasingly reliant on reputation and interaction gained through 'personal networks' (Duranton 1999: 2185). Duranton notes, with logical precision:

> The concept of personal networks allows us to capture the fact that 'proximity' is synonymous with A wanting to be close to B willing to be close to C and D. For instance, A is a close colleague of B. B and C play tennis together, whereas C and D are married to each other, and so on. This string of personal interactions, all requiring physical proximity, is what may keep these people together in the post-industrial city. (1999: 2185)

But is the metropolis the primary source of personal contacts and meeting places? Wired workers and knowledge entrepreneurs are among the most widely connected or mobile people, always on the move and dependent on distanciated connections sustained by telephone, fax, email, the internet, teleconferencing, and the like. Theirs is a spatially dispersed and mobile string of personal connections. These are connections of intense interaction, and not dependent on local face-to-face contact alone (see chapter 2). It is this very geography of interpersonal relations through mediated communications and travel that has freed the knowledge entrepreneur/worker from the 'tyranny of proximity' in chasing business opportunity. How else do we explain the explosion of business travel, so evident from the congestion of briefcase-clutching travellers demanding ever more flights and trains from continuously enlarged airports and railway stations (five London airports shift more than 100 million passengers a year – Barley 2000)? How else can we explain the gigantic volume of work transacted, both from fixed locations and by the mobile workforce, through telephone conversations and internet exchanges? It is hard to accept that local personal contacts are of primary importance for business in the knowledge economy.

Even Flores and Gray, who believe in the powers of the knowledge economy, question the role of localized networks:

> In this new environment, relationships of trust are built out of increased transparency in costs, frankness about interests, assessment of performance, and recognising and respecting unfamiliar identities. Familiarity is no longer the basis of trust. Local networks are less and less the ground of a career. Local knowledge has a shorter shelf life. As industries change rapidly, skill in coping with new social contexts is often more useful than slowly built-up understandings of established social milieux. (2000: 19)

The knowledge entrepreneur/worker clearly does not rely on local knowledge alone. Perhaps their desire to be in the city is explained by a more subtle sociology of belonging, the desire of cosmopolitans for a fixed point. Richard Sennett (1998) argues that the desire of the supermobile for local familiarity in the public spaces of a city is a reaction to the intense volatility and mobility that marks their economic geography. This kind of local belonging has little to do with the localized economies of trust and reputation.

To come back to the new economic localism, a second current of thought sees local proximity as a source of *tacit* knowledge. A belief among commentators on the geography of innovation is that the growing ubiquity of codified knowledge, through its formal scripting and rapid spread due to globalization, is putting a premium on tacit knowledge environments (Maskell et al. 1998; Nooteboom 1999). The latter are said to facilitate, *inter alia*, the interpretation of ideas, learning in doing, the sharing of information, and organizational agility. Adherents of this view – inspired by the experience of Marshallian industrial districts and high-tech regions such as Silicon Valley – believe that tacit learning is achieved through ties of reciprocity and exchange within localized business networks. Such 'untraded interdependencies' (Storper 1997) may even spill over from the business networks into the wider social fabric of these places as collective conventions and social practices. This is when locality most matters as an economic asset:

> the intensity of instability associated with hypercompetition suggests that place-based 'anchors' of open networks may more readily facilitate social capital because of pre-existing localized social relations. Localized clusters of firms have the potential advantage of frequent face-to-face interaction and social cohesion . . . thereby providing opportunity to transfer tacit knowledge. . . . It is the combination of social cohesion and openness to new knowledge . . . followed by ability to integrate that knowledge and reconfigure existing knowledge that defines competitiveness, notably under hypercompetition. (Ettlinger 2000: 27)

The claim is that local proximity is a vital source of innovation-based competitiveness. There are, however, three problems with this claim. First, rarely does tacit knowledge work in isolation from codified knowledge; competitive advantage is normally the result of how the two are combined (Amin and Cohendet 1999). Codified knowledge is effective when it is interpreted through a variety of tacit measures and understandings (such as conversations to decipher and disseminate new science and technology), while tacit knowledge only too often relies on codified knowledge (manuals, instruments, qualifications, specialized publications). It is because of this inseparability that the sociology of science now prefers to think of knowledge as a continuum in actor-networks enrolling cognition, bodies, conversations, technologies and artefacts.

Second, local business networks are not the only source of tacit knowledge. How could they be in our era of corporatization and corporate branding of knowledge? Multinational corporations, international banks, global business consultancies are not spaces of ubiquitous knowledge pumped out of central R&D sites and HQs. Instead, they are constellations of distributed know-how and reflexivity within communities of practice operating at different spatial scales, from managers linked up with counterparts across the world, to process workers in national and local teams. The organizations, in their various sites, possess a varied repertoire of technologies, soft and hard, to combine tacit and formal knowledge for competitive advantage (Amin and Cohendet 2000).

Third, in an emerging 'soft capitalism' (Thrift 1997), whatever counts as tacit is becoming incorporated as organizational assets for competitive advantage. This ranges from the reliance on family ties and traditional loyalties by overseas Chinese business networks to manage their globally dispersed ventures (Yeung 2000a), to the mobilization of cultures of performance and enactment by 'fast companies' as a means of branding, bonding and encouraging creativity (Thrift 2000b). If there is anything 'local' about such usage of tacit conventions, it is as an organizational endowment, not as a place property. The local circumstances described by Ettlinger, we would argue, have to be seen as unique to localities in which industry and society coincide (such as districts specializing in a single industry). The majority of cities are not like this.

Other knowledge economy specialists, however, propose the city as a rich source of *codified* knowledge, rooted in the city's corporate HQs, research establishments, universities, arts and cultural organizations, and print and media industries. Therefore, Richard Knight (1996: 9) notes that cities could develop 'territorial clusters of related knowledge-based activities' (clusters linking up medical and biomedical research with education, health care and medical services, or international financial centres linked up with related producer services such as public relations and management consulting). Knight explains:

> Cities can play a significant role both directly and indirectly in conserving knowledge resources. Directly, by investing in knowledge by improving the intellectual-infrastructure and building a knowledge-infrastructure. Indirectly, by creating conditions and a milieu which is stimulating and conducive to citizens in a learning-based society, innovation, and knowledge-based development. Conserving the knowledge-base and improving the milieu and attractiveness of the 'city' is becoming increasingly critical; cities which are not aware of the development potentials of their knowledge resources, and which do not develop policies to strengthen them, run the risk of a 'brain drain', or being unable to retain and attract talent, and seeing their knowledge resources erode. (1996: 10)

Here we have it all. In the knowledge city the ugly scars of industrial cities must be replaced by the aesthetic and intellectual charm of preindustrial European cities, through a combination of science policies to stimulate innovation and learning, cultural policies to improve the urban milieu, and social policies to encourage local linkage and 'the transformation from production to knowledge cultures' (Knight 1996: 11). The city can be re-engineered as a brains trust for localized clusters.

Here too, however, there is systematic underrecognition of codified knowledge located in wider corporate and institutional networks. Urban centres of knowledge within firms (R&D labs, training centres, market test centres) are almost always linked with other sites elsewhere, tied into a corporate mission that sees no obvious reason for local spillage. Similarly, the mark of excellence in the world of science and education is peer recognition and international impact; local linkage alone can be a sign of parochialism. Then, as Leadbeater notes, the mass availability of codified knowledge in the new economy through media such as recipes, software and scientific journals has allowed its rapid global diffusion and replication/manipulation by users in distant settings, serving to re-place 'an old inefficient social division of labour which enshrined [a] tacit, traditional way of learning' (1999: 33). Leadbeater is right to re-cognize the stretched geographies of knowledge production and acquisi-tion. Take the fashion industry as an example. Suppliers will often want a strong presence in cities in order to track market trends by being close to consumers. In some niche markets, especially those of a highly cus-tomized or innovative nature (such as designer clothing, new fashions), the proximate consumer is also a rich source of knowledge, helping not only to test preferences but also design the product or service. Interest-ingly, though, it is the need for proximity to *consumer* knowledge that seems important. Urban presence is not an expression of clustered *pro-ducer* knowledge, tacit or otherwise – this is gathered from designers and consultants scattered around the globe, from distributed centres of re-search excellence, from the skills and experience of specialized workers who might be located in inner city districts but are also to be found in abundance in low income regions (McRobbie 1999).

Cities as Sites

Can we see cities as something other than localized economic systems or the forcing houses of (knowledge) capitalism? In the rest of this chapter we wish to show that once we replace the idea of the city as a territorial economic engine with an understanding of cities as sites in spatially stretched economic relations, a rich ecology of urban economic life opens up for consideration. This ecology, we argue, is supported by varying urban institutions and circulatory flows, which, however, never quite return the city as an economic unit.

Sites in near–far networks

Let us examine the geography of three spaces to illustrate the varied role of urban sites within now routinely distanciated networks of economic organization: the space of transnational corporations; the geography of supposedly place-based creative industries such as advertising; and electronic space.

There is a vast body of literature on the economic power of transnational corporations (TNCs). According to UNCTAD, there were in 1997 some 44,000 TNCs with almost 280,000 foreign affiliates. The world's top 100 TNCs employed nearly 6 million people worldwide and raised the equivalent of 7 per cent of global GDP. They constitute a gigantic international production complex that straddles national boundaries and forms a trade network in its own right. 'Around one-third of world trade takes place within transnational corporate networks', with 'about two-thirds of international transactions . . . associated with the international production of TNCs' (UNCTAD 1997: 18). These corporations dominate industrial life. For example, in the European Union, more than 25 per cent of the value added in the major manufacturing industries is produced by a handful of corporations (Amin 2000).

Through the TNCs, the corporatization of economic life across territorial boundaries is taking many forms. Alongside traditional hierarchies of centrally coordinated but globally distributed activities have arisen varied heterarchies of decentralized management and decentred production. These are complex, with firms involved in strategic alliances, licensing agreements and co-production arrangements with a multitude of other firms, managing long supply chains spread around the world, relying on self-governing units along a chain of distributed competences and negotiating for influence at different spatial scales of governance.

Global firms have become a 'constellation of network relations' (Yeung 2000b), incorporating entire social worlds of production, trade, organization, negotiation and power play. They are extraordinarily powerful, and importantly, their power is located in a very particular kind of economic space: one that is not reducible to the powers of place. Their space

> can include localised spaces (e.g. financial districts in global cities) and inter-urban spaces (e.g. webs of financial institutions and the business media that bind together global cities). The firm is made up of social actors engaged in relational networks within a variety of 'spaces'. The analytical lens we adopt can thus vary widely. It may be geographical, it may be sectoral, and it may be organisational. It may be a combination of these. (Yeung 2000b: 26)

Firms have become circulatory networks. Any attempt to theorize the geography of economic power has to be based on an understanding of this ontology. Flow and mobility are increasingly assumed into the system, with elaborate schemes in place to ensure the rapid transfer of people, goods, money and information around the world. How else do we explain the explosion of business travel and infrastructure around the world, or the corporate ownership of fleets of jets, trucks and ships, to keep supplies on the move? How else do we explain the crucial role of logistics, with the location of distribution centres considered as vital when production is located? Key considerations for corporate location choices now include the availability of warehouse complexes, access to transport routes, and proximity to major logistics companies or their distribution centres.

We cannot claim territorial integrity for cities in this context. In one city an airport or restaurant might suffice as the site for international meetings, while in another city the financial district might be implicated. Somewhere else, a production facility might link up workers commuting from the urban periphery to supply chains drawing in cities thousands of miles away. Other cities might be key nodes for distribution outlets and logistics management. A network site displays no distinctive pattern of spatial connections. Nor does it perform a fixed function, as was the case in older urban hierarchies, when capital cities were centres of administration and research, intermediate cities were sites of special-ized production, and peripheral or less developed cities were sites of cheap labour for unskilled work. All we can generalize is that, in the network economy, cities are points of translation and transmission (Castells 1989).

The firm seen as a circulatory network forces a non-territorial under-standing of economic knowledge. Firms routinely look for ways of managing distributed knowledge. These include the use of sophisticated centralized computer systems to manage information flows; corporate training programmes and higher educational qualifications as a way of standardizing and distributing local knowledge; databases, archives and other means of coding and storing knowledge for wider access and for further manipulation; knowledge managers and brokers, as well as corporate away-days and meetings, as a means of assimilating new know-ledge; and placements of scientific and technical staff at points along the supply chain, to generate common understandings. The tools of cor-porate knowledge management have expanded enormously, involving a varied geography, from one-off locations chosen to build consensus, to the movement of knowledge-bearers and the wired transmission of digitized information.

Even urban clusters find their significant connections in a wider network, which brings us to our second example. A widely held view is that the creative industries (such as publishing, media, advertising, fashion) cluster in fashionable inner city areas which provide firms with their resources, inspiration, contacts and social enjoyment. The tale, told and retold, of the media and advertising cluster in Soho in Central London is typical (Nachum and Keeble 1999). In this cluster, concept-based companies are said to put together teams of talented young people around specific projects; they work late into the night and spill over into Soho's many twenty-four-hour bars and dives of one sort or another to feed their creativity, exchange ideas and soak in the state-of-the-art. In turn, the branding of Soho as the place for designer media products, fast creativity and hypersociability is said to attract customers, more talented people and consumers of the Soho lifestyle. Soho's strong sense of place and its networks of creativity are paid to reinforce each other to make the district a significant economic space.

But this is only a partial tale. It leaves out another significant organizational aspect that is not reducible to place. Gernot Grabher (2001) has shown that the leading firms are international heterarchies, also dependent on project teams scattered around the world, linked up virtually and through placements. The international space of these heterarchies of affiliates and alliances matters, because it is a space of internal rivalry, changing ownership and financial mobilization, as well as a space of creativity and brand reputation. Soho without its role in this wider economic space makes no sense. If it has a power of place, this has little to do with the economics of agglomeration and local association. Grabher questions whether Soho can be seen as an industrial district. There are no systematic linkages between local firms. What seems to matter instead, is the *combination* of the global corporate reach of some firms and the economy of time that local proximity provides to highly mobile project teams. Stripped of the power of its international heterarchies, Soho would deliver limited economic returns. Its pull as a brand name for reputation, customers, creative people and investment would diminish without its instantiation through the firm as a circulatory network.

Finally, building on the last chapter, let us consider the urban implications of economic life conducted at a distance owing to the rise of electronic space. While the rise of telematics does not represent the end of older forms of technological and human communication, or the dematerialization of the city into a space of bits and flows (see Thrift 1996a), the significance of a new electronically mediated time-space should not be missed. As Mike Crang notes, 'telematics do not occur in or between urban spaces but produce a new form of space-time. . . . now urban space is not a space and time that contains action, but an inter-active, real-time cityscape' (2000: 303).

Telematics enable real-time interaction at a distance. Through this, they constitute a stretched space-time reaching into suburbs and beyond, linking households, offices and parts of cities to sites around the world (mediated by call centres in other parts of the world and satellites in space). The con-nections involve meanings of significance that are no less authentic, no less intimate than proximate or face-to-face links within the city (Graham 1997). Telematics join a multitude of devices, such that 'being there' no longer requires physical co-presence. Telematic space allows contact with distant suppliers and customers, the ebb and flow of distant commodity and money markets, decisions of organizations and elites located elsewhere, and the daily global circulation of information, data and know-how.

Viewed from within the city, this new space enables economic transac-tions and routines to be spatially and temporally stretched, so that proxi-mate actors are no longer reliant on economic relationships with each other. We are back to the city as a site of isolated happenings. In addi-tion, the new virtual spaces are economic circuits in their own right, composed of traded signs, images, information and knowledge. This is how we must interpret the rise of internet markets for music, company ratings, property markets, share prices, images, and so on. What is the city in these markets, other than the wired terminals of the producers, intermediaries and consumers of the services and digitized goods? If it features as a place, it does so as a virtual place that attracts, labels or orients the digital visitor, or as a distribution outlet or node for the goods and services ordered over the wire (see box 3.1).

All three examples above show that once we consider the growth of eco-nomic organization – corporate and virtual – the city breaks down as a place of strong local interdependencies, as a site of economic power.

Circular consumption

If cities are not engines of competitiveness, they are certainly generators of demand. They possess the economic power of consumption and circu-lation. This power is largely neglected in contemporary theorization of urban economic life. As Glaeser, Kolko and Saiz note:

> [The] basic viewpoint – that cities are good for production and bad for consumption – colors most of urban economics and has influenced most thinking on the future of cities. The critical questions about the future of cities have always been (1) whether cities can maintain their productive edge in the world of information technology and speedy transportation,

and (2) whether the service industries that currently drive urban employment will stay in cities or follow manufacturing plants out to the non-city areas. . . . But we believe that too little attention has been paid to the role of cities as centers of consumption. (2001: 27)

Box 3.1   Distribution centres

Eastman Kodak Singapore is one of only five central distribution centres (CDCs) responsible for supplying the full range of Kodak products from around the world to marketing operations in the Asia Pacific region (Gilmour 1997). Kodak deems central distribution on a world scale to be more efficient and economical than supplying local markets from local factories and distribution centres. CDC-Asia in Singapore receives shipments from Kodak manufacturing plants in the US, Australia, Brazil, Mexico, Germany, France and the UK. Each Kodak marketing company in the Asia Pacific region sends an electronic order on Friday night for stock items, as well as daily orders for non-stock items. The orders are shipped out within a week, and two weeks at the latest. In turn, regular shipments by air and sea arrive from Kodak plants from around the world. The complex logistics are handled by sixty employees located in an office on Alexandra Road or working from the massive 11,500-square-metre warehouse located in the duty-free zone of the Port of Singapore.

The Singapore operation is of crucial importance in a multibillion dollar business. For the city of Singapore, it provides revenue associated with warehousing and international logistics, some local employment, and consumption of the two truckloads per week destined for the Singapore market (Gilmour 1997). But the real economic significance of Singapore lies in its function as a global logistics and distribution centre. Its failures would affect supply and consumption in a worldwide value-chain.

This example is not atypical in the distanciated economy. Increasingly, the role of cities, through the miles of distribution complexes located near major transport nodes, is to keep produce from around the world 'on hold' for customers well beyond the city. These are sites neither of production nor consumption. The rapid rise of such distribution centres in recent years is related to the growth of dominant business corporations, global supply chains, time and cost saving logistics, IT-based management systems, and minimized storage at factories and retail outlets. For example, in the late 1980s and early 1990s, major UK supermarket chains such as Tesco and Safeway moved to sales-based ordering (allowed by barcode scanning at checkouts) of stock held at their own distribution centres (which replaced wholesalers and direct store deliveries from manufacturers). But rarely is the stock held for long. For 'current logistic systems are so sophisticated that, whereas a one-hour delay in a delivery used to be a problem, now a ten-minute delay appears as an exception report to the IT Director of Tesco. Fork-lift trucks in warehouses are fitted with a computer terminal . . . Deliveries are scheduled throughout the day and night, so goods spend the minimum time in the stores' (Seth and Randall 1999: 221).

The imperative of rapid and flawless provision has stimulated the rise of powerful independent logistics corporations with their own transport fleets, IT systems and distribution centres, to further complicate the geography of supply and demand. Excel Logistics in the UK is a typical example. According to Valerie Bence, 'in the four years from 1989 to 1993 Excel Logistics grew to be a market leader in distribution and supply chain services. . . . With a turnover of almost £600 million in 1992, Excel Logistics were operating 3700 vehicles, 1.6 million m² of warehousing and almost a million m³ of cold storage capacity. Its companies employed over 14,600 staff and operated out of 220 distribution centres across the UK, mainland Europe and North America' (1997: 327). Excel was the beneficiary of the increased use of third-party or outsourced distribution by major manufacturers and retailers, for the reasons given above. It managed the entire distribution chain for its customers, from IT systems to inventory and physical delivery. In the UK in the period described by Bence, it was the company behind the bulk of newspaper and book distribution, and distribution for the main food and drink producers, the chilled and frozen food industry, major automotive and electronics companies, and major department stores such as Comet, Woolworths, Boots, BHS, Habitat, Marks and Spencer, and Mothercare. Distribution centres for operations on this scale are carefully scattered around key urban gateways and transport nodes, marking a geography of delivery that has virtually no connection with the original geography of production and the final geography of consumption (for instance, cars produced and sold in one region, via a long journey to and from a distribution centre located a thousand miles away).

Cities are, if nothing else, agglomerations of people, buildings, technologies, communications networks, offices, homes, parks, services. This dense ecology of presence cannot be explained in terms of the economics of (international) competitiveness. Instead, it is to the economics of consumption that we need to turn. Glaeser, Kolko and Saiz identify four urban amenities that mark the city as a consumption site:

> First, and most obviously, is the presence of a rich variety of services and consumer goods. . . . restaurants, theaters, and an attractive mix of social partners are hard to transport and are therefore local goods. [. . .] The second amenity is aesthetics and physical setting. We have little evidence on the role of architectural beauty, but it does seem that more attractive cities have done better since 1980 (e.g. San Francisco). [. . .] The third critical amenity is good public services. Good schools and less crime are also linked with urban growth. [. . .] The fourth vital amenity is speed. In a sense, the range of services (and jobs) available in a metropolitan area is a function of the ease with which individuals can move around. (2001: 28)

While the nature of the urban amenities they select is open to debate (for instance, the importance attributed to the aesthetics of the built environment), the central issue is that if the city exerts a certain territorial pull, it is as a large centre of consumption (Krugman 1997). The demand is generated, as encapsulated in the concept of cumulative causation, by market opportunities generated by agglomeration, resulting in further spin-off and specialization. A growing population sustains varied markets for consumer goods, housing, leisure and recreation, and so on, while the proliferation of firms and institutions generates diversified markets for producer services. In turn, the social and cultural heterogeneity of the city, together with its spatial expansion and subdivision, supports an extraordinary range of markets, from new products and services sold in shopping malls, high street shops and open markets, to second-hand and recycled products exchanged through a similarly varied set of outlets. It is hardly surprising that listings of these commercial activities take up the lion's share of the Yellow Pages across different cities of the world.

But, in the arena of consumption too, the city has become a site in wider circuits of provision. Demand resulting from agglomeration and population density is not met through local supply alone. Local consumption does not return the city as a closed economic circuit. The dynamics of food consumption and supply provide a vivid reminder of the importance of cities as circulatory sites. First, the sheer scale of demand is staggering. In Mexico City, 50,000 trucks loaded with 25,000 tonnes of food roll into the city every day, while a city of 10 million people imports on average 6,000 tonnes a day (Stetter 2000). Second, there is nothing particularly local about the supply chain. For example, the 56-acre New Covent Garden wholesale market in London afore-mentioned employs 2,500 people and buys in a massive range of fruit and vegetables a year, 70 per cent of which are imported.

Rightly, Stetter notes:

> A vast network exists to feed cities; to grow, distribute and sell food to people who cannot grow their own. . . . Every step of the journey involves a different form of transport, a new layer of packaging or type of con-tainer, another place where the goods can be chilled, sorted, packed, stored and eventually sent off again to the next station. Prices are negotiated, demand is assessed, orders are placed and deliveries are made, until finally, the produce appears, as if by magic, in our local shop. This intricate net-work is not controlled by governments or official bodies, but is made up of many private businesses and individuals. . . . If the network came crashing down, the world's major cities would find themselves short of food within a matter of days. (2000: 41)

This complex network links together farmers and distributors around the world, international transport and logistics firms, warehouses, hauliers, supermarkets and shops in destination countries and cities. It is a network of vast profits, rewarding the firms and intermediaries which constitute it. So, as we saw in box 3.1, while much of the trade may be transacted within individual cities, the revenues feed the global network, with only modest circulation and retention within the city and its 'locally owned' firms. The city no longer experiences self-expanding growth based on local consumption.

If local circuits do exist, they are likely to be found in the non-profit sector. For example, in the interstices between the private and the public sector lies the social or non-profit economy, which finds its rationale in the under-met needs of the city. Cities abound with third-sector, volunt-ary and community organizations, as well as micro-credit networks and local trading schemes set up to deal with exclusion from the formal economy or to support alternative lifestyles. Thus we find religious organizations providing food or shelter for the poor, voluntary groups catering for the needs of elderly people, charities working for the unem-ployed, drug addicts and the disabled, communities getting together to clean up the neighbourhood or provide child-care facilities, squatters reclaiming empty property, communes setting up to provide mutual sup-port and shared resources, and low-income groups establishing non-monetary trading networks. These too are economic activities, generating and redistributing resources, meeting consumer and welfare needs. They too are part of the urban economy. They too need to be incorporated in a theorization of the urban economy.

Similarly, the economics of the everyday city includes the demand for public and welfare services. There is a large public goods economy that citizens, firms and institutions depend on, but which also spawns its own markets. Cities are places of large-scale demand for utilities, communications, public works, libraries, green spaces, nurseries, schools, hospitals, nursing homes, medical centres. Each sector relies on research, know-how, skills, services, supplies and maintenance, some of which is generated, or traded, within the city. These public goods are, of course, also supplied by private racketeers and profit-making organizations in many cities of the world, but in others, provision is regulated or secured through state organizations. While such state involvement does not guarantee local supply, in principle public sector decision-makers are in a position to select the providers of services. They can therefore influence the degree to which the public goods economy can be used to stimulate local provision.

We do not wish to overstress the third sector or local state as sources of increasing returns to place. What they do show, however, is the need to look beyond the profit-based marketplace for an economics of local returns.

The density of light institutions

If cities are not local economic systems, do they support firms in other ways? We wish to claim a role for specific institutionalized practices within cities. These involve sturdy institutions offering collective assets through organized activity (meeting places, common services, associations, state support) as well as 'petty' institutions of no formal constitution (such as informal contact networks). We see both as sources of 'light' institutional support: not central for core business activity, but advantageous for tracking opportunity. In addition, we see them as institutions of translation, not territorial embedding: relay points for dispersed network spaces, not sites of economic containment.

Cities are replete with organized activity. The rich and varied ecology of life in cities presses for institutionalization, through the opportunity for collective organization offered by scale and density, but also the need for orientation and rules in a bewilderingly complex and varied environment. The outcome (see chapters 4 and 5) is an institutional intensity, captured in rules and sites of urban administration and government, codes of public behaviour, technologies of control and orientation (traffic signs, surveillance, policing), and presence of organizations and associations. If clustering is to be found in cities, it is as an amalgam of institutions of regulation, power, representation and sociability, some of which are specifically urban (such as local government), while others are translocal institutions with a presence in cities (such as political parties, crime squads, industrial relations agreements).

Some of this organization keeps the economic machinery moving. Access to urban services is one example. Firms can find in cities the full range of business and financial services, transport and communications services, educational and training opportunities, commercial and retail services, legal and administrative services, and so on. And here, familiarity with locally known/trusted organizations could matter, as does the option that alternatives can be found elsewhere in the city through personal contacts, reputation and business directories. But the service base need not be local. Firms locked into long supply chains, or those surfing the net or able to afford the services of larger suppliers, may well look beyond the city.

Another example of organization comes through the meeting places offered by cities. Restaurants, football matches, musical events, golf clubs are places where ideas are developed and deals are struck, deliberately, or through casual socialization. They are places where standards are tracked, gossip is exchanged, rivals are noted and disputes are aired, rather as they are in business associations and interest groups. But these meeting places are not Marshallian spaces of interchange between members of the same community of interest (say, furniture makers in an Italian piazza). Instead, they are more broadly constituted centres of sociability or professional gathering with a light economic touch; mixing pleasure, voice, search and business opportunity in emergent ways. Without being there, business will not collapse, but the anxiety of potential loss might grow. This is why soft indicators, such as the nature of social amenities, have become a significant factor in urban investment decisions (see box 3.2).

A third light institution is the synthesis of different types of formal knowledge in the city. The city, to return to the earlier discussion on the knowledge economy, is not a source of contextual or tacit knowledge rooted in particular kinds of business practice (for example, trust in clusters). Nor is it an uncommitted reservoir of creativity to be found in the market of knowledge workers. Instead, it can be seen as a site of *varied compositional* knowledge, situated in schools, colleges and universities, workplaces, night classes and voluntary gatherings, libraries and cultural centres, learned societies and certification agencies, and so on. How the knowledge generated in each setting translates into local economic benefit is almost impossible to theorize in advance. What could

Box 3.2   City ratings

Business ratings of cities have exploded in the last two decades, as a consequence of the increased global mobility of capital, professionals and migrants (Rogerson 1999). Consultancies and the business press now routinely rank cities around the world for their business climate, from evidence gathered from executives, economic development organizations and independent surveys. A broad range of factors are taken into consideration, including the economic opportunities offered by a city, its cost regime, communications networks, labour market characteristics, the availability and cost of premises, the regulatory environment (such as corporate tax) and the quality of life.

In 1999 (20 December), the business magazine *Fortune* ranked, in descending order, the following as the top ten US cities: Dallas, San Jose, Austin, New York City, Atlanta, Seattle, San Francisco, Denver, Boston and Chicago. Worldwide, the ranking for Asia was Singapore, Sydney, Melbourne, Hong Kong and Taipei; for Europe it was London, Amsterdam, Budapest, Munich and Stockholm; while Monterrey, Mexico City, Buenos Aires, Santiago and San Jose were ranked the top five business locations in Latin America. The magazine comments with surprise that the non-US cities are among the most expensive places for business, but they are rated as top locations due to their able labour forces, good communications networks, pro-business legal systems, and a *high quality of life*. These same reasons are listed for the top US cities.

Quality of life matters, even though it may not be ranked by business executives as the most important location factor. For example, in a survey of European cities (which ranked London, Paris, Brussels, Frankfurt, Milan, Amsterdam, Barcelona, Madrid, Zurich and Munich as the top ten) the quality of life for employees was ranked below market access, availability of staff, transport and communications, cost of staff, business regulations, availability and cost of office space, language spoken and ease of travel within the city (Healey and Baker 2000). However, businesses have also become sensitive to the role of 'soft' factors such as the quality of schooling, shopping, housing, leisure and entertainment opportunities. These are considered to be significant not only in terms of maintaining staff commitment, but also as sites affecting business location (see Dziembowska-Kowalska and Funck 1999 for evidence on the role of the arts sector in Karlsruhe in Germany).

The business surveys reveal urban sociability to be particularly significant in the business services and knowledge industries. These are industries in which the core assets are the capabilities of the mid/high-ranking or creative knowledge-workers – professionals, consultants, analysts, scientists and technologists. They are a mobile transnational elite, ever circulating between globally dispersed offices. And, as a transient elite, the quality of life offered by a city of temporary residence matters a lot, for hedonistic compensations for a relative absence of local ties, and because of the need to ensure that assets such as education and cultural opportunities are not endangered by continual mobility.

But there is more. There are business-related uses of urban social amenities in these industries, as shown by Beaverstock and Bostock (2001) in a fascinating account of the lives and working practices of British expatriates in Singapore's financial sector. They reveal an intensive usage by expatriates of bars, restaurants, clubs, sporting clubs and events, parties, sponsored events and business asssociations. Sociability in these places is the basis on which contacts and opportunities are made, trust and reliability is tested, knowledge and jobs are exchanged, business deals are tested or scaled, reputations are tracked and business is made sociable. Beaverstock and Bostock cite one expatriate, for whom doing business in a social context 'is essential . . . you wouldn't be particularly successful in Asia given the fact that all business is about networking here . . . at the end of the day people will do business with people that they also know in a social context and that means basically you're on call twenty-four hours a day seven days a week.' The reason cited is not peculiar to business in Asian contexts, but is typical of contexts in which networking is a core business activity. There, the sites of pleasure in the city come alive as business institutions.

be significant, though, is the sheer variety of types of institutionalized knowledge available, as a pool of diversified and redundant know-how. This is a pool with unpredictable effects in the space economy, both in terms of its generative effects, and where these effects are manifested (as when a local invention is turned into a commercial product elsewhere).

The city's institutional base also includes important petty or unstructured activities that support economic life. In cities many small enterprises competing with each other in local markets often rely on informal institutions in order to survive. For example, ethnic minority businesses, based in immigrant areas, often rely for their trade on specific consumption norms (such as customer preference for particular types of food) and opportunities made available through local kinship and cultural networks (denominational schools, community associations, religious organizations – see Kesteloot and Meert 1999). The mainstream small firm economy, too, draws on the city's petty institutions. Typically, the corner shop relies for its business on certain local rhythms, from the shopping patterns of parents with young children and the lunchtime habits of office workers to the daily invasion of schoolchildren, and perhaps also the desire of some local residents for light chat. A similar petty institutionalization underpins the many informal and semi-legal ventures that service the city, from neighbourhood trading schemes to credit networks to cash-in-hand for gardening, household repairs and car purchases. All these ventures are crucially dependent on the institutionalization of local reputation and turf, as well as ties of support and familiarity located in circumscribed parts of the city (Duneier 1999; Fleischer 1995; Mingione 1996).

Conclusion

Cities cannot be read as economic machines, as a bounded economic space with special properties of place. Instead, we have argued in this chapter that cities have to be seen as a site in distanciated economic networks, with site effects that have more to do with the light sociology of urban institutions than with the nature of ties between proximate trading partners. Whatever power they exert occurs through firms and institutions located within them, but not necessarily working for them. Their economic life is constituted through the role they play in a wider global space of circulatory flows and economic organization. Rarely does this economic space break down into localized networks.

This difference in interpretation has significant practical implications. First, our perspective leaves little room for policies which assume urban competitiveness, on the grounds that it is firms, not cities, which compete. Thus, competitiveness-based policies (now the mainstay of urban economic policy everywhere, see World Bank 2000) are not likely to deliver self-sustaining local economic development. For example, cluster programmes aimed at strengthening ties between firms might well end up with a poor uptake, while policies to improve the knowledge assets of a city might well serve to sustain business ventures with limited local effects. Second, our perspective tends towards action at other levels, for example, through the institutional base of the city which underwrites economic activity in non-obvious ways, or national strategies to improve the resource base of firms (for instance, via national credit or fiscal reforms), or demand-based regeneration programmes focusing on local needs which are of limited market interest to non-local suppliers (such as the renewal of green spaces, or care for the elderly in specific parts of the city).

Finally, throughout the last two chapters, the reader will have noticed that we have had problems in working with some of the distinctions current in the urban literature, which assume fixed scales of analysis and which, when they write of circulation, feel the necessity to anchor it back into these scales. Can we find another vocabulary with which to describe the city, one which takes circulation, hybridity and multiplicity as key urban moments, and fixed boundaries as temporary allegiances and alignments? That is the task we set ourselves in the next three chapters. Our intention is to attempt to redescribe the city as an ecology of circumstance, as an ordering of uncertainty, so producing lines of power, and as a political arena full of potentialities able to be mobilized and fought/ thought through. What we are attempting to do is to redraw the map of the city in such a way as to show up new channels of disempowerment and empowerment. Crucially, this task involves charting spatialities which exceed the old territorial stereotypes in which one scale intersects or nests within another. In other words, a good deal of what is needed in order to understand the modern city consists of the invention of new sociospatial vocabularies that can unlock new insights.

4 THE MACHINIC CITY

Introduction

The first step in building the new sociospatial vocabulary is to understand the city as a *machine*. But in using this term, in this chapter, we do not mean to imply that the city can be understood through mechanical metaphors – with inputs, mechanisms and outputs – but rather as a 'mechanosphere', a set of constantly evolving systems or networks, machinic assemblages which intermix categories like the biological, technical, social, economic, and so on, with the boundaries of meaning and practice between the categories always shifting. This Deleuzo-Guattarian conception has a crucial consequence: the technical is not seen as separate from the social or the natural. This is a constant refrain of much recent work in the social sciences and humanities (as in, for example, actor-network theory (Latour 1993)), but the main tenets of the approach still bear repeating. Thus, to begin with, humans are defined by their use of tools: they are technical from their very origins as a species. Tools and machines are therefore best thought of as extra organs growing into existence, rather than as something outside the compass of the human body. Technics is originary. So second, and at the same time, machines are not seen as something 'other'; they are a fundamental fact of *life*; 'artifice is fully a part of nature' (Deleuze 1988: 73). Their strengths are crucial to how the mechanosphere evolves (as Latour has remarked, we wouldn't want or need machines unless they were stronger than us). Third, technics understood in this way problematizes the distinction between subject (organism) and objects (environment).

Instead, then, human beings must be seen as just one part of a symbiosphere – a set of different species living in physical contact with one another. For one thing, this conception short-circuits the kind of species-specific arrogance that the environmental movement has spent so long criticizing; we need to think of ourselves as 'animated water' (Margulis 1998), not god-like beings: 'No evidence exists that we are "chosen", the unique species for which all the others were made. Nor are we the most important one because we are so numerous, powerful and dangerous. Our tenuous illusion of special dispensation belies our true status as upright mammalian weeds' (Margulis 1998: 119). For another, we cannot construe the organism as if it were something readily present-to-hand. That kind of (Darwinian) reasoning leads nowhere. Instead we need to turn to an ethological approach which integrates organism and environment (Ingold 2000).

> The problem in Darwinism is that it construes the animal as if it were something present at hand. As a result, it loses sight of the 'relational structure' between the animal and its environment. It fails to appreciate, therefore, that the 'environment' is an intrinsic feature of the becoming of the movement of the organism. In this rethinking of the becoming of life Heidegger's thinking comes close to Deleuze's emphasis on ethology, although Deleuze's analysis takes place on a much more molecular and machinic level which renders the notion of the organism hugely problematic both philosophically and politically. A Deleuzian-inspired reading of the will-to-power would point to its attempt to conceive reality in dynamical and processual terms in which the emphasis is placed on a centred system of forces, and in which 'evolution' is seen to take place without fidelity to the distinctions of species and genus. (Ansell-Pearson 1997: 117)

These strictures apply equally to the rest of the biological realm as well. The idea of a fixed, or neatly evolving, organism must be jettisoned in favour of a 'geographical' notion of becoming in which the dynamics of evolution must be conceived of

> not in terms of organs, organisms, and species, and their functions, but in terms of the affective relationships between heterogeneous bodies. This is to define things not in terms of determinate organs and fixed functions, not in terms of either substance or subject, but in terms of lines of longitude and latitude. As Deleuze points out, a 'body' can be anything – an animal, a body of sounds, a mind or an idea, a social body of collective, and so on (Deleuze 1989: 127). Deleuze is attracted to the so-called 'mystical vitalism' of a biologist like von Uexküll because of the attempt to describe animal worlds in terms of overlapping territories in which becomings take place in terms of affects and capacities for affecting and being affected. Since an animal cannot know in advance which liaison will be good or bad for it (Is this poison or food I am eating? Poison can be

food! Etc.), this means that evolution speaks, in fact, of an involution, that is, the dissolution of forms and the indeterminacy of functions, as well as the freeing of times and speeds (Deleuze and Guattari 1988: 267). (Ansell-Pearson 1997: 117)

Thus, 'community' becomes a multiplicity of beings – rather like the lichens.

The desert valleys of Antarctica's Victoria are an icy hell. Gusts of wind periodically blow over rock and instantaneously freeze the melting ice of summer. Nonetheless, hidden two or three millimetres away beneath the rock thrive communities of lichens, a symbiotic mix of fungi, algae, and bacteria that even inhabits porous sandstone. As long as this community can sun itself through the crystalline grains of quartz, it lives. An estimate of the global weight of such fungus-lichen rock dwellers is 13×10^{13} tons, a biomass greater than all life in the ocean! (Margulis 1998: 108–9)

Such a view can be seen as part of a general turn to an immanent, desubjectified or impersonal *life*, inspired by the rediscovery of Nietzsche, Bergson, Deleuze, Foucault and others (May and Thrift 2001), which is perhaps best summarized by Agamben, discussing Michel Foucault's last text 'Life: experience and science':

What characterises these pages, which Foucault conceived as a great hom-age to his teacher, Georges Canguilhem, is a curious inversion of what had been Foucault's earlier understanding of the idea of life. It is as if Foucault, who, with *The Birth of the Clinic*, had begun under the inspiration of Xavier Bich's new vitalism and definition of life 'as the set of functions that resist death' ended by considering life instead as the domain of error. 'At the limit,' Foucault writes, 'life ... is what is capable of error ... With man, life reaches a living being *who is never altogether in his place*, a living being who is fated "to err" and to be mistaken.' This displacement can be seen as further documentation of the crisis that Foucault, according to Deleuze, experienced after the first volume of the *History of Sexuality*. But what is at issue here is surely something more than disappointment or pessimism, it is something like a new experience that necessitates a general reformulation of the relation between birth and the subject and that, nev-ertheless, concerns the specific area of Foucault's research. Tearing the subject from the terrain of the *cogito* and consciousness, this experience roots it in life. But, insofar as this life is essentially errancy, it exceeds the lived experiences and intentionality of phenomenology. 'Does not the en-tire theory of the subject have to be reformulated once knowledge, instead of opening on to the truth of the world, is rooted in the "errors" of life?' (Agamben 1999: 220–1, emphasis added)

In other words, there is an immanent force of potentiality.

> A life is everywhere, in all the movements that traverse this or that living subject and that measure lived objects – immanent life carrying events or singularities that effect nothing, but their own work actualisation in subjects and objects. This undefined life does not itself have moments, however, close to one another as they might be; it has only inter-times (*entre-temps*), inter-moments (*entre-moments*). It neither follows nor succeeds, but rather presents the immensity of empty time, where one sees the event that is to come that has already happened in the absolute of immediate consciousness. (Deleuze 1997: 23)

In such a perspective, modern cities become spaces of flow and mixture, promiscuous 'meshworks' (De Landa 1997) and hierarchies of different relations, rather than patchworks of different communities; hybrids involving almost continuous improvisation in which the 'in-between' of interaction is crucial. And they are best described, therefore, in terms of a language of forces, densities, intensities, potentialities, virtualities. Everything is piled in and from this high-density mix, this strange brew, new potentialities can constantly emerge, for example, practices intended to produce certain goals are adapted to produce new ones (destratification, in DeLanda's terms). Thus 'what truly defines the real world . . . are neither uniform strata nor variable meshworks, but the unformed and constructed flows from which these two derive' (De Landa 1997: 260).

However, we do need to be careful with depictions of this kind. There is what we might call a flowsy-flowsy depiction of the city doing the rounds currently, especially in cultural studies, which seems to end up arguing that flows are good, and fixity is correspondingly bad: proliferation is all. While we have sympathy for the productive energies of the position, it clearly runs the risk of simply producing a mirror image of that which it criticizes. We therefore need a more nuanced argument which we will build around the notion of circulation.

Circulation

We certainly take circulation to be a central characteristic of the city, as we note in chapter 3: cities exist as means of movement, as means to engineer *encounters* through collection, transport and collation. They produce, thereby, a complex pattern of traces, a threadwork of intensities which is antecedent to the sustained work of revealing the city minute on minute, hour on hour, day on day, and so on. These forces are distinguished in four ways: by what they carry, by how they carry, by their stretch in space and by their cyclicity. It follows that these forces are at once local and distributed, natural and artificial, objective and constructed, material and semiotic. In turn, it follows that, from earliest times, the city has never been able to be defined by definitive boundaries since much of the purpose of the city consists of traces which spill over its boundaries as a matter of course: what seem to be bounded spaces are actually gatherings of traces which cross boundaries, and the city's integrity is not necessarily compromised by this fact in the way portrayed by many humanist theorists concerned with the impact of technological changes (such as Virilio 1991).

Henri Lefebvre continually made this point: bounded spaces are spaces of transit. He took the example of the modern house, whose boundaries are crossed by all manner of conduits – electrical wiring, water pipes, gas pipes, telephone lines, radio waves, television signals, and so on. That quintessential space of privacy is actually open to the world. It functions because of travelling. Further, because traces may flow does not mean that they lack order. Quite the contrary, much of the city's existence is concerned with energy flows taking place on different levels: from water and sewage through to electricity and information, from people and animals, to machines and vegetables; and, in turn, engineering these flows themselves requires a series of encounters. Smooth displacements require the machinery of placements (instruments, metrics, labourers), as Latour has constantly emphasized. To think otherwise is to court ontological disaster.

What happens if, instead of attending to instruments (rigid bodies, laboratory sites, changes of scale, institutions in charge of time and standards and the know-how that goes into experimental trials) we attend only to the results of smooth displacement? To continue with my favourite example, what happens when the man in the 1st class compartment of the TGV ignores not only the famous 'man on the embankment' but also the inhabitants of the story of aligned stations and cities, the whole machinery and administration of train companies? He really will think that there can be something like a displacement in time-space that does not require any ageing, any transformation – something that is paid for moreover by costly network building. He may even come to think that isochronic time – measured by his watch in relation with the train's clock – and isotropic space – signalled by the number-bearing milestones that flash regularly along the track – are normal features of the world. This will not happen if he boards an Italian train, let alone an Indian train, and it will not happen either . . . if there is a strike or other incident, or even if the air conditioning malfunctions slightly. But if all goes smoothly, this traveller will take the result of the railway companies' labour-smooth travel across space in time as its normal course. After having discarded as irrelevant the tracks, the train, the switches, the bureau of standards, the clockwork, the regulations, the time-tables, and the whole attendant menageries, he will then be tempted decisively to believe that this system of isochronic and isotropic co-ordinates can be located in his mind! That is the real great danger of train trips; they are too comfortable (at least in Switzerland). Epistemology is a professional hazard of first class, air-conditioned train travel. (Latour 1997: 187)

In the rest of this chapter, we want to bring out what this perspective might mean for considering cities. Roughly speaking, we want to argue that it is only by moving beyond the slower times of the city's built fabric – which seem to form a container – to the constant to and fro of the movements which sustain that fabric that we can begin to understand what a city is and how it constructs us through the medium of 'everyday life'. We will begin by considering the city as a set of flows by drawing on the Spinozan notion of *passions*. Our intention, first, is to consider the city as a field of movements; a swirl of forces and intensities, which traverse and bring into relation all kinds of actors, human and non-human, in all manner of combinations of agency. The city becomes a kind of weather system, a rapidly varying distribution of intensities. This is a seductive way of understanding the city but it can be, as the quotation from Latour makes clear, a little too seductive. We also need to think about how cities are *orders*, and this ordering is often exacted through the design of flows as a set of serial *encounters* which construct particular spaces and times. Thus, second, we look at the dynamic ordering processes which have produced our chief senses of urban space and time. As we will see, these have mainly been produced through the design of mundane instruments of encounter which themselves became the proof of the existence of particular spaces and times.

The City of Passions

'Passions' often conjure up images of Carmen, or Romeo and Juliet, or at least the grizzly suburban murder of an unfaithful partner. Passions are thought of, in other words, as extremes; as peculiarly intense intensities. But we need to be very careful here. For a start, many passions are, of course, rather less incandescent: the kind of passion that goes into Civil War re-enactment societies, or the showing of dogs and cats, or trainspotting. And then there is the constant swirl of emotions that takes us through the day: the petty jealousies, the moments of paranoia, the quiet love of a parent for a child. It is not all excitement. What are we trying to get at, then, in seeing the city as an ethology made up of 'instincts'? What might that mean? In using the word 'instinct' we might seem to be suggesting an animal-like stimulus–response model. In a way, we want to keep this mechanistic image; but we will temper it by using Spinoza's formulation of the organization of the passions.

Spinoza's thought can best be conceived as a kind of physics of bodies in which the human body is not a self-contained whole but is built out of other bodies with our own. Thus the importance for Spinoza of emotions or 'affects'. 'Where bodies are like our own – human bodies which undergo similar modifications – this experience of other bodies can intensify our awareness of our own desires, joys and pains' (Gatens and Lloyd 1999: 14). This experience is amplified because 'the human body is of a higher degree of complexity than other bodies, incorporating a greater number of subordinate unities, and this greater complexity makes it capable of acting and being acted upon in many ways at once' (p. 18). What emerges from Spinoza, then, is an associative logic which

> could just as appropriately be described as a logic of emotion, and especially of desire, as it can be a logic of imagination. The conjoint operations of imagination and emotion are not to be seen as mere dysfunctions of reason. The interactions of imagination with the central emotions – desire, joy and sadness – yield systematic variations in intensity of attachments and aversion. These fluctuations are different from the ordered relations between clear ideas of reason; but they have none the less an order of their own which lends itself to rational investigation.
>
> The rational understanding of this affective logic of the non-rational becomes the core of Spinoza's analyses of the forms of political life – analyses which centre on understanding the organisation of the passions, rather than on the deliberations of a supposedly rational will. Spinoza sees the passions as generated in conjunction with images, around which they are organised; and he sees these organised patterns of affect and image as changeable through challenging the appropriateness of the images at their core. (Gatens and Lloyd 1999: 26)

What this depiction of life – and Deleuze's development of it – means is that the city should be seen as a kind of force-field of passions that associate and pulse bodies in particular ways.

What this means, in turn, is that we want to see the city as a kind of force-field: 'behaviour can no longer be localised in individuals conceived of as preformed homunculi; but has to be treated epigenetically as a function of complex material systems, which cut across individuals . . . and which traverse . . . organic boundaries. This requires the adumbration of a *distributed* notion of agency' (Ansell-Pearson 1999: 171, emphasis added). So what then are the chief sources of agency-intensity in the city? We argue that there are three.

The first and most obvious is the *human body*, which is usually conceived of as a centred cognitive being, as the chief source of agency in the city, setting plans and carrying them out. But, in fact, very few bodily actions require motive (attribution of intent, justification, accounting). Nearly all the activity of the human body takes place in what Lakoff and Johnson (1999) call the 'cognitive unconscious'. Thus, for example, actions fire up in the body before we are consciously aware of them; some 95 per cent of bodily activity is automatic, based on embodied descriptions; which is also the way the body conforms and deals with the city without having to rationalize every movement/moment. This is the embodied knowledge that allows us to drive a car several kilometres without remembering how we got from A to B, that allows us to walk along crowded streets without bumping into people, and that allows us to remember the city from one city space to another without maps. Much of our knowledge of the city is stored in this 'unconscious' way, which goes to prove that 'there are many skills that we best exercise when we do not think about what we are doing' (Nörretranders 1998: 141). In other words, these are not trivial skills. Indeed, it might be argued that the ability of this unconscious knowledge to translate our experience is much greater than that of conscious knowledge.

> Millions and millions of bits are condensed to a conscious experience that contains practically no information at all. Every single second, every one of us discards millions of bits in order to arrive at the special state known as consciousness. But, in itself, consciousness has very little to do with information. Consciousness involves information that is not present, information that has disappeared (along the way). Consciousness is not about information but about its opposite: order. Consciousness is not a complex phenomenon: it is what consciousness is about that is complex. (Nörretranders 1998: 125)

In other words, cognition might be thought of as something that is distributed across many actors and parts of actors, as an 'ecology of mind' (Bateson 1973). This distribution takes place through passings of various kinds. To begin with, there are embodied actions and reactions which, after all, are usually carried out to affect others. Thus action should not be seen as 'individual', but as a repertoire of practices, often concerned with the particular bodily organs. The *hand* is a particularly crucial organ, able to carry out many operations. Though there are clear problems in defining what the hand is – 'we can no longer say with certainty where the hand itself, or its control of influence, begins or ends in the body' (Wilson 1998: 9), hands are crucial means of *thinking* the world, pathways of understanding. Take piano-playing: 'I sing with my fingers, so to speak, and only so to speak, for there is a new "I" that the speaking I gestures toward with a pointing at the music that says: It is a singing body and this I (here, too, so to speak) sings' (Sudnow 1978: 152).

Hands are crucial elements of the life of the city and the city has provided an opportunity for those hands to grow in influence. There is almost no urban practice in which hands are not richly implicated. Frank Wilson, in his classic book *The Hand* (1998), lists just a few: making jewellery, printing, puppetry, controlling mechanical diggers, building skyscrapers; as well as the continuing cultural evolution of pastimes like eating, stacking, drawing, copying. Yet the urban literature is all but silent on what is (quite literally) right in front of its face. Though we write incessantly of a city of sight and screens, we forget the city of a forest of hands, picking their way across keyboards, clicking mice, gripping steering wheels . . . (McCullough 1996). Though we write about the history of writing as a crucial element of urban life, we forget that it takes the hand and unsung objects like the pen and pencil (Petroski 1989) to bring it into being. We simply forget the mundane experiences of punching a keyboard in disgust, or pressing too hard on a pen in our anxiety. 'Hands feel. They probe. They practice. They give us sense . . .' (McCullough 1996: 1). And we certainly will not be able to understand the future of cities, which will depend in large part on the *craft* of the practised digital hand (McCullough 1996), the hand with which so much of what initially looks like an abstraction takes place.

The second characteristic of the body is *talk*. The city is a constant cacophony of talk. But talk has to be seen in a particular way, as a means of doing something, rather than as a means of representation. This way of seeing talk is important for three reasons. First, because it characterizes talk as a toolkit of utterances (words in their speaking) which are there for doing things. This is the Bakhtinian city. Second, because it sees us as having in common 'not a set of agreements about meanings, beliefs or values, but a set of intrinsically two sided "topics" (Greek *topoi* = places) or dilemmatic theories of "commonplaces" for use by us as resources from which we can draw the two or more sides of the object' (Shotter 1993: 14). Third, in such a conception, talk involves both 'finding' and 'making' successive speculations on states of affairs that are about making those states of affairs both intelligible and legitimate to those around us. Cities, then, hum with talk which is based on shared conversational contexts in which categories and identities are constantly articulated: local understandings which often very elegantly exploit the possibilities of ordinary talk. Fine grain is still the chief grain of the city. Such an interpretation is aided by recent work on affect. Affect provides an artful dimension to interaction through arrangements of body stance, a corporeal social logic which adds *texture* to the social moment in all kinds of situations, a 'temporary flesh for the passage to an altered state of social being' (Katz 1999: 343).

The third characteristic is improvisation. There is good evidence to suggest that improvisation is a crucial element of embodiment (Thrift 2000a) which is, under certain circumstances, able to go beyond its situation. We know that children first gain the ability to improvise meaningfully at about the age of eleven. Equally, there are elements of social organization that seem to be means of fostering improvisation, in particular those to do with play (Sutton-Smith 1998). Improvisations are clearly made up of dispositions which are part of a learnt repertoire (Bourdieu 1999). But they consist of more than that. Improvisation also has a performative element which cannot be reduced to the refuelling of learnt behaviour; it is a partial and temporary resetting which consists of attempts to make something new in the moment, something stemming in part from processes of separation and individuation, especially in early childhood (Stern 1998), and in part from the productivity of the social setting.

As mention of the pencil implies, the second chief source of agency-intensity in the city is *objects*. Objects are a vital part of passions. They are not simply passive relays, maintaining human life. They are part of the transhuman world. Two classes of objects are particularly powerful elements of the constitution of passions in cities. The first of these are objects whose very presence implies passionate action: the knife or the gun, for example. Some objects may, indeed, have their own effectivity, an irresistible call to action: take the end of G. B. Pabst's film *Pandora's Box*.

> Jack the Ripper looks dreamily into Lulu's face in the light of the lamp, suddenly sees the gleam of a bread knife over her shoulder; his face, in close-up, gasps in terror, his pupils grow wider, 'the face has become a paroxysm', then his face relaxes as he accepts his destiny, given the irresistible call of the weapon, and the availability of Lulu as a victim. This scene, Deleuze suggests, can be grasped in two ways. On the one hand, it defines an 'actual' state of affairs, localised in a certain place or time, with individual characters (Lulu, Jack), objects with proper uses (the lamp, the knife), and a set of real connections between the objects and characters. On the other hand it can also be said to define a set of qualities in a pure state, outside their spatial temporal co-ordinates, with their own ideal

singularities, and virtual conjunctions. Lulu's compassionate look, the brightness of the light, the gleam of the blade, Jack's terror, resignation and ultimate decisiveness. (Smith 1997: xxxi)

The mention of film leads on to a second set of important objects of passion, those that are concerned with representation – texts, film, certain images. These are objects which live, for three reasons. First, because they portray life and in doing so, make life run. Second, because it is these representations that people often act to. They become the world. Third, because these objects are able to create coherent spaces and times. For example, Latour notes how certain sets of objects when brought together are able to produce perspectival space:

Mobiles that are becoming immutable – painted scenes, planets, account books, anatomical plates, printed books, etched plates – are tracing a new space that has the strange characteristic of establishing new continuous links with each of these discrete and heterogeneous novelties. Of course, neither perspective, nor painting, nor etching, nor Copernican astronomy, nor double-entry book keeping are enough to explain any of the others. Serious historians can always point out the gap between those discontinuous innovations and they are right. What they miss, however, is that each of these inventions, of more immutable, more mobile elements, is creating a new specific type of space that allows them to merge with the other in a specific homogenizing way. (1988: 127)

Apart from the object world, there is one more source of agency-intensity. This is the rest of the *biological realm*, a realm of 'general intelligence' we cannot gainsay (Budansky 1998). The prevalence of animals in cities has been remarked on often enough. Many animals have adapted to urban living in the strangest of ways. There is to begin with the host of 'companion' animals. Such animals have their own passions and often raise considerable passions in their owners. Then there are all the feral and wild animals, for whom the city is often a viable habitat. 'Generalist' species, like pigeons, rats (6.7 million of them in British cities alone), racoons, possums, foxes – even cougars – have all thrived, as well as a host of insects. Recently, for example, foxes, and now seagulls, have spread into European cities in some profusion (box 4.1). Similarly, in US cities mountain lions may now be in transition from highly specialist niches to a more general opportunism as they learn to feed off pets, small wildlife, or even the occasional jogger. 'What we are witnessing may not be any less than a behavioural quantum leap in the emergence of mountain lions with a lusty appetite for slow, soft animals in spandex' (Davis 1998: 249).

Box 4.1 Urban foxes rework the city

The ecologies of cities are often surprisingly functional. Indeed, as Shoard (1999) has pointed out, many sites on the urban fringe are ecologically more diverse than sites in the countryside (and especially those rural areas that have been subjected to industrial farming methods). Certainly, it is the case that the animal populations of many cities around the world have expanded mightily. The result is that all around us, sometimes unnoticed, all kinds of dramas are being played out in which both animals and humans have a role (Philo and Wilbert 2000).

A good example is the red fox (*vulpes vulpes*) population in the large British city of Bristol. This population has been studied since 1977 and it has therefore been possible to build up a detailed picture of the behaviour of this animal in this city. By the early 1990s, Bristol's foxes had become remarkably common, with thirty-three adult foxes per square kilometre. This density was possible in part because of interaction with humans. For example, many residents put out food and 'the amount of food deliberately supplied by the residents appeared to have had a profound affect on the social organisation of the fox population' (Baker et al. 2000). The large number of foxes meant both that the average size of social groups was large (increasing from two adults in the 1970s to seven in the 1990s) and that territories were accordingly small: often just a fraction of a square kilometre. On one estimate foxes visited 60 per cent of their territory each night. Not surprisingly, foxes became a common sight in Bristol, appearing regularly in gardens, even strolling along streets – apparently unconcernedly.

But then, disaster. In 1994, an outbreak of sarcoptic mange, caused by a mite (*sarcoptis scabiei*) that burrows into the skin, killed off the majority of the population. Perhaps less than 3 per cent of Bristol's foxes survived.

What followed was a puzzle. Ecology textbooks would forecast that the population should have recovered rapidly and gone back to its old habits. But that has not happened. One of the reasons may be that half of the adult foxes still have mange, but the seriousness of the infection is less than in the past and mortality rates are correspondingly lower. Another reason may be that far fewer households were deliberately feeding the foxes – in part because there were so few foxes to be seen.

Even so, foxes seem to have dramatically changed their behaviour. The population density remains less than 5 per cent of that seen before the outbreak and there are now only 1.3 adult foxes per kilometre. Their territories are seven times larger than before, even though these territories are more difficult to defend. Social groups are now much smaller, with pairs the norm, making it more difficult to raise cubs. And the territorial behaviour of the foxes is entirely different. Their behaviour is more purposeful, and they visit only about 40 per cent of their territory each night, 'rarely re-crossing their route. Large areas are hardly visited. So while some people frequently see foxes in their garden, others ponder where they've gone' (Baker et al. 2000).

Tracking the foxes shows that there is no apparent logic in the distances they travel or the amount of energy they expend. What has changed is ranging behaviour. More time is spent defining and defending the peripheries of (still contiguous) territories.

In other words, after the outbreak of mange, foxes changed their behaviour in Bristol, producing a new urban ecological reality that is not easily explained. Though reduced population density is an obvious factor in the new behaviour patterns, it seems unlikely that that alone can explain all the change. It might even be that, fuelled by the new post-mange landscape, the foxes' *social* reality has changed – an adjustment relying on changed behaviour by humans as well. In other words, increasingly mites, foxes and humans form a complex hybrid ethology tied together by the city, an unfolding over time that is part of a new concept of vitality.

The biological realm hardly stops here, however. There are also the urban flora to count in, to be found in pubs, gardens and streets, from 'native' weeds growing up between the paving slabs, to practised botanic invaders like buddleia (only introduced into British cities one hundred years ago), to grand trees dying of pollution. Then there are all the swarming colonies of bacteria and viruses, which are often quite as dangerous as wild beasts, for whom the city, and all its inhabitants (revealing the fact that most human and animal bodies are seething zoos of microbes), is the ideal habitat. Indeed, De Landa (1997) traces the emergence of new diseases to the densely packed association of humans and domestic animals that characterized ancient and medieval cities. And since the early cholera maps, which have now themselves become urban icons, the spread of diseases has clearly been associated with the concentration of population as well as with travellers moving from city to city and with the sexual passions of urban inhabitants.

In other words, cities have to be seen less as a series of locations on which categorical attributes are piled, and more as forces and intensities which move around and from which, because of their constant ingestions, mergers and symbioses, the new constantly proceeds. Just as many of our new and useful body parts may have begun as life-threatening infections, so we can see how seemingly redundant combinations brought about by cities can gain performative status. This multiplicity is what enables us to argue that life in the city contains magical powers; it is full to brimming with an abundance of life, which, in turn, provides many strange thoughts and knowledges. But we should not make too much of this. Though the city might in some senses be framed as a curved and sinuous baroque entity, which can never be entirely known, we also need to understand the other side of the coin. For example, texts may be instruments of passion but they are also very often ordering devices. Alongside a fancy magical realist novel, an Oulipo conceit, a murder mystery or even a fairy-tale, which themselves are, of course, attempts to impose a kind of order, there are gazetteers, A–Z's, and geographical information systems. These latter texts may be mundane, certainly, but they may well be no less important for how we structure and attend to our imaginative capacities.

If we live in a world of artifice, then this means thinking especially about the little things that escape our attention because they have become so much a part of everyday life, yet are constantly directing us here and there, often without us noticing because we have adjusted our bodies to their imperatives; we take on an appropriate posture without recognizing we are doing so (Lingis 1998). Latour's (1988) famous examples of the weighted hotel key and the automatic door closer are just two among many such examples. Think only of the paraphernalia of driving – the traffic signs, the road markings, the pedestrian crossings, the bollards and speed bumps. Or think of all the signs and objects that shepherd our bodies in particular directions – entrance and exit signs, push and pull signs on doors, seats, public toilets, cash registers, credit card swipe machines. Or think of all the machines constantly measuring how the city is going on, various computers, pollution meters, atmospheric meters. These are all things that run us as much as we run them; they are rules incarnated. Or maybe we need to make a different set of distinctions altogether and see such items as a part of the circulating entities to which we are hooked up and which provide cues for particular modes of consciousness and subjectivity to operate (Gil 1998; Latour 1999).

In turn, this leads us to understand the modern city as a whole series of circulating networks of command and control. But these networks do not add up to any definitive panoptic order, able to make the city open and transparent to the gaze of the powerful. Rather, they produce what Latour has called an 'oligopticon', a series of partial orders, localized totalities, with their ability to gaze in some directions and not others. The city becomes a series of observatories – in which many of the objects of the gaze have themselves been created as registers of the efficacy of that gaze – which enable the city to be overlooked, but also overlook many things. Thus de Certeau's tactics and little stratagems – a favourite theme of so much current writing on the city – can be seen as a demonstration of the non-additive and experimental nature of the city, which means there are always spaces and times left over and spaces and times which are neglected.

A precondition of the modern city is that it cannot be totally conditioned. Why? To begin with, the city is a complex imbroglio of actors with different goals, methods and ways of practice. Then, precisely because of this complexity, the city can never be wholly fathomed. There always remain parts that can never be reached because the instruments (devices, organizations, subject practices, etc.) created in order to reach and bring back particular locations are representations which must exclude to include/intrude – and are themselves acted to – and because new contributions are continually coming into being which will in any case outrun these instruments. Thus the city provides not only a set of objectives and knowledges but also a set of *ecologies of ignorance* (Luhmann 1998): gaps, blind spots, mistakes, unreliable paradoxes, ambiguities, anomalies, invisibilities which can only ever be partially taken in, since they are, to an extent, one of the means by which knowledge itself is created and justified. Even as the city creates objects to be governed, these are exceeded: in a sense, organizations in cities create problems to be solved:

> Organisations are not goal-realising but rather goal-seeking systems. They are constantly involved in interpreting (observing) their own operations and seek goals, or even new goals, that make what happens or has happened understandable and determinable. Planning is for the most part a writing of the system's memoirs . . . All planning, programmes, and directing consist in operations that must be accomplished within the system; that is, they are also observed with the system. What happens on the basis of planning does not come from the planning itself but the observation of the planning or even from the momentum of the observer of the planning. Reality functions according to the model of second order cybernetics. Organisations are organisations of observing systems. (Luhmann 1998: 105)

Indeed, increasingly much modern knowledge, guided by cybernetic and similar principles, assumes a deficit of knowledge. Then again, many problems a city may face cannot be forced into a framework of organized tasks, although it is often the case that it is assumed that this is possible, promoting an illusion of control.

There is one more point to make. Most of the activity that goes on in the city is unconscious (or rather conscious in different ways). One of the problems with writing the city has been that so much of that writing assumes that the city is a site of cognitive operations, motivated, planned, based on rules and principles, intent on accumulating knowledge. But so many of the relations in the city are unconscious. As we have pointed out, already there are all kinds of objects and devices whose efficacy is not cognitive but is, nevertheless, active. And perhaps 95 per cent of human action is non-cognitive. On a purely factual level then, most of human activity is cocooned in a system of practical knowledge which depends on bodily disposition rather than formal procedure. Then again, so much human activity does not require motives (attributions of intent, justifications, accounts) to be understood adequately. In other words, what we 'know' as the city is much more than we can tell (Polanyi 1956).

However, this does not of course mean that no fixed knowledge exists in the city or that formal knowledge is unimportant. The problem is the assumption that knowledge is stored in human heads when, in fact, it is stored in devices which form a part of a transhuman system, an ecology of mind which is distributed around networks rather than being held in just one place. In the final section, we therefore want to consider these devices in more detail. We will argue that the modern city has been constructed in large part by two – or now perhaps three – great waves of 'devices' (mediaries and intermediaries understood as cultural practices) which have constructed much of the fabric of what we now regard as everyday life. This is not, of course, to argue that everyday life can be reduced to these devices. But it cannot exist without them, for they are what provide the rhythm of the 'everyday' in each and every day (May and Thrift 2001). Nor is it to argue, as so many have done, that the manifestation of these devices represents a narrowing of experience: one could as well argue the opposite.

The Engineering of Certainty

As the city grows in size and, more importantly, as it adds in new entities, so its circulation becomes more complex, and so practices need to

be invented to cope with the complexity of the uncertainty that is in-
duced. These practices are clearly to do with the management of *encounters*, especially as a settlement moves beyond face-to-face interaction as
the only means of such management. Above all, this management of
encounters requires the invention of new spaces and times that regiment
and therefore direct bodily energies in productive ways.

> Each and every day we make ritual gestures, we move to the rhythm of
> external cadences, we cultivate our memories, we plan for the future. And
> everyone else does likewise. Daily experiences are only fragments in the
> life of an individual, far removed from the collective events more visible to
> us, and distant from the great changes sweeping through our culture. Yet
> almost everything that is important for social life unfolds within this minute
> web of times, spaces, gestures and relations. It is through this web that our
> sense of what we are doing is created, and in it lie dormant those energies
> that unleash sensational events. (Melucci 1996: 1)

The invention of new spaces and times? In a world which we understand as events located in a container defined by space and time, this
may seem an odd statement. But in fact, the comings and goings of
encounters have had to be constructed and located through mediaries
and intermediaries which register and are aimed at providing very different possibilities. As these spaces and times lie thicker on the ground, so
they have produced what we tend to call *everyday life*, a space of to and
fro which depends on the establishment of sites and means of return
(Seigworth 2000).

The exact status and content of everyday life remains, of course, a
matter of considerable debate (Gardiner 2000). After all, this is the space
of the mundane in which nothing much happens – and yet an awful lot
happens as well (Blanchot 1993). The realm of the quotidian has often
been written out or underplayed and yet it is in this realm, perhaps more
than any other, that cities have been so successful at rendering secure
and securely rendering. In a sense, everyday life may be the city's great-
est invention (Lefebvre 1991). But this realm includes so much that is
familiar but not necessarily known (to paraphrase Hegel's maxim which
Lefebvre was so fond of quoting) that we can only begin to list its
characteristics: the lived experience of spatiality and temporality; the
force of embodiment; the manifestation of subjectivity, affect and
desire; the importance of the 'event'; the ethico-aesthetic movement of
the encounter; and the importance of the precognitive, to name but a
few (see Thrift 2000a, 2000c). And the realm forms a sense (or senses)
that we find difficult to describe.

But what sort of sense is constitutive of this everydayness? Surely, this sense indicates much that is not sense so much as sensuousness, an embodied and somewhat automatic 'knowledge' that functions like peripheral vision, not studied contemplation, a knowledge that is precognitive and sensate rather than ideational. As such it not only challenges all critical practice, across the board, of academic disciplines but is a knowledge that lives as much in the objects and spaces of observation as in the body and mind of the observer. What's more, this sense has an activist, constructionist bent; not so much contemplative as it is caught *in media res*, working on, making anew, amalgamating, acting and reacting. (Taussig 1992: 16)

Perhaps Lefebvre's notion of 'everydayness' (spaces of representation, the lived) best captures the necessary project, those modes of existence that come to 'precede (and recede and exceed) . . . actualisation in representational spaces' (Seigworth 2000: 251) – an everydayness located in Lefebvre's other two terms of the equation of everyday life (spatial practice, the perceived) and the everyday (representations of space, the conceived) which both embrace it and make it possible. Straightaway, the connection to more general notions of life that we have prefaced in this chapter becomes clear, for the vitality of the virtual to be found in everydayness can be equated with, for example, Deleuze's notion of the lived as a set of virtualities, events and singularities, endlessly making waves, the 'fiery line of the world's breathing' (Scigworth 2000: 252). And it is the notion of life to be found in Guattari's notion of transversality and of 'being before being' (Guattari 1995, 2000). In both cases, life is a mutant, undisciplined creativity that is worked out through the properties of existence. In other words, everydayness captures 'the desires that bleed out from within and around the repetitions and cycles of modern life' (Seigworth 2000: 255) – but also depends on those repetitions and cycles to provide the working material through which these devices can be generated.

Everyday life was born in the city through the invention of a world of objects and texts which could present and re-present the present in such a way as to make it (or at least make it seem) replicable, likely to produce certain known outcomes. Of course, this process of the 'detailing of circumstances' (Sherman 1997) has been going on for a long time. Clanchy (1991) and Goody (1996), for example, note the growth of lists and the parallel growth of bureaucracies in the early medieval period. Later in history, in late medieval cities, we can make a tour of tally sticks, double entry book-keeping, account books, more and more sophisticated metrics, even simple maps, as means of providing replicable spaces and times. But perhaps the first period in which the modern western city was clearly *designed* as a known and knowable entity was in the seventeenth and eighteenth centuries. Here, what we find coming into existence is a series of devices which enable the city's encounters to be recorded and ordered; a new choreography and chronogeography thereby develops (Thrift 1996b).

To begin with, there are new means of *marking* time. The *watch* allows the inhabitants of the city to construct finer grained time. Though at first watches are largely ornamental objects, indicators of the wearer's power and wealth, as pocket watches telling minutes (not very accurately until the later seventeenth century) become widely available, so a truly accessible private source of chronometric information comes into being; one which produces in the likes of Samuel Pepys a wonderful glee for a new apparatus that can measure out his motion in time and space:

> To the Change after office, and received my watch from the watch-maker; and a very fine (one) it is . . . given me by Briggs the Scrivener. Home to dinner; and then abroad to the Attorney General . . . So home, and late at my office. But Lord, to see how much of my old folly and childishness hangs upon me still, that I cannot forbear carrying my watch in my hand in the coach all this afternoon, and seeing what o'clock it is 100 times. And am apt to think with myself: how could I be so long without one. (cited in Sherman 1997: 77–8)

A few months later Pepys's glee has turned to a means of measuring out the city: 'up, and walked to Greenwich, taking pleasure to walk with my minute watch in my hand, by which I am now come to see the distance of my way from Woolwich to Greenwich. And do find myself to come within two minutes constantly to the same place at the end of each quarter hour' (cited in Sherman 1997: 79). The minutes became a means of measuring the city anew. Thus:

> In Pepys's short record of his experiment, details of space become secondary to those of time. Pepys names only his point of departure and of destination (and those confusedly; still unaccustomed to moving in those precincts, he begins his entry in the manuscript, 'Up, and walked to Woolwich', before crossing out the final word and replacing it with 'Greenwich'). Despite his opening announcement that 'I am now come to see the distances of my way', Pepys delineates no 'distances' reached as number of miles or the fixed points on the route. Instead, he tells time. What interests him both in the walking and the writing is the relation of his movement to that of the watch, which he gazes at continually as its hands advance steadily through large spans and small. Even for those durations he offers no absolute numbers, nor does he say how long the journey takes him; he recites them only relative to each other and to his progress, and gleans

from them a layered self-knowledge: of the fundamental regularity of his pace (and by reciprocal influence, of the watch's), of the inevitable and idiosyncratic variations of tempo within that steady structure, and even of the exact range of those variations ('within two minutes'). By writing up 'the distances of my way' in minutes rather than in miles, Pepys manages both to make good on the odd plural in that phrase, and to give singular force to the possessive. The space he traces along the public road belongs to all, but the timing of his trek belongs to him alone. 'My' way consists of multiple temporal 'distances' that vary from each other from day to day and from span to span: some occupy thirteen minutes, some seventeen and some durations in between. (Sherman 1997: 89)

Then there is the invention of new means of *recording* time. For example, the *diary* was, in certain senses, a textual analogue of the watch, a means of gridding everyday life via a calibrated narrative with its imperative to fill each dated blank space with prose. At the same time, the diary heightened skills of observations of everyday life, since the event now could be routinely noted down. The diary went hand-in-hand with items of textual comprehension like the memo books, the making of 'minutes' by clerks, and the use of shorthand ('tachygraphy' or rapid writing) to produce a textual comprehension much closer to that of the present, which, indeed, begins to produce a different kind of present, but compressed and, through these new possibilities now offered, opened out.

Then, finally, there is the invention of new means of *circulating* urban times. In particular there is the *newspaper*. From the time of the publication of the first daily newspaper – at the beginning of the eighteenth century – we see running accounts of the public realm offered which in turn define the public realm as a sealed time and space in which an hour can profitably be spent keeping up with the print-out. The newspaper leads to another closely linked invention, the *post*. Until the end of the seventeenth century, most countries had no regular postal service other than the 'occasional' porter for hire, ready to carry what needed carrying. 'Now the post assured the papers a means of delivery, the papers guaranteed the post a steady source of income (then as now, there were special newspaper rates), and the symbiosis between the two affected not only the papers' timing, but also their form and meaning' (Sherman 1997: 120).

The net result of these inventions was to produce a city which could be attended to in new ways because of a layer of *mediation* which provides new means of achieving immediacy (Bolter and Grusin 1999). In turn, it can therefore be argued that these inventions stimulated new cultural forms – like the novel. Thus:

In 'Course in the Novel', his seminal account of novelistic heteroglossia, Mikhail Bakhtin established that what he calls the 'everyday genres' . . . 'diaries, confessions, journalistic articles and so on' – 'play an equally significant role' in the making of the novel, 'bring(ing) it into their own language'. He posits a modern chronotype (i.e. a time-space matrix) grounded in 'everyday life' as a defining feature of the novel, 'such elements . . . as food, drink, the sexual act, death . . . enter everyday life, which is already in the process of being compartmentalised. (Sherman 1997: 211)

As a single word, the term 'everyday' operates as a kind of mass noun and (if such a thing existed) mass adjective; it identifies phenomena – habit, practices – which have become familiar by frequent use over extended time. When compartmentalised – separated into 'every day' – it points to something completely different: the successive but separate units of time in which such familiarity develops. It is in this form that the term best incarnates the new compartmentalisations – in clocks, calendars, texts and consciousness . . . (Sherman 1997: 225)

During the late eighteenth and early nineteenth centuries, these kinds of devices were extended and made more complex by developments in communications like the coach, the railway and the telegraph, and by the organizational templates needed in order to cope with the more complex timings and spacings they made possible (and not least the railway companies themselves) (Thrift 1990). But we could argue that, for the bulk of the population, these developments only started to bite into the organization of everyday life in the latter part of the nineteenth century. From then on and into the early twentieth century there is a wave of re-mediation of everyday life, in which the very fabric of presence and absence, departure and return is reworked into a new productive banality. What Seigworth calls a new 'rhythmic soak' (2000: 255) comes into existence and defines what existence is. And this re-mediation takes place through the medium of cities which now begin to transform life in myriad ways (see Kern 1983; May and Thrift 2001). The spaces and times prefigured by the inventions of the seventeenth and eighteenth centuries are now inculcated into networks of devices, thereby confirming the existence of these spaces and times, extending them into more and more aspects of human activity and allowing human beings to be present in several activities at once. In other words, the city becomes a vast narrative structure that constantly re-presents itself. In particular, everyday life is distributed over a much wider area: the city thereby itself becomes a kind of clock and map writ large.

This distribution takes place through four main inventions. The first of these is the model of *commuting* that springs up at the end of the nineteenth century based on horse-drawn carriages and trams and then on the automobile (box 4.2). This phenomenon – which has enormous consequences in its impact on the growth of the city – produces a basic rhythm the length and breadth of the city, in the constant ebb and flow of people and traffic supported by continuous design innovations. (Take just the case of the humble roundabout, an idea that was invented in France and imported into Britain – to the garden city of Letchworth – in 1907. By 1925, there were 'gyratory systems' in London – at Parliament Square, Hyde Park Corner and Marble Arch among other locations. In 1966, 'give way to the right' became mandatory in order to promote smooth flow, followed by new 'mini-roundabouts', designed to produce efficient flow on minor roads (Martin 2000).)

The second invention is the growth of reliable and fast means of *transmitting and storing information*. This was reflected in the rapid growth of the postal service (which already by the end of the nineteenth century, in larger cities at least, could mean eight or nine deliveries a day). The service inspired all manner of territories and temporalities. Then there was the use of the telegraph, which provided flows of information with unprecedented speed and regularity. And there is the growth of the telephone in the twentieth century, with its own particular rhythms and cadences (see de Sola Pool 1981; Thrift 1990; Katz and Katz 1998). But these devices were the tip of an informational iceberg. As important was the growth of means of analysing, recording and storing information, taking in a vast array of mundane devices that mechanized writing, the adding machine, the typewriter and also filing cabinets and card files (Yates 2000).

The third invention is the growth of *reliable means of supporting everyday actors*: the growth of gas, electrical and sewage networks, for example. These networks begin to produce a vast underground realm of urban services (Gandy 1997; Kaika and Swyngedouw 2000). Finally, there is the growth in the *means of mass representation*. The newspaper and the novel are joined by the radio, the gramophone, mass photography, the cinema and television, producing an enormous symbolic economy of mechanized images which redefines the sense of a location which a person inhabits as being more than the area they inhabit. The city becomes a set of elsewheres that test the notion of where to set its limits.

These four developments are supported by an iconography of devices which are both essential parts of reproduction and, at the same time, a means of communication of their existence. Thus, in the case of commuting, the chief icon is probably road signage and markings, a landscape of movement so obvious to us now that we hardly notice it at all. For example, much of the modern motoring landscape of Britain today took shape in the 1930s: the first pedestrian crossing, white centre-lines

Box 4.2   Cars

Until quite recently, cars have been the city's unmarked epiphany: so important that they seem to be almost invisible. Yet, as Urry points out, even simple facts are startling in their implications: there are now 500 million cars worldwide – most of them concentrated in cities – and that figure is expected to double by 2015. Cars make up the single most important industrial system and they have produced an enormous associated machinic assemblage consisting of the 'car's technical and social interlinkages with other industries, including car parts and accessories; petrol refining and distribution; road-building and maintenance; hotels, roadside scenic areas and motels; car sales and repair workshops; suburban house building; new retailing and leisure complexes; advertising and marketing; and so on' (Urry 2000: 58). Cars are one of the key moments in individual consumption, and thereby a potent cultural icon: there are numerous 'car cultures' (Miller 2000). Cars are the predominant form of mobility in most cities, and the key environmental issue facing cities. The 'culture of automobility' is surely Weber's iron (or steel, or aluminium) cage of modernity incarnate.

In cities, we can say that cars have four main presences in everyday urban life. First, they represent millions of 'little times' which have displaced one objective clock time. Cars represent the ability to produce personalized prescribed timetables, but at the same time that flexibility is coerced 'because the moving car forces people to orchestrate in complex and heterogeneous ways their mobilities and socialities across very significant distances' (Urry 2000: 59). This is active passivity. Second, they are a key form of social interaction. Within the car there are accepted roles (back-seat driver, passenger as navigator, etc.). Between cars, there are also various forms of interaction. Encounters can be civil or aggressive as drivers literally mobilize their anger in a V-sign. Katz shows that the road is one of the most potent sources of everyday urban moral philosophy:

> Drivers monitor the interaction content of the vehicular form that they inhabit, managing their thing-selves from within and without. What the angry driver seeks to defend, when he or she is cut off, is not the trajectory of the car but the intertwining of the body and the car. Anger's enemy is in the first instance an effort to hold onto an inhabited form. When one is cut off, the offence lies precisely in the

understanding that other drivers would treat 'one's' car as an impersonal thing, without harming the car, of which the driver is intensely
aware, that what is cut off is the driver. (1999: 45)

Third, and relatedly, what cars produce is a driving body, seated,
hands on steering wheel and handbrake, feet on pedals, which is
able to deal quickly with many risky situations. This is a hands-on
sensual verification (Katz 1999: 94) which cars are increasingly
designed to elaborate: cars are designed so that the driver's hands
and feet naturally fall on buttons and controls. Fourth, cars are a
means of habitation, of dwelling (Urry 2000). They inhabit the
road – and there is a genuine ecology of the road itself. Then, they
are a habitation in themselves.

> The environment beyond the windscreen is an alien other, to be kept
> at bay through the diverse privatising technologies which have been
> incorporated within the contemporary car. These technologies ensure
> a consistent temperature, large supplies of information, a relatively
> protected environment, high quality sounds and sophisticated systems
> of monitoring which enable the car driver to negotiate conditions of
> intense riskiness on especially high speed road. (Urry 2000: 63)

Then again, as this quotation implies, increasingly what is being
inhabited is an intelligent machine which points to the hybrid person-
machine nature of the car.

Cars, then, have become one of the key means of timing the
spaces and spacing the times of the city. They take up much of the
space of the city (Horvath 1973). 'They have replaced watches as
the micro-engineered personal possession that, like a miniature
world's fair exhibit, displays the latest technological achievements
to the masses. Also like watches, cars can be readily constructed as
a reassuring touchstone for the assessment of messier segments of
one's life' (Katz 1999: 44). Indeed as Katz goes on to argue.

> The marketing of cars and watches has set up a kind of cultural
> competition between metaphors of space and time, and cars are now
> winning decisively in this struggle. Cars commonly have clocks in
> them that display time more visibly than any wristwatch. And cars
> now contain other devices (phones, fax machines, CD players) that
> allow one to conquer time and space by maintaining several lines of
> actions and identities at once. So far, time pieces have not yet been
> made into machines for moving their wearers. (1999: 352)

on the road (in 1931), dotted white lines (in 1936), coordinated signs; and then in the 1950s and 1960s, yellow lines (in 1956), white lines to mark the road edge (in 1966) and box junctions (in 1966). These icons create their own spaces and times; parking times, traffic-light cycles (usually between 24 and 120 seconds), queues. In the case of means of transmitting and storing information, the ring of the telephone bell arrives, the clatter of the typewriter, and so on. In the case of the support networks, it is the things we take for granted, the oven, the toilet, the plug socket, and so on. And in the case of the growth in the means of representation, it is those mundane signifiers that constantly tell us where we are, the television channel's logo, the local radio station's jingle. These are the banal locational cues that affirm that place, that make us exercise our existence (Billig 1995).

It may be that we are currently passing through a third major phase in the constitution of everyday life, as a cloud of informational devices begins to descend over the city, bringing with them another informational re-mediation (Castells 1996; Sassen 1999b). Thus the computer screen, the internet, the mobile phone, the personal digital organizer, and a host of other devices, all provide means of structuring the life of the city in new ways, by combining heterogeneous spaces, by providing new support networks that provide further kinds of immunity to disorder and by producing new means of representation which are media-saturated (or hypermediated) attempts to erase all traces of mediation (Bolter and Grusin 1999). We should not exaggerate (what, after all, is one of the key applications in so many of these devices but a diary?), but nor should we downplay the inventiveness of the cultural uses to which these devices can be put (as, for example, in the case of the unexpected growth of text messaging, which is initiating new kinds of social swarming across the city (Townsend 2000). There are, in other words, important new 'informational ecologies' which are being born in the city at present (Nardi and O'Day 2000) and which may well provide important sources of diversity in modern cities, if the discourse of technological neutrality can be surmounted.

Most particularly, the growth of ubiquitous and wearable computing has the potential to produce cities which constantly compute. Such developments – which are more important than the overhyped internet – provide, through the combination of computing and wireless, for a whole new era of 'informational devices' (Norman 1998) which will allow computing to become a pervasive part of the urban environment, with even the most mundane device having some computing power and some ability to communicate with other devices, so producing a constant informational hum. In turn, this computing power will become better and better at responding to or mimicking human bodies, through a greater and greater capacity to recognize voices and faces, and even work with and simulate affect (French and Thrift 2002).

In turn, this re-mediation produces its own iconography. There are the obvious icons that inhabit computer screens, all the way from bins and bookmarks to the musical bars that signify that the computer has booted up, which now means that screens have taken on a kind of life of their own as part of a 'postsocial' realm (Knorr-Cetina 2001). More to the point, increasingly there is an expectation that the world will be structured on the same lines as a technical substrate like the screen, an expectation of a certain technical presence, which is on a much greater scale than in the two previous constructions of everyday life. Clough (2001) even writes of a new technological 'unconscious' which is predicated on globalized technical networks (exchanging information, capital, bodies, abstract knowledge and media events) which are beyond any single user's ability to control and which presage a new postpersonal imaginary.

The point is, of course, that all these different timings and spacings directly make up everyday urban experience, the sound of the radio news, the thud of a letter coming through the letterbox – or the chime signifying new email – the click of the kettle for the morning coffee, the taste of that coffee, the smell of exhaust fumes, and so on. And, more than this, these different timings and spacings of immediacy produce a structure of *expectation*: we are often put out if they do not happen; it is abnormal, unusual, out of the 'ordinary'. In other words, through the detailing of circumstances these different timings and spacings have *produced the ordinary*.

So far we have said very little about the role of embodiment in the construction of everyday life in the city; the account has all been about devices. There are varying reasons for this. To begin with, the body is very often only a trace in the city, its authority and 'humanity' depending on the bodily extensions we have outlined above (Latour and Hermant 1998). Then, it is possible to argue that this has become more and more the case: the subject is, in a sense, becoming object (Boyne 2001), as some of us live in more and more technologized cities in which the body comes heavily equipped as part of a more general assemblage. But most importantly, the absence of bodies is because we have yet to add one more element into our story: body disciplines.

Cities are means of mass producing and acculturating bodies. And in the nineteenth and twentieth centuries we have seen this insight incorporated into institutions which strive to govern the production of bodies (Segel 1998). These institutions are ways of life. There are institutions of education. There are institutions of discipline and punishment (concerned institutions, police, etc.). There are institutions of health and hygiene. In the more extreme Foucauldian manifestations, these institutions form a normalizing machine complete to itself, extruding well-disciplined bodies which are complicit in their own discipline through the interaction of what counts as the norm (and the abnormal). But such a gigantic design process is too severe a vision for at least three reasons. First, Foucault himself drew back from it, by searching out self-fashioning modes of signification which might provide a space of resistance and by identifying a new mode of governmentality – the so-called pastoral mode – which attaches more importance to the formation of a confessional self that is allowed more agency in return for making more of the self available. Second, it too often confuses systems of allocation with efficiency. It is quite clear that discipline does not always produce availability. Then, third, and again a characteristic of Foucauldian thought, bodies are reduced to embodiment degree zero: shorn of many of their performative capacities, unconscious thought, emotions, passions, even violence, they present a peculiarly passive stance to the world. Even so, it is clear that everyday life also consists of many unconscious body movements which have been inculcated into us from an early age (Thrift 2000c). To a large degree, expectation of what happens next resides in the body and increasingly that expectation is engineered by various abstracted systems which strive to produce replicable results across large spaces and times. Seen in this way, order is able to be obtained without explicit rules, through routine invocations which call forth our mastery of a situation (or lack of it).

However, the detailing of circumstance and the vagaries of bodily disciplines have not necessarily made the world appear more deterministic. Lingis has argued that 'we have in modern Western culture, for the conduct of our lives, only a science of determinism and chance and an ethic of freedom and decision. The archaic discourse of luck and destiny survives only in the disqualified columns as astrological charts in our newspapers' (1998: 167). Still the growth of ideas of complexity and of the creative power of chance (Lestienne 1998) may be producing a much less rigid sense of the way of the world – one which plays to the joys of cities. But this sense is only now starting to become widespread. And that in a context of the establishment of very widespread order and certainty (though as the phenomenon of writing shows, not that widespread). On the whole, as we have shown, inhabitants of cities like to believe that the world will show up at something approaching the right time and at something approaching the right place (and given the vagaries of previous cities in history, who can blame them?). In the next chapter we want to take up this issue again, but in a rather different way, by reconsidering notions of power and domination.

5   POWERFUL CITIES

Introduction

Cities are rarely the site of disinterested practices. They are full of subtle, and not-so-subtle, acts of brutality. Even (or especially) in transhuman cities, certain ways of life gain priority over others – often at their expense. The city is as much a means of shutting down possibility as it is a means, through the openness of some (and only some) encounters, of opening it up. We come, in other words, to the 'hard' issues of power, domination and oppression – and to the role of cities in defining who or what is normal and who or what is abnormal, who or what is appropriate and who or what is inappropriate and who or what can be conceived and who or what is inconceivable. One thing has to be said at the outset. Though we have argued that cities do not add up and that in the gaps and overlaps cities offer means of seizing the new through their capacity for recombination, we do not mean to suggest that cities do not produce additive, even totalizing, projects, intent on seizing the right to the city.

Our interest in power is of a very particular kind in this chapter. Rather than focusing on the conventional interest in urban studies on the domination and oppression by certain kinds of actors and institutions, our concern is with power as a mobile, circulating force which through the constant re-citation of practices, produces self-similar outcomes, moment by moment. This is power based on momentum, rather than inscription. It is power conceived as power to, rather than power over. It is power 'as the relation of', force to the other forces it affects, or even to forces that affect it (inciting, exciting, inducing, seducing, and so on, are affects) (Deleuze 1986: 17). So to begin this chapter we will focus on the chief ordering projects of western cities. Obviously, we will have to paint with a broad brush, and the way that we will do this is through the Foucauldian concept of the diagram as revealed through the various urban utopian projects of the eighteenth, nineteenth and twentieth centuries.

But, then, in the second part of the chapter we will discuss the ways in which the city escapes lines of power through the production of institutions that bypass at least some of the dominant imperatives. Our argument is that the city is able to produce this escape in three interrelated ways. First, through providing space-times where practices of power either do not reach, or are heavily contested. Second, through providing sensory registers that practices of power do not have much purchase on. And, third, through stimulating practices of imagination and fantasy that quite literally escape dominant orders. In the first case we will concentrate on the night. In the second case we will concentrate on senses other than vision, especially sound. And in the third case we will concentrate on the city's dreams of itself. However, in none of these cases are we trying to provide a naive view. 'Escape' is always a matter of degree, as we will argue in the final part of the chapter, where we will show that there is a constant process of co-option, by reference to the theming of urban experience, which allows all manner of urban imaginations and fantasies to be turned into commodities, and to the writing of software which sets practices in stone.

Diagrams of Power

The bare outlines of power, domination and oppression are what will concern us in this section. These are not to be thought of as underlying structures, but rather as *lines of flight*; accumulations of a *passion to construct the world in particular ways*; impulses which constitute how and therefore what things are to be controlled, modes of practice which are also modes of thought. Such a notion is perhaps best captured by the Foucauldian idea of the diagram, understood as an impulse without determinate goals, a 'functioning, abstracted from any obstacle . . . or function [which] must be detached from any specific use' (Foucault 1979: 205).

For Foucault, the diagram was an 'informal' dimension, an abstract machine which stamps a particular form of conduct on a human multiplicity: 'the imposition of a form of conduct is done by distributing in space, laying out and serialising in time, composing in space-time, and so on' (Deleuze 1986: 35). The diagram does not have 'goals' as such; an unstable and fluid affair, 'it is almost blind and mute, even though it makes others see and speak':

> Every diagram is inter-social and constantly evolving. It never functions in order to represent a persisting world but produces a new kind of reality, a new model of truth. It is neither the subject of history, nor does it survey history. It makes history by unmaking preceding realities and significations, consisting of hundreds of points of emergence or creativity, unexpected conjunctions or improbable continuums. (Deleuze 1986: 35–6)

Thus the diagram produces what might be called 'immanent cause', that is cause which is 'realised, integrated and distinguished in its effect'. How to describe this 'here–not here state'? First of all:

> the diagram is the map of relations between forces, a map of destiny, or intensity, which proceeds by primary non-localisable relations and at every moment passes through every point, 'or other in relation to every relation from one point to another'. Of course, this has nothing to do with either a transcendent idea or with an ideological superstructure, or even with an economic infrastructure, which is already qualified by its substance and defined by its form and use. None the less the diagram acts as a non-unifying immanent cause that is coextensive with the whole social field: the abstract machine is like the cause of the concrete assemblages [schools, workshops, army, etc.] that execute its relations and these relations between forces take place 'not above' but within the very tissue of the assemblages they produce. (Deleuze 1986: 36–7)

Second, the diagram is, in effect, a kind of selection mechanism. Assemblages are selected by diagrams. For example, prison may have only a marginal existence in sovereign societies and becomes important only when a new disciplinary diagram directs attention to it and makes it into an exemplary collective machine. Third, the diagram can indicate to only a limited degree what form an assemblage takes. They may be sharply segmented with well-constructed insides, and outsides, and quite different principles of generation, or they may form a continuum, all coming to resemble one another because they are run on similar principles, or they may be crossroads accommodating the complete diagram and making exchanges with other diagrams.

In the modern western city, many diagrams coexist. We will catalogue just four of the most important of these and we will do this by reference to the literature of urban utopia, which provides exemplary cases of how these diagrams might be assembled. In each case, the diagram provides an important map of a particular social field, illustrates its productive and passionate possibilities as a formation of power, and also points to new problems: 'there is no diagram that does not also include, besides the points which it connects up, certain relatively free or unbound points, points of creativity, change and resistance' (Deleuze 1986: 44).

The four diagrams we will outline come together in various combinations and with varying intensities in systems of governance that we will call, after Foucault, forms of 'governmentality'. Foucault's chief concern was with an analysis of government which took as its central concern *how* we govern and are governed within specific regimes, and the conditions under which such regimes are able to emerge, continue to persist, and are transformed. According to Dean (1999: 23), an analytics of government therefore works through four dimensions of problematization:

1   Characteristic forms of visibility, ways of seeing and perceiving.
2   Distinctive ways of thinking and questioning, relying on definite vocabularies and procedures for the production of thoughts (for instance, those derived from the social, human and behavioural sciences).
3   Specific ways of acting, intervening and directing, made up of particular types of practical rationality ('expertise' and 'know-how'), and relying on definite mechanisms, techniques and technologies).
4   Characteristic ways of forming subjects, selves, persons, actors or agents.

However, in using the term 'governmentality', we need to take care. Foucault's inclination was to think of such systems of governance as all-encompassing – not panoptic, but certainly close to it. Because he wanted to show how governmentalities constructed subjects who in turn constructed practices which frame the world in confirmatory ways, he was clearly pessimistic about the room for manoeuvre to be found within technologies of government, and sceptical about what might lie 'beyond' power (Deleuze 1986: 109). For example, he would probably have been pessimistic that modern systems of surveillance, in which we are often undisturbed 'by the fact that our own observations are being observed' (Luhmann 1998: 62), could generate practices which work with or go round that observation in qualified ways – even given his earlier work on resistance, countermemory and the like. In partial contradiction, our intention is to think of forms of governmentality as much looser operations, which can even be overwhelmed – precisely by their own impulses. In other words, forms of governmentality may be totalizing *projects*, but they are not totalizations. Thus city populations can escape some of their inclinations and find new angles of declination. This ability to escape these projects is the subject of the following section.

Bureaucracy

The first impulse is bureaucratic. While it is problematic to characterize bureaucracy as just the unthought practices of institutional rationality – indeed it may be that a state bureaucracy is essential to the maintenance of democracy (du Gay 2000) – still we may say that the bureautic impulse is a crucial element of the city, whether that impulse is manifested on clay tablets, in filing cabinets or in databanks. The mention of 'bureaucracy' tends to conjure up images of a dry-as-dust world of here reconstructed in files as there. But we need to see the impulse to record and categorize as much more than this, as a passion of a much stronger kind:

> a sensual pleasure in classifications, the same mania for cutting up (the body of Christ, the body of the victim, the human soul), the same enumerative obsession (accounting for sins, tortures, passions and even for accounting errors), the same image practice (imitation, tableau, seance), the same erratic, fantasmatic fashioning of the social system. (Barthes 1976: 3)

To begin with, the bureaucratic impulse consists of the obsessive multiplication of categories, sometimes amounting to a fetish for enumeration. For example, the inventor of the utopian paradise of Harmony, Joseph Fourier, divides mankind into 1,620 fixed passions, combinable but not transformable. Cabet encourages the recording of accounts and facts in absolutely objective 'minutes', rather than in newspapers, minimizing errors and speculation. And so on. The desire is to produce an irreducible articulation, a summation of intelligibles in a metrical order which means that *nothing is left to be said*: everything has been captured. Then there is the emphasis on cutting up and naming territory. Space has to be planned so that it can be named, weighed up and elaborated. Thus nearly all urban utopias are distinguished by an extensive spatial order in which all life is laid out: form and function coincide as a kind of glue of asocial relations.

Production

The second impulse is production. The productionist impulse is also often to be found, naked and unadorned, in urban utopias. Usually this impulse simply mimics capitalist production in its desire to produce an effective machine, but in some versions of urban utopias, production becomes a kind of orgy of excess, prefiguring career capitalism. Certainly we can see how production is figured as a desiring machine in three ways. First, as a vast army of bodies, marching towards the thoroughly planned industrial millennium. For example, in Bellamy's *Looking Back* of 1888, cities are run by industrial armies of workers who are mustered into industrial service for twenty-four years. There they become part of diverse trades on the basis of their aptitudes.

> Every man for himself in accordance with his natural aptitude, the utmost pains being taken to enable him to find out what his natural aptitude really is. The principle on which an industrial army is organised is that a man's natural enhancements, mental or physical, determine what he can work at most profitably to the nation and to himself. While the obligation of service in some form is not to be evaded, voluntary election, subject only to necessary regulation, is depended on to determine the particular sort of service every man is to render. As an individual's satisfaction during his term of service depends on his having an occupation to his taste, parents and teachers watch from early years for indication of special aptitudes in children. A thorough study of the national industrial system with the history and achievements of all the great trades, is an essential part of our educational system. While manual training is not allowed to encroach on the general intellectual culture to which our schools are devoted, it is carried far enough to give our youth, in addition to their technical knowledge of the national industries, mechanical and agricultural, a certain familiarity with their tools and methods. Our schools are constantly using our workshops, and often we take on long excursions to inspect particular industrial enterprises. In your day a man was not alarmed to be grossly ignorant of all trades except his own, but such ignorance would not be consistent with our idea of placing every one in a position to select intelligently the occupation for which he has most taste. Usually, long before he is mustered into service a young man has found out the pursuit he wants to follow, has acquired a great deal of knowledge about it, and is waiting impatiently for the time when he can enlist in its ranks. (Bellamy 1996: 31–2)

Second, production is figured as a vast generalized web of exchange. Fourier, for example, subverts the notion of the stock exchange by producing a much more social body, a 'negotiation assembly' in each canton which deals every day with the disposition of meals and tasks, meetings for work and pleasure, borrowing of cohorts among the various cantons, and with all manner of meetings and travels. In turn, this giant filofax produces a 'great entertainment' since:

> There are functionaries of all kinds, and dispositions, by means of which each individual may follow thirty or so intrigues at once; in such a way that the exchange of the least canton is more animated than those of London or Amsterdam. There one negotiates principally through signals by means of which each director-trader may, from his office, enter into

debate with all individuals and deal, through his acolytes, on behalf of twenty groups, twenty series, twenty cantons at once, without racket or confusion. Women and children also trade as well as men in order to fix meetings of all kinds, and the struggles that arise each day in this subject among series, groups, individuals form the most piquant game, the most captivated intrigue . . . (Fourier, cited in Mattelart 1996: 140)

Then, third, production is a vast landscape of ordered flows, a body productive, which is able to put everything in its place. For example, in Chayanov's utopia of 1924:

> The concept of the city – a self-sufficient place, with the countryside serving as its pedestal – has completely disappeared. Towns and villages are no more than 'points of application of a node of social connections', gathering places, the central points of a district, places full of colour, culture, theatres, museums, cafeterias, leisure and public services. Although Moscow still has a hundred thousand inhabitants, there are hotels for four million outside visitors, and lodgings for a hundred thousand visitors in each district of ten thousand inhabitants. Factories have moved to the country and fields are run as co-operatives. Technical inventions linked to the new land management plan have allowed for the installation of 'metaphors', a network of 4,500 stations of magnetic flows capable of mastering atmospheric conditions.
>
> The rural habitat is dispersed. But an intelligent policy of communication has placed each peasant at one to one and a half hours from his town. And he goes there often. The administration of these routes is, along with justice, one of only two items belonging to a central power, to state control (a state that has become a means and not an end in itself). What is essential to the organisation of social life is found elsewhere; not only in the co-operatives but in different associations, congresses, leagues, newspapers and other organs of public opinion, academics and clubs. (Mattelart 1996: 160)

Sensuality

The third impulse is sensual: the city is both a focus and a producer of bodily experiences and desires which can touch on each of the senses and combinations thereof in all kinds of unexpected ways (box 5.1). In many urban utopias sensual impulse is reined in – except for the obsessive visual gaze. But in a few utopias the cities become maximizers of all the senses, generators of a heightened state of bodily awareness. Perhaps the most obvious example of this tendency is the work of Fourier.

At the age of 27, Fourier himself hit upon what he believed to be God's plan in assigning sensory proportions and passions to everything in the

Box 5.1   The gardenscape

Many cities around the world are studded with gardens or yards. Yet this quintessential suburban activity has received remarkably little attention, perhaps because it is so suburban and therefore out-with the imperious and belittling gaze of the intellectual (Silverstone 1996; Baxandall and Ewen 1999). Certainly, the continuing neglect of gardening now seems downright odd. First, there is the sheer size of gardening as an economic circuit. In Britain, for example, garden-ing is now a £3.6 billion per annum industry (Lee 2000). Second, gardening has formidable environmental consequences, some good (gardens as wildlife corridors), some bad (excessive water use in arid areas). Third, gardening is a major activity of urban residents, not because they are all incipient garden designers desperate to give their garden a makeover (although the garden is a sign of a practical aesthetics), but for quite other reasons. To begin with, gardening is a major focus of sociality, a source of everyday tasks and a means of access to all manner of clubs, shows, competitions, and so on. Then there are the sheer sensual pleasures of gardening: gardening is a way in which the body can become immersed, committed, in touch. And then there is the matter of gardening knowledge. Garden-ing is perhaps one of the key urban circuits of knowledge. Formal sources of knowledge like books, television programmes and videos amplify what is already an extraordinarily widespread set of prac-tical skills. Fourth, gardening is a key source of cultural-technical innovations. From the pond to the summerhouse, from the patio to the shed, from decking to the introduction of new flowers and shrubs, each year gardening is a key cultural site.

Take the lawn, a quintessential aspect of British cities which takes up a large part of their overall area. No one knows quite when the grass lawn was first invented. The Romans may have had them. They may have originated in Benedictine monasteries. The word 'lawn' is first found in the English language in the mid-sixteenth century, but then only to refer to a clearing in woodland. It seems likely that the craze for bowling greens in Tudor times led to the first true 'lawns' (as in later times, the quintessentially suburban game of golf would become a similar lawny icon) (Fort 2000). But until the end of the eighteenth century there were only two ways to manage cultivated grass – by animal (cow, sheep, deer) or by scythe. It was the invention of the mowing machine (bulky and of use only to a few, then made general through the offices of the push mower and the petrol mower) in the nineteenth century that made management possible and with this the democratization of the lawn. The lawn became the basic canvas of the suburban garden (Fort 2000), and lawn mowing became the archetypal sign of suburban masculinity.

The idea and practice of the lawn moved out to the cities of other countries too, most notably to North America.

> Among early Presidents, both Washington and Jefferson were lawn experts. The house Jefferson built at Monticello, with its vistas of immaculate turf, overlooks his University of Virginia, known familiarly as the Lawn. As time went on, however, the American domestic grass patch became a site for puritanical bullying. You could judge a man's character by the state of his lawn, or so the pioneers of the garden suburb movement taught. Neat lawns reflected family virtue. They also upped property values, so righteousness and profit went hand-in-hand. Privacy was suspect. It was 'unChristian' to hedge your garden from the sight of others decreed Frank Jessup Scott, prophet of the suburban paradise. Lawn care became a national issue, with Congress voting thousands of dollars to the study of grass cultivation. (Carey 2000: 40–1)

So the lawn has managed to make its way even into patently unsuitable environments like Los Angeles where the sprinkler-induced hissing of summer lawns is a crucial part of the city's sensory experience.

> universe. He decided that all things, including humans, were linked through bonds of natural attraction. Civilisation (a foul word in Fourier's vocabulary) attempted to repress and divert these natural attractions or passions, thus disrupting the social and cosmic order. In the ideal world, however, the carefully orchestrated accommodation of all passions would lead to an harmonious and just world order. (Classen 1998: 25)

Fourier's ideal urban society of Harmony, ruled by taste and touch above sight, hearing and smell, has eliminated material poverty and so can devote itself to the perfection of the sensory faculties. Thus:

> everyone in Harmony will be guaranteed employment suited to their temperament and will have access to a wide range of sensory pleasures . . . children will have their senses educated from an early age . . . The sense

of taste will be trained through the study of cuisine, thus taking advantage of children's love of food and turning them from gluttons to gourmets. The senses of sight and hearing will be educated through the presentation of operas, allowing children to indulge in their passion for singing, acting, dressing up, and painting. Touch will be educated through enjoyable manual activities.

Furthermore, where the senses are repulsed and repressed in civilisation, they will be attracted and cultivated in Harmony. The sense of hearing will, on the one hand, be flattered by daily concerts, and on the other, no longer be assaulted by noise: carpenters will be confined to isolated quarters and croaking toads will be exterminated. The architecture of Harmony in turn, will create curved spaces where the voice will resonate, allowing conversations to be carried out at a distance. Harmony will also be pleasing to the eye. The openness of the architecture will allow the eye to range freely over the city without constantly being obstructed by brick walls. The colours of Harmony will offer both sensuous and spiritual delights to the subject, as every colour will be employed in keeping with the symbolic meaning . . . (cited in Classen 1998: 27–8)

Such ideas of maximizing the senses were taken up in turn by other writers. For example, in the twentieth century the Situationists were concerned to produce playful models of social organization in which each of the senses could thrive and grow. They even adopted Fourier's model of a unitary architecture (the phalanstery) which could embody and fulfil passionate social harmony.

Of course, the passions and senses are often automatically associated with freedom, but they must also be seen as a will to power. For example, in Fourier's notions of the phalanstery, the passions are channelled in order to be maximized: 'The imbrications of the passions were primitive analogies based on the machine, formed in the material of the psychology. This machinery, formed of men, produced the land of Cockaigne, the primal wish-symbol, that Fourier's Utopia had filled with new life' (Benjamin 1983: 160). Indeed, this machinic aspect can be regarded as having overtones of Sade: it represents a channelling of the flesh into numerous combinations which are meant to multiply ecstasies in such a way as to leave 'nothing outside . . . and to concede nothing ineffable to the world: such it seems is the keynote of the Sadian city . . .' (Barthes 1976: 37). Thus the city can be a sexual multiplier but its variations must be strictly controlled.

Imagination

The fourth impulse is the imagination, the ability to imagine what is not there and to keep hold of that 'image'. Urban utopias are themselves evidence of this impulse, but in this case they are boosted by all manner of imaginative writings which have appeared since the birth of the novel in particular, and which are constitutive of how we approach and hold cities as cities. Indeed, as a model of the generation of address, this world of writing is often regarded as the urban world.

Apart from the obvious example of the multiplying world of writings, the imaginative impulse is found most often in cities in two sources. The first is dreams, which Foucault once described as the opening into and precondition of imagination (Weigel 1996), and as a key moment in experience and cognition. Dreams are, of course, a key element of social theory, not least because of their place in the literature on cities where the complexity and profusion of cities is often depicted in dream-like terms. For example, Benjamin's *Passagen-Werk* project was at the threshold between dreams and wakefulness, with dreams remembered in the waking consciousness of the city itself. The second source is play. Play, as experimental activity, is often regarded as a key constituent of, and stimulant to, the imagination. It is also of crucial importance in the city's activities, and in programmes to free up the city's spaces. For example, much of the Situationist political programme can be interpreted as the production of new modes of play and correspondingly playful spaces within which the imagination could roam free.

Like the senses, the imaginative impulse can be regarded as a wild card, constantly providing path-breaking experiments. But that is too easy. In the contemporary world, the imaginative impulse can be seen, through the enormous resources provided by evolution of the media – stories, novels, film, television and so on – as enjoying a new freedom to roam. Yet at the same time the media also provide quite sharp limits on what it is possible to imagine. Thus Appadurai notes that:

> The world we live in today is characterised by a new role for the imagination in social life. To grasp this new role, we need to bring together: the old idea of images, especially mechanically produced images (as in the Frankfurt school sense); the idea of the imagined community (in Anderson's sense); and the French idea of the imaginary (*imaginaire*), as a constructed landscape of collective representations, which is no more and no less real than the collective representations of Émile Durkheim, now mediated through the complex prism of modern media.
>
> No longer mere fantasy (opium for the masses whose real work is elsewhere), no longer simple escape (from a world defined principally by more concrete purposes and structures) and no longer mere contemplation (irrelevant for new forms of desire and subjectivity), the imagination has become an organised field of social practices, a form of work (both in the sense of labour and of culturally organised practice) and a form of

negotiation between sites of agency ('individuals') and globally defined fields of possibility. (1996: 73–4)

It is more difficult to find the urban utopias that fit this impulse (except in that, in a certain sense, they are themselves manifestations of it). In part, this is because the number of possible utopias has now been multiplied. For example, science fiction has produced numerous utopias over the last sixty years – though often with very definite downsides included in the package. And in part it is because the idea of a one-size-fits-all utopia seems increasingly at variance with the multivalent nature of modern urban societies; utopias are much more easily perceived as a means of forcing particular cultural mores on to groups who are growing their own.

But if the urban utopia is under threat, so is the imaginative impulse that undergirds it, from new technologies which attempt to produce utopian social relations through a kind of mass mimesis which adjusts what people feel themselves to be: an exercise in self-construction thereby becomes an exercise in self-expression. This mass mimesis takes three forms.

To begin with, the limited imaginings of most urban utopias have been replaced by a host of more attractive media imaginings which activate and boost the imagination but also channel and limit it, precisely through the spread and utilization of the media in everyday life. Stars we want to be like, and enthusiast relationships like fandom, even the constant susurrus of daydreaming, all too often seem to be suffused by models of media performance (Abercrombie and Longhurst 1998). Then, human interaction is increasingly taking on new, more hygienic and instrumental forms in which events are increasingly preset so as not to give offence or provide any kind of jolt. For example, spoken interaction is becoming increasingly formulaic as the codification of talk takes place.

> The norms of written language have been codified and taught for centuries; literacy has always been an acquired skill – albeit in modern times one that is expected of almost everyone. In the case of spoken language, by contrast, only the most formal and ritualised instances have been extensively codified and their rules explicitly taught. Judgements of skill have undoubtedly been made, but the criteria have been variable and largely implicit. Now it seems that things are changing. (Cameron 2000: 2)

Thus we are led towards globalized communication which can apply without regard to persons or contexts. Spoken interaction becomes stabilized as a set of *skills* which are meant to present a person and what they say in the best light. Such 'synthetic personalization' (Fairclough 1992) is often justified in terms of 'empowerment', providing a more caring, communicative and cooperative person but, as Cameron makes clear, it is, if anything, the reverse:

> Communication training tends to valorise the speech styles that facilitate those activities (e.g. egalitarian, co-operative, non-judgemental) and to teach the associated discourse strategies (for instance, 'mirroring', asking open questions, giving verbal reinforcement). It would be wrong to suggest that these styles and strategies have no value, but it might well be argued that the value is most limited in the contexts and activity types where the connection between language and power is most obvious. They are not calculated to 'empower' speakers in a legal contest or political debate, for instance, or in any kind of confrontation with authority. These are cases in which the goal of using language is not to produce self-knowledge and intimacy (real or imagined) with others, but to influence others, and thus to shape the course of events in the world. (2000: 179)

But, to move to the last point, developments like these can be seen as part of a more general change in the social landscape of the western city being produced by an emphasis on a therapeutic model of the self, a continuous self or body which can be narrated into existence at any time (Giddens 1991; Rose 1995, 1999). Arising out of the continuing interaction of post-feudal state centralization and the dispersion of an ecclesiastical/pastoral power (Foucault 1979) which manages population through particular techniques of the self, this 'therapeutic ethos' (Nolan 1998) has three core elements: the notion of an emancipated self which becomes 'the touchstone of cultural judgement' (Bell 1976: xxi), an emotivist ethic, in which 'the truth is grasped through sentiment or feeling' (Bell 1976: 72), and the emergence of new elites skilled in articulating the demands and pathologies of the self. 'The important point here is not that everyone is sick or that everyone finds himself or herself to be sick . . . What is important to recognise is that it is increasingly acceptable to speak of oneself according to these categories' (Nolan 1998: 14). Thus, in many countries, and in the cities of many countries, key indicators such as the rise of therapy, and of judgements based on the pathologies produced by therapy, are on a marked upturn. In other words, what is increasingly being practised is a New Harmony based on a state and citizenry united in their desire to institutionalize the therapeutic ethos, in the state's case as a cornerstone of legitimation (the state feels your pain) and in the citizenry's case as a means to produce successful normalizations (feeling good about yourself). The city therefore becomes a repository for all kinds of projects on and of the self.

Thus everyday life becomes a space in which new transcontextual discourse technologies of disclosure (interviewing, talking, counselling, advertising) become toolkits, refined by constant research, for burrowing into the psyche (a description which is itself a part of the toolkit). It is, in certain senses, a rather terrifying practice of a new kind of nice governmentality, one that in its own way is as oppressive as much that has gone before.

In turn, these new practices of mimesis may be a part of a more general and more major sea change in modern societies, a move away from society based on systems of tight discipline (which is not to say that such systems no longer exist!) towards societies based on performance and performativity which perform new kinds of value and meaning and new kinds of dominance. Whether the change heralds the 'rise of global performance', as Jon McKenzie (2001) claims, we doubt (see Thrift 2000b). But they certainly presage new post-personal strategies and normativities which have not been available before, which depend on 'decentred subjectivities and highly unstable object fields' (McKenzie 2001: 179). So:

> Just as discipline's subjectivity and objectivity do not pre-exist its power arrangements, performative subjects and objects do not perform as much as they are performers. As Judith Butler stresses, there is no agent behind performance, rather agency itself is an effect of performative citationality. Across the performance stratum, hybrid hyphenated subjects rapidly emerge and immerge, passing through a variety of subject positions and switching quickly between innumerable language games. Multitasking, channel-surfing, attention deficit disorders, these portend the emergency of fractal (N-1) dimensional subjectivities . . . It may well be that theories of social construction are already in the process of becoming an ideology in need of deconstruction (along with the concept of ideology itself). Similarly, the constructedness of even the most 'natural' of objects is also becoming readily apparent in performative societies. (McKenzie 2001: 179–80)

Thus, for McKenzie, because of the interference of the mass media and education we now 'know' that objects are constructs, not givens. The patently artificial nature of nature becomes clear, as does the artificial nature of societies because of debates around topics like multiculturalism. In other words, knowledge of the world is increasingly characterized by simulation rather than representation.

According to McKenzie, the advent of such a performative social principle can be seen to be the result of the confluence of 'techno performance' (based especially in the rise of new writing systems like software), 'performance studies' (based especially in the rise of the media but with a more general culture application) (Abercrombie and Longhurst 1998) and 'performance management' (based on the idea that organizations and employees must perform) (Thrift 2000b). This is performance as programming, based on a cultural politics of constant reterritorialization, rather than fixed territorialization. And its upshot is clear: potential points of emergence are radically attenuated.

Escape Attempts

In the urban literature, as we saw in chapter 1, the city is often seen as a place of escape, a place to get lost (and to lose oneself) within, a way to side-step the cold (and) spreading embrace of commodity capitalism or a rampant (and growing) attachment to the self. But how might the city become a means of escaping the institutions, especially once power is seen as productive, even performative? The putative solutions are of three kinds. First cities can provide actual spaces where the workings of such regimes do not reach. These spaces may be quite literally places where the laws and conventions of these regimes do not hold. Then there are spaces which, though primarily intended to enact certain practices, are able to be bent to others. These are the spaces that writers like the Situationists, de Certeau and others, make so much of. Then, finally, there are spaces that allow subjects to unfold in unexpected ways by providing various cognitive capacities. Such spaces may be actual or virtual (texts and various other media), though the distinction is not an easy one to make in a field where the actual and the virtual constantly inscribe each other.

These thoughts are best amplified through a concrete example. In this case, building on chapter 1, we want to look at the literature on the city at night, a literature which first surfaced in the late 1970s (Melbin 1976, 1978; Parkes and Thrift 1980). This literature shows that it was not until the eighteenth century that something approaching a distinctive night-time set of activities began to appear, chiefly based around enter- tainment, and that it was not until the nineteenth century that a distinct- ive 'night-life' evolved, based especially on the growth of gas and then electric lighting and on new leisure institutions, as well as the continuing expansion of night-time workforces based on night life and the increase in shift systems. By the end of the nineteenth century, therefore, a number of urban industries were already stretching into the night: security and watch services, transport and delivery, water, gas and electricity com- panies, newspapers, hotels and restaurants, and night cleaning, as well as various large industrial enterprises. In the twentieth century, this night- time activity has expanded again, with the further growth of all kinds of incessant activity, twenty-four-hour opening of stores, twenty-four-hour radio and television stations, and so on; all signs of an increasingly urban population awake and active at night.

Thus the night-time city becomes increasingly visible and increasingly regulated as this gradual expansion takes place. But it also provides spaces of escape. For example, it provides spaces into which the forces of law can only extend a tentative and unsure hand: certain downtown areas, some low income housing estates, many parks and cemeteries, all places which elude surveillance. Then at night the city's spaces are transformed in ways which make them anew. For example, the streets at night will contain more young people, more men. And spaces may be more easily subverted to other uses: by drunken, boisterous behaviour, by ease of gathering, even by cultural expectation. Of course, not all these subversions and transgressions will be good. They may be violent, they often exclude women, and so on. Then, finally, the night provides a fertile source for the imagination. It may cause people to feel less restrained in their stance towards the urban world, correlated as it often is with leisure, pleasure and sexuality. It may also act to make them feel more restrained, correlated as it also is with fear and danger (Valentine 1989). And it can provide a general perceptual disposition:

> it presents 'images' which often condense into solid metaphors, into signals for a particular attitude towards the city, and it challenges perceptual capacity in special ways. At the same time it also offers an opportunity to tie the imagination closer to practical knowledge, experience and everyday life. (Schlör 1998: 19)

For example, night walks have, since Dr Johnson (Holmes 1996), provided a rich vein of images and metaphors concerning the city which have been endlessly replicated, becoming a part of how we now experience the city at night.

The second way in which the city offers escapes from the prevailing designs of power is through the very simple fact that each mode of governmentality tends to privilege certain sensory registers over others. In particular, until recently, nearly all modes of governmentality have tended to privilege vision over the other senses. The practice of government has depended on a gaze which can produce objects to be governed. This gaze was often assumed to be of a panoptic kind, intent on making the city over into a totally surveyed environment. Certainly, the classically modernist city plans of the 1920s and 1930s show this kind of totalizing ambition; out of an ordered gaze will come order. More recently, this kind of ambition has been carried forward through technologies. To begin with there are webs of cables which transport the gaze of camera lenses to observers. The spread of CCTV, video cameras on ships and so on is clearly of a panoptic sort, but it is worth remembering that their images have to be processed, recorded and, most of all, watched. Then there are all manner of other instruments that sense the urban environment: weather observatories, pollution meters, and so on (Barry 2001). In turn, these technologies produce their own sense of the city etched out in images of what previously went unrecorded. To add to all this there is information technology which increasingly provides a currency of urban re-presentation which has become a presentation in its own right: so maps come alive in GIS systems; traffic is tracked through the streets; water-mains bursts are located; electricity, gas and telecommunications networks are etched on screens, and so on. The flow of 'information' is constant and unrelenting, a desperate attempt to light the ways of the city by creating lighted representations of them. In turn, this 'informated' city has its effects, in the repositioning of traffic lights and road signs, in the constant circulation of bills and accounts, in the embodied stance of those working with and on information.

Obsessed with the capture of movement, imbued with the values of precision and caught up in its own representations, the visual is clearly the chief register through which the governance of the city is registered. But we should not make too much of this for three reasons. First of all, governance does not just take place in the visual register – think only of the hum of conversation on telephone lines or mobiles as the city is constantly *talked* into being. Second, the visual register cannot be easily detached from the other sensory registers: a visual identification is nearly always an identification in other sensory registers as well. Third, the visual register is constantly transgressed, for example by fly-posting, graffiti, even the sheer complexity of some landscapes.

Still, it is undoubtedly the case that other sensory registers are neglected – not ignored – in the contemporary city. The engineering of smell in supermarkets, the use of muzak, the press of buttons on lifts or at crossings: these are all elements of certain forms of governance, but they usually provide only a light touch compared with the imperatives of the visual. These other registers therefore provide means for escaping the gaze.

For example, there is the case of sound. Sound is a constant in cities, marking out time through the daily to and fro of traffic, conversational noise (Lefebvre 1996), providing all manner of often unnoticed lines and intensities. The 'soundscapes' of cities often elude visual representation. For example, the steely gaze of video cameras does not capture individual conversations or the hum of the word; it catches only the part of gesture, so vital to conversation, that is available to the camera angle. Then, much of the sound produced in the city has never been subject to governable codes. Though sound itself might be the product of codes (as in turn-taking in conversation or the play of music), the city's jumble of sounds still often remains unsorted so far as the projects of government are concerned. But this is, of course, changing. Sound is becoming one of the new landscapes of urban governance, increasingly treated and programmed. For example DeNora (2000) documents the careful use of music in shops to establish buying moods. Activities like clubbing are often interpreted as oceanic experiences (Malbon 1999), floating away from the imperatives of everyday life, but they are just as easily interpreted as commodified musical workouts directing bodily energies in utterly predictable directions, ably assisted by the economic circuits of alcohol and drugs.

Then the third way in which the city offers escapes from prevailing diagrams of power is through the exercise of fantasy. All modes of governmentality have distinctive fantasies of control which they interiorize. For example, the disciplinary mode of government would want to bend the body into shape, into specific embodied graphics of obedience, which are then to be interiorized. The pastoral mode interiorizes discipline by attaching it to the formation of the self, conceived as a means of expression of expression. Its fantasy is an emotion-racked perfect confession. But these dreams of order can only partially hold, for three reasons. First, dreams and fantasies are, by their nature, only partially controllable since they are only partially conscious. Of course, through the rise of the therapeutic state the unconscious is increasingly being worked on (via different means of socialization of embodiment, various drills, therapy and so on). But these workings are hardly exact. Second, dreams and fantasies are amorphous multiplicities; they are therefore difficult to operate on in ways which guarantee particular effects (though, of course, they *can* be worked on, via texts, advertisements, spectacles, and so on). Third, dreams and fantasies conjure up the problem of who is dreaming what. Thus one of the continuing themes of writing on the city – from Baudelaire through Benjamin to Jacques Réda – is that the city dreams itself through its inhabitants. In a sense, the city itself becomes an enormous dreaming.

This latter point demands expansion. For the city does not exist just in the 'minds' of the individual bodies that navigate its highways and by-ways. It is carried on images like postcards and holiday programmes and photographs, and it is pressed into texts. And these images and texts are themselves actors performing different species of spaces which, though they may use the same city name, are radically different imaginaries. The different species have common motifs, textures and traditions. Wolfreys, for example, argues that in the series of modernist texts of the nineteenth and twentieth century that he examines, the city of 'London does not have a location or base. Instead it names a multiplicity of events, chance occurrences and fields of opportunities' (1998: 7). The city as an enormous confluence of relationships without fixed sites is necessarily difficult to know; it cannot be visualized, deciphered or depicted. In turn, chance and hidden recesses become keys to this ineffability, locations able to be temporarily pulled out of flow and from which it is possible to get some hold on the flow. The city, then, takes on a spectral quality of indefiniteness. For Wolfreys, for example, Baudelaire comes alive in London, not Paris, because there is a much less definite sense of this city. Thus:

> the writers of the city of London are not merely documentarists; or, rather, their writing, responding to the nature of London, cannot help but be transformed into something other than a mimetic or realistic medium. Representable verisimilitude is not an issue in the writing of London. Instead, it is important to recognise that the writing of modern London is a writing which acknowledges what Carol Bernstein calls 'the transformation of city into text. The city becomes the scene of writing . . .' (Wolfreys 1998: 25)

In turn, however, precisely this indefiniteness is used to suggest a space shot through with anxiety arising out of a threat to a stable identity, a threat which can only be overcome by writing it down, and so out. For example, in certain nineteenth-century city texts:

> This quality has already been noted by Raymond Williams. There is, writes Williams, 'a failure of identity in the crowd of others which worked back to a loss of identity in the self, and then, in time, a loss of society itself, its over-writing and replacement by a procession of images'. No immediate danger presents itself as such to the writer in question. There are no anarchists or terrorists, no criminals or murderers, no 'perverse' or 'monstrous' individuals who are to be encountered in other fictions of the city. There is not even the specific threat of institutions such as the law courts or government offices, such as we encounter in Dickens, Collins or Trollope. There is merely the city with its crowds, its poor, its liminal and marginal figures, its lights, and anonymous masses, its locomotion, all of which give rise to the crises of identity and a range of anxious responses. (Wolfreys 1998: 99)

But . . .

But we need to be careful with the notion of spaces of escape. Most such spaces are only brief respites. Most such spaces do not light the way to another land; at best, they give hints of another kind of future. And some of those spaces are either generally dangerous or they are dangerous to particular groups of the population. In other words, the idea of a romance of escape – which is sometimes hinted at in the writings of authors like de Certeau – needs to be firmly resisted (Bennett 1999).

This is even more the case because these spaces can be co-opted by the new performative developments. Let us take just two of them to make clear what we mean. There is now a concerted attempt to re-engineer the *experience* of cities, one which is on a par with the construction of Haussmann's boulevards – but happening in many cities around the world – and one which is just as ambitious, but perhaps less known because it is the result of many different plans rather than one single masterplan. In turn, this reorganization challenges nearly all the categories which have been picked to cope with the so-called city of modernity, from 'flâneur' through to stranger. This development is the attempt to 'theme' cities in such a way as to make them into a series of urban experiences which are commodifiable, which are sources of economic value. Now in a sense this is hardly new – the entertainment industry and the tourist industry have done this for many hundreds of years, from Vauxhall Gardens onwards (see Ogborn 1998). What *is* new is the general pervasiveness of this phenomenon and the construction of a systematic body of knowledge – of what spaces entertain how – which informs it.

The beginnings of this theming of urban experience are probably best traced to three events – the opening of Disneyland in Anaheim in 1955, the construction of the first shopping malls in the United States in the 1950s, and the rise of mass tourism in the 1960s (Urry 1991).

What we see in this concatenation of events is that consumption and entertainment become both increasingly indistinguishable and increasingly large-scale. Today's commercial spaces are not only increasingly themed, they are also actively entertaining. The creation of entertaining events that are based on popular culture symbols increasingly characterizes the material forms of our society (Gottdiener 1997: 7). People are no longer depicted as passive consumers of the goods and services they are offered by such spaces, they actively perform their presence in specific motile milieus. The parameters of agency have been changed (DeNora 2000). The commercial spaces that are specifically designed to entertain include not only themed and karaoke pubs and very large malls, but also shops and even garden centres. Spaces compete with each other by promoting their performativity across a whole set of activities formerly set apart, such as shopping, dining, recreation and even education (in visits to increasingly 'hands-on' museums). As this process of theming has happened, so new spaces have been laid down across cities which are spaces of concentrated and systematic imaginative 'escape'. These spaces have a number of characteristics. To begin with, they are highly interactive. That is, both bodies and objects within the spaces are likely to act back in certain characteristic ways. Second, they explicitly appeal to an aesthetic which can capacitate in a particular manner. The spaces are theatrical, intended to stimulate the exercise of certain forms of imagination through carefully scripted performances. Third, they are omnisensory. Because they tend to rely on a multitude of media, they tend to reach across the senses, using not just vision but also touch, smell, taste, hearing and kinaesthetic (movement) senses in order to produce strong bodily reactions. Finally, these spaces are adaptive; that is, they are spaces which are constantly monitored and adjusted to data gathered on audience reaction (box 5.2).

Thus, in these spaces, the impact of the imagination and fantasy becomes a major part of the conduct of business, to be traded on and turned into profit. Of course, this has always happened – what, after all, of books and music? – but what distinguishes these moves is the sheer spatial scale of the activity and its dependence on growing a body of systematized knowledge to create a new set of 'experience' commodities which are, in effect, the spaces themselves and those goods that can be allied to them. This, then, is the new experience economy: a set of living, embodied geographies which provide a new source of value through their performative push (Pine and Gilmore 1999; Thrift 2000c).

The other way in which spaces can be co-opted is both more widespread and more insidious. That is the invention of a new form of writing which goes under the name of *software*. There is, of course, much work in the urban literature on digital cities, but remarkably little attention has been paid to the millions of lines of code that have come to run cities as computing power has increased and as many former bodily practices have been written in to code. The modern city exists as a haze of software instructions. Nearly every urban practice is becoming mediated by code. There are more lines of code in some modern elevator systems than there were in the Apollo spacecraft. So many software programmes exist in cities that audits carried out to counter the Y2K problem at the turn of the millennium could not locate many of them.

This odd neglect of a new and highly animated form of speech may be because code is in some sense invisible compared with its computer carapace. It may be that, in all its complexity, it is difficult to comprehend. Yet increasingly code has a still-living history, with legacy systems buried deep in many programs (Gelernter 1992). It may be that we are schooled in ignoring software, just as we are schooled in ignoring standards and

Box 5.2   Roller-coasters

So what does the theming of experience mean? To begin with, it means understanding *space* as an active determinant of what the commodity is, not just a passive context. Second, it means deploying this understanding in ways which heighten *anticipation*. Third, it means building up a *vocabulary* able to describe the experience produced, even though much of it is not cognitive, in order to reflect on and amplify it.

Let us take an example: the roller-coaster. 'Amusements' and theme parks have become an important component of urban leisure. There are more than thirty major parks in the world which can each, according to *Amusement Business*, expect more than 3 million visitors a year, some nearly six times as many. In 1999 they included:

Tokyo Disneyland, Japan (top at 17.5 million)
Magic Kingdom, Walt Disney World, Florida (about 15.2 million)
Everland, Kyonggi-Do, South Korea (8.6 million)
Blackpool Pleasure Beach, England (7.2 million)
Hakkejima Sea Paradise, Yokohama, Japan (5.6 million)
Ocean Park, Hong Kong (3.3 million)
Tivoli Gardens, Copenhagen (3.1 million)
Santa Cruz Beach Boardwalk, California (3 million)

Most of them will have a roller-coaster, often more than one (one park in Ohio has fourteen). The first proper roller-coaster – little more than a switchback railway – was built in the 1890s in New York. But they spread rapidly around the world. Globally, there are currently about 960 registered roller-coasters, with more coming. (The roller-coaster is not a static technology. There is a constant need to outrun the competition: more and more investment is demanded to come up with something bigger, better, more thrilling and more terrifying, so that the customers don't get tempted to go elsewhere.) No wonder that seventy-five new rides were expected to open in 2000 around the world based on relentless technology innovation in search of more and more visceral experiences – with a maximum of 4.5g being pulled. This is the era of the gigacoaster, the coaster more than 300 feet high, able to provide maximum 'airtime' where riders are momentarily weightless.

Yet describing these proprioceptive experiences is remarkably difficult, not helped by the wide variety of rides on offer. Some coaster operators have started to use dance notation as the best approximation of the thrills on offer. Others use fan feedback. Around the world there are devoted bunds who spend much time on the internet recounting their experiences to each other. For example, the London-based European Coaster Club has 1,200 members while the Roller-Coaster Club of Great Britain has 1,500 members. The names that have evolved for types of ride are evocative: Tower, for a ride where passengers are shot up into the sky, Dark Ride for interior rides, maybe through a haunted house, Flume for hurtling through or into water, Wild Mouse, where the nose of the car juts perilously out over the drops and corners of the track – they add up to a comprehensive vocabulary of experience.

classifications (Bowker and Star 1999). Whatever the case, code will increasingly be responsible for the future of cities, from attempts to produce 'emotional computing' that will respond more closely to users, to attempts to produce 'thinking cities' in which all software is linked up by wireless or landline into one vast adaptive system.

Whether this burgeoning ecology is a new form of 'informational life' joining the numerous species that already exist at the leading edge of digital capitalism (Schiller 1999), or a set of 'writing acts' rather like speech acts (French and Thrift 2001), or simply a slavish set of machine stimulus-responses, what seems certain is that increasingly code is responsible for how cities go on, producing its own new spaces and adding new components of action into the tracery of familiar urban space. In a sense, it acts as a new form of dictation, the problem being – who is dictating what? In turn, it follows that there is a politics of software. Thus Lessig (1999) argues that software is a filter which may increasingly reduce our choice by acting as a series of 'models of constraint'. He argues we need 'open code'. Similarly Boyle (1996) advocates a new Declaration of Independence, a constitution for code, to prevent code from becoming just another language of power.

Whatever the case, it is certain that we can no longer think of cities in the old, time-honoured ways. The advent of software signifies the rise of new forms of technological politics and new practices of political invention that we are only just beginning to comprehend as political: politics of standards, classifications, metrics, and readings (Barry 2001). These orderings – written down as software – are becoming one of the chief ways of animating the city. They must not be allowed to take us unaware.

Such new spaces as we have described here might suggest that there is no way out of modern governmentalities: they might seem to be gradually closing down all attempts at escape, producing cities which provide free space in name only. Modern cities are increasingly spaces of categorical saturation, in which every element is named and narrated (Bowker and Star 1999). Stories like these are beloved of certain doomsaying academics who have made pessimism into a high art form. But we need to be careful not to be tempted by them into believing that no spaces of escape remain: what we need to do is to understand that there are always countervailing tendencies. These tendencies are of five kinds. First, urban life is not made up of (larger) social categories pressing down, slab-like, on (small) everyday life. Rather such life is made up of (sometimes risky and often quite hesitant) networks which are longer or shorter but do not reach everywhere and constantly interfere with each other. For example, the capitalist market should be understood as a set of emergent calculative agencies which constitute 'a many-sided, diversified, evolving device which the social sciences as well as the actors themselves contribute to reconfigure' (Callon 1998: 51), and capitalism itself as an experimental rather than a fixed system.

In turn, such a description means that the networks of control that snake their way through cities are necessarily oligoptic, not panoptic: they do not fit together. They will produce various spaces and times, but they cannot fill out the whole space of the city – in part because they cannot reach everywhere, in part because they therefore cannot know all urban spaces and times, and in part because many new spaces and times remain to be invented. Then, second, nearly all networks look tighter than they actually are. All networks are held together by the activities of mediaries and intermediaries, armies of delegates which roam the networks, keeping them going. But, in fact, networks *do* often shatter and break down. Indeed, a key urban skill is the negotiation of these breakdowns – from the failure of a traffic light to a wholesale power cut, from a train being late to a train strike, from an annoying misdelivery to a whole set of records unable to be found. Repair is a major urban industry in its own right. Third, especially because so many urban spaces depend on the improvisation of the chance encounter, they often contain within themselves the ability to go beyond routinized response. Though urban inhabitants will usually tend to improvise in routine ways, sometimes they will also produce something quite *new*. So urban spaces have the ability to produce new forms of interaction, to mutate and so exceed themselves.

Fourth, nearly all systems of governance in effect acknowledge that they are dealing in part with the unknown and ungovernable; they do not just tell their inhabitants what to do, they learn from them. Thus, to begin with, they often depend on activities outside the norm to constitute what is to be governed. Then, nearly all systems of governance in fact depend on improvisation to keep functioning day on day: they are only partly rule-based (Thrift 2000a). Governance, in other words, is as much a context-dependent anthropological activity as it is a rule-based systemic activity. And then again, systems of governance have evolved technologies (interviews, focus groups, etc.) whose whole raison d'être is to try to understand what is going on, implying not just a new society of control (Deleuze 1992) but also genuine ignorance. Fifth and finally, to put these four points in a different way, urban networks are complex: they interact and interfere with each other in ways which are not predictable and which produce *emergent* forms of social organization in ways which cannot be foreseen. Cities are still virtual entities that can 'start without presuppositions', to use a Deleuzian phrase (Rajchman 2000).

In other words, urban spaces are not predictable machines for reproducing bounded and controllable relations. Rather they are engaged in a struggle with an often unknown end-point, in which corporations and other assemblages constantly try to modulate the environment in order to realize gain. But they do not necessarily succeed. So far as the growth of themed spaces is concerned, corporations have to deploy a whole panoply of technologies – the interview, the focus group, the poll – which will inform them about what consumers 'want'. But consumer 'wants' are hugely variable and not available to easy capture. Thus themed spaces are often used in unpredictable ways by consumers, ways which have little or nothing to do with the maximal consumption they are designed to unleash. And, indeed, these spaces can sometimes be the focus of explicit resistance, all the way from taking packed lunches to actual protest. Similarly, the spaces of code – the screens, the keyboards, the actual lines of code – are not easily controlled. Microsoft does not rule all – even though it might try. The advent of freeware like Linux shows one alternative model. The advent of heavily contested file-sharing software like Napster, Gnutella and Freenet is another. What these developments show is not only a commitment to free digital spaces, but a commitment to craft (McCullough 1996) and also to something else, what can best be described as a kind of aesthetic sense. After all, 'whenever people experience a piece of software – whether it be a spreadsheet or a physics simulation – they have natural human responses. They experience beauty, satisfaction, pleasure, or the corresponding opposites'

(Winograd 1996: xix). In other words, the city still contains objects (and contexts) that can agitate thought and change practices.

Conclusion

In this chapter we have argued that we must see cities as nexuses of systems of discipline – certainly and undeniably. But we must also ensure that we keep a vision of cities with all the uncertainties and risks left in, and especially the recognition that the cities' inhabitants get the chance to redefine, though rarely on their own terms, what it is to be ordered about and interrogated by these systems. The city, in other words, always contains a necessary contingency without which it would be an impossible project (Luhmann 1998).

A large part of this contingency consists of what is often called politics. However, we need to be careful about what we define as 'the political'. On the one side, there are all those practices and institutions which have come to be regarded as the stuff of politics. In the urban sphere, this includes the world of states, political parties, social movements, and all the other elements of political appeal, conceived in part through the urban spaces they occupy. On the other side, there are those numerous elements of urban practice and representation which fall outside what is regarded as political. These will often include certain types of space, which may well be at the edge of legibility because, for example, they exist prior to prepresentation: mundane signs such as the brand which dwell in the interstices of our attention, ways of bodily comportment, which can often speak volumes without speaking at all, and visual frames of representation which dictate what we see as public. Such practices and representations are often no less fiercely political because they do not reach the discursive register. In other words, Lefevbre's (1996) right to the city needs to be understood as encompassing a very large number of 'rights', many of which dwell outside of what is conventionally regarded as the urban. It is this expanded sense of the political that we will explore in the next chapter.

6   THE DEMOCRATIC CITY

Introduction

An expanded urban democracy? How can we imagine, yet alone achieve such a goal? One thing we are clear about is that the goal cannot be prescribed or an end-point legislated. But this does not mean that we can leave things entirely to the free play of the current political system. In other words, we need to be normatively non-normative. That means, we argue in this chapter, an extension of universal rights in order to allow citizens to engage actively in politics. This is not a romantic vision of agreement and consensus. Rather, it is an attempt to make a space for agonistic politics, where the democracy lies in the democratization of the terms of engagement. Such a democratization must include the active encouragement of subjectivities, for it seems to us that politics is increasingly being measured through performative display. This is one consequence of life after a democracy of representation and acting on behalf of others. These days citizenship is often asked to be demonstrated in order to be recognized: through focus groups, displays at school, media intelligibility and good old-fashioned mass demonstration.

Our interest thus lies in a particular form of democracy – civic empowerment and participation – which has always been associated with cities. In theory, cities as repositories of institutions, associations, public spaces and social vitality seem perfect places for participatory democracy. They *are* the sites of everyday participation, intermingling with others and daily confrontation between the private and the public, between the citizen and institutionalized power. Whether in reality the city encourages active citizenship has been a matter long disputed among urbanists. In the early decades of the twentieth century, Lewis Mumford lamented the destructive effects of the large, sprawling US city. 'Megalopolis', he wrote, breeds 'anonymity' and 'impersonality' which act as 'a positive encouragement to asocial or anti-social actions' (1938: 266). Its 'pseudo environment of paper' (p. 255) – newspapers and statistics – produces 'a world where the great masses of people, unable to have direct contact with more satisfying means of living, take life vicariously, as readers, spectators, passive observers' (p. 258). Wholesome human contact is perverted by the 'acquisitiveness of the sick metropolis' and the 'poison of vicarious vitality' spreading through mass consumerism and commodification. The sense of civic democracy negated in the modern city runs through the work of the majority of the great urban thinkers of the last hundred years.

It should have become clear by now that we do not share this portrayal of the effects of modern city life on democracy. There is much participation that takes place through work and association, in spaces of consumption and recreation, in friendship and care networks. But of course such participation cannot be read automatically as democracy enhanced. How then to link it to civic democracy? This is the question we explore in the chapter. We begin from the premise that cities are no longer a self-contained political space. Part of the political history of modernity has been the expansion of institutions and movements beyond the urban arena, weaving local politics into a wider net of national and transnational domains of power and struggle. Local government, for example, is nested in rules and resources distributed by central government, and local struggles (over housing proposals or the closure of a school) often depend on wider institutional connections (national media, Parliament, global corporations, political parties, international issue coalitions). We want to work, therefore, with a distanciated model of urban democracy, one which combines universals aimed at restoring the commons with city efforts to institutionalize democratic participation. Our model differs from the trend in much contemporary writing to see the city as a unique or formative political space (a place for struggles over local issues, or a site of politicization for 'bigger' campaigns). It also differs from the current fashion of imagining the urban public sphere as an arena of deliberation (deliberative democracy) or one of healthy disagreement between different groups and identities (radical democracy).

In this chapter we first lay the foundation of our approach by summarizing the efforts of reformers at the turn of the last century in the US to encourage direct democracy through educational and other institutional reforms to encourage political deliberation. We then outline our misgivings with contemporary models of urban democracy, before developing our own alternative in the second half of the chapter.

'Creating a Democratic Public'

Creating a Democratic Public is a book by Kevin Mattson (1998) on the Progressive Era (1890–1920), a period of extraordinary experimentation in US cities with participatory politics through educational centres and grassroots debate. This was a time of rapid industrial and urban expansion during which a mass working class was forged through waves of European immigration. It was a time of people on the move, geographically, socially and culturally; an undereducated mass, overwhelmed by corporate America, harsh working conditions, urban poverty, urban congestion, gang warfare and an authoritarian state. It was a mass that had yet to become a public.

Intellectuals and activists such as John Dewey, Charles Zueblin, Frederic Howe and Mary Follett were convinced 'that community-based forums and discussions play a constitutive role in making the public judgements necessary for a democracy' (Mattson 1998: 4). Here was a conviction that 'a democratic public should be a goal in and of itself' (p. 8), that 'local publics should become the basis of the American nation' (p. 8); putting pressure on the state and other institutions through informed discussion, debating societal alternatives and, most importantly, developing its own capacity to decide and act collectively. Theirs was a vision of 'real democracy' rooted in practical effort, a democracy from below, fashioned and controlled by activists and citizens; but with institutions to sustain the project.

Enter cities. While some intellectuals such as Dewey idealized the city's neighbourhoods as places of face-to-face democracy, others saw in the city a rich set of institutions to make, inscribe and interpret the public experience. At the start of the Progressive Era, leaders such as Charles Zueblin looked to build *agora* spaces – public spaces for cultivating civic pride and social interaction. Through the American Park and Outdoor Art Association (APOAA), founded in 1893, and the American League for Civic Improvement (ALCI) founded in 1902, the City Beautiful Movement campaigned for public parks and squares as well as public sculpture and vernacular art (such as murals). Zueblin also saw the need for direct access to learning and he pioneered the University Extension Scheme which offered lectures on public issues of the time. There were many other similar mass education schemes, for example, through the People's Institute, founded in 1897, which set up Tent Meetings in working-class communities, or the Forum Movement, which spawned over a hundred sites in different cities by 1916. Both hosted lectures on pressing issues of the day, attracting audiences of over a thousand.

The high point of the Progressive Era was the formation of the Social Centers and Civic Clubs in Rochester (New York) in 1907, which spread to 101 cities by 1912. The centres were run by citizens, not activists or intellectuals, and focused on active debate, with citizens deliberating on political reforms. They drew working-class people from a mixed background, gathering to debate local issues such as housing, property speculation and public services, as well as national questions such as 'race relations', 'women's suffrage', 'public health' and labour unions. It was here that 'citizens learned crucial lessons about democracy and about the importance of open public discussion' (Mattson 1998: 56), by debating controversial topics and by encountering strangers. All of this was buttressed by leisure and recreation facilities offered by the centres and clubs. By the 1920s, however, the Progressive Movement, had begun to unravel. For Mattson, this was for two reasons. First, it became the stamping ground of social workers keen to tackle local welfare problems through their own centres. This conversion of active citizen to professional client alienated a working class still keen to meet and deliberate on its own terms. Second, with historical prescience, the roaring twenties generated a new form of participation – consumerism – as a counterweight to education and public deliberation.

What are the contemporary implications of this experience? Clearly, many of the reasons for direct democracy have disappeared with the rise of representative democracy, the expansion of basic rights, universal education and the rise of mediatized communication. However, for us, seven principles of the Progressive Era continue to be relevant for a society of active citizens. First, the initiatives responded to real need through a combination of vision and pragmatism. They were bold and experimental, and for that they mobilized considerable interest. Second, they came with explicit normative goals to encourage a civic culture and social autonomy. They were not procedural experiments. Third, they were projects of social transformation, with the public realm seen as a place to change attitudes through education. Fourth, the Social Centres and Civic Clubs gave control to participants. This helped to generate relevance, commitment and creative energy. Fifth, they combined sociability and political activity. Sixth, the Progressive Era institutionalized real democracy by drawing on new and existing formal and informal institutions. Finally, for some movement intellectuals such as Mary Follett, the urban ventures were part of a wider political project: no parochial celebration of local community, but a recognition of the resonance of local issues with wider federal politics. We shall invoke these principles in our understanding of rights to the contemporary city later in this chapter.

Political City

Today, a century on, there is no shortage of interest in urban participatory democracy. For some commentators participation promises a return to community, a 'panacea for all the main illnesses of modern society – alienation, isolation, excessive anarchic and individualistic capitalism, social disintegration, and political indifference' (Tamir 1998: 214). For others, after the crisis of universalist, nation-centred politics, the cosmopolitan city promises a politics of difference based on plural cultural expression and identification (Sandercock 1998; Dear and Flusty 1999). We discuss below three influential visions of urban democracy.

Public space/public sphere

One distinguished tradition centres on the public usage of open or shared spaces – streets, squares, parks, cafés, libraries and malls. Since the 1930s, the emphasis has fallen on the construction of a civic public through mingling and interaction. Thus Simmel (1950), and more recently Sennett (1970, 1977), envisage anonymity and casual contact among strangers as part of the replacement of traditional ties of family and kinship with new ties of civic association. Another line of interpretation, encapsulated by the City Beautiful Movement and the writings of Lewis Mumford (1938, 1998), celebrates the civilizing effects of everyday mingling in spaces of recreation such as parks, fairs and squares. Today the call for urban public spaces open to all has intensified – rightly so – against a background of encroaching privatization and urban dereliction. The complaint is a familiar one, with warnings especially from the US of the perils of gated communities, public surveillance, secluded zones, dereliction of inner city spaces and segregation of once communal areas. The erosion of public spaces is seen to threaten the public sphere. And so urban leaders are pressed to rehabilitate derelict spaces, reintroduce cafés, fairs and bazaars in public places, pedestrianize streets, plan multifunctional spaces (such as medical clinics in shopping malls) and recognize the importance of vernacular moments such as parades and street festivals.

The aesthetic desire cannot be faulted, but are the above necessarily civic spaces? For some, yes. Sennett expects 'a public realm in which people think about themselves and act socially other than as economic animals, their value as citizens not dependent upon their riches' (1997: 163). He does have citizenship in mind in public spaces seen as 'a site that offers relief from the burdens of subjective life' facilitating 'mutual engagement, and so mutual obligation and loyalty' (Sennett 1999a: 23–4). For others, the city's spaces are potentially the generator of new shared meanings and hybrid cultures arising from intermingling. This is the account we get from cosmopolitan readings which note the rise of hybrid cultures (Hannerz 1996), new transnational diaspora claims (from international business elites or migrant communities – Sassen 1999a), and urban spaces used for cultural experimentation (for instance, selected streets in Seoul to display a new youth subculture that mixes Rodeo and traditional Korean values – Shields 1997). The link with democracy is explained by Kian Tajbakhsh:

> The hybridity of identities can further radical democratic public policies because the complex differentiations characteristic of the city and the multiple groups and identities that it concentrates provide the setting for a social learning process that creates citizens who possess a reflective, mature, and contingent sense of self, tolerant of a high degree of ambiguity and difference. This hybrid sense of self is capable of envisioning, formulating, and supporting more enlightened and more rational preferences and collective decisions regarding a range of pressing social problems, which will lead to a more effective and socially just set of public policy outcomes. (2001: 176)

A progressive 'politics of propinquity' (Copjec and Sorkin 1999) in urban public space? We are not sure if what goes on in public spaces can be seen as a conduit of democratic change. First, it is not clear why 'public space' and 'public sphere' are treated as the same. For Bruce Robbins, the 'public is a phantom' (1993: ix), as both space and sphere, if it is meant to signify the common good or a single public: the city has never been 'open to the scrutiny and participation, let alone under the control, of the majority', and besides, 'where were the workers, the women, the lesbians, the gay men, the African-Americans' (p. viii) in most evocations of the public sphere? Then we would echo Nancy Fraser's (1993) concern that once we accept that the public realm is not a civic arena that brackets difference and private interests, any lingering notion of a shared citizenship emerging out of co-presence or exchange in the public sphere becomes questionable. Besides, what makes us sure that the *piazza* is the space of effective politics, so long as the real political decisions are made in the *palazzo* (Martinotti 1999)?

The distinction of the public as civic sphere from the state as institutionalized power and the market as private realm is a problematic one:

the civic realm is as political and private as violence in the family, say, is a public matter. It follows that there is no reason to suppose that civic virtue will emerge from mingling in public spaces. Take walking in a park as an example. We often wander with a pregiven attitude towards others, carrying learnt rules about what to do with dog litter and sweet wrappers. Our contact with strangers is fleeting; a smile from someone might reassure or repel, depending on past experience, attitude and mood. Some people want to be in the park to be alone or even anti-social! Casual contact with strangers in public places may on rare occasions yield life-changing leaps through the serendipity of contact (Delaney 1999), but it is naive to think that parks, buses and cafés nourish 'the eroticism of city life, in the broad sense of our attraction to others, the pleasure and excitement of being drawn out of one's secure routine to encounter the novel, the strange, the surprising' (Sandercock 1998: 210).

The thesis of a new cultural politics rooted in urban mixture is unconvincing. That cosmopolitan lifestyles and plural subject positions exist in the global city is undeniably true, but are these not forged out of (local and translocal) associative connections, with public spaces no more than a site in these networks? There is a limit to how far the new cosmopolitanism can be tied to the city's public spaces. Cultural hybridization requires meaningful and repeated contact, the slow experience of working, being and living with others, and the everyday fusion of cultures in what we consume, what we see, where we travel, how we live, with whom we play, and so on. At best, public spaces can be seen as spaces of tolerance and sociability, perhaps gathering points on particular occasions. They are not the formative spaces of hybrid identities and politics.

Deliberation

A second tradition holds that the recovery of urban democracy lies in agreement between different groups through rational communication. There has been an explosion of literature on deliberative democracy in recent years (Elster 1998; Bohman and Rehg 1997; Gutmann 1998), building on the Rawlsian concept of justice through association and Habermas's belief in a public sphere of moral agreement through rational communication. Jon Elster (1998) defines deliberative democracy as:

> collective decision making with the participation of all who will be affected by the decision or their representatives: this is the democratic part. Also . . . it includes decision making by means of arguments offered *by* and *to* participants who are committed to the values of rationality and impartiality: this is the deliberative part. (1998: 8, original emphasis)

Democracy here is institutionalized debate to solve collective problems through argument and disagreement (Gutmann and Thompson 1996), and deliberation is the practice for conflict resolution and problem solving. The claimed effect is a more inclusive and lasting democracy, for deliberation is a 'process of public discussion and decision making that includes and affirms all particular social group perspectives in the society and draws on their situated knowledge as a resource for enlarging the understanding of everyone and moving beyond their own parochial interests' (Young 1997: 399).

For Iris Marion Young, discussion motivates claimants to appeal to arguments of justice rather than self-interest and teaches them to see their own position in relation to that of others. What is required are the right rules of engagement. Accordingly, Amy Gutmann and Dennis Thompson recommend 'extensive moral argument about the merits of public policies in public forums' (1996: 12); regulation of the political process by the principles of reciprocity, publicity ('making public') and accountability; governance of the content of policies by the principles of basic liberty, basic opportunity and fair opportunity; and cultivation of 'moral reasoning' in schools and other cultural sites.

Our worry with this position relates to the perfectibility of deliberative techniques. As Susan Stokes notes, deliberation has its own 'pathologies' which can yield

> normatively unpleasant results: it may allow policy to be driven by special interests that manipulate common citizens' notion of what they want the government to do; it can displace real citizen preferences with preferences that politicians, coaxed by interests and the press, mistakenly impute to citizens; and it can instil identities in citizens that they would probably otherwise not hold and which by any commonsense measure are not in their interests. (1998: 136)

Then, the principle of rational consensus does not deal on its own with the problem of entrenched inequalities and differences (Amin 1997): 'not all civil society is civic-minded. Some associations have the contradictory effect; they threaten social cohesion, erode the social capital, frustrate social equality and equal opportunity, and violate individual rights' (Tamir 1998: 215). Take, for example, the politics of Residential Community Associations (RCAs) in the US, home-owner associations that have mushroomed in recent years to provide local services on a private basis. The RCAs have spread like wildfire, and as they grow they demand local tax reductions on the basis that it is they who provide the services, not the local state. For Daniel Bell, the RCAs are a far cry from the commons, because they teach members 'to act *in opposition* to the interests of the wider community and to evade their responsibility for a fair share of the burdens (e.g. housing the mentally ill) that political communities normally undertake' (1998: 245, original emphasis).

If the normative ideals of deliberative democracy are compromised by flawed assumptions about communicative rationality, so too are the related suggestions for urban democracy. Significantly, Young (1999) has proposed four types of urban action/orientation: social differentiation without exclusion via associational pluralism, spatial openness and hybrid spaces; eroticism of the new and unfamiliar via the fecundity of 'disorderly' streets and bazaars; the publicization of difference and strangers via open public events such as festivals and games; access to public institutions and well-being in place (physical spaces that are well looked after). These are wonderful ideals, but we cannot ignore the fact that spaces such as bazaars and streets are riddled with power inequalities of one sort or another. And, ironically, action to check abuses of power may even necessitate giving the disempowered and excluded (such as gays, children, ethnic groups, older citizens) their own spaces in order to *strengthen* democracy (Iveson 1998).

In urban planning theory and practice the idea of communicative or deliberative planning has gained considerable influence (Friedmann 1987, 1992; Forester 1989; Healey 1997; Sander-cock 1998). Deliberative planners reject universal, state-driven solutions, preferring community-based, negotiated decision-making. Leonie Sander-cock (1998) argues that this is essential in the contemporary multicultural and multiethnic city, since difference and diversity can no longer be reconciled through universalist projects. Enter a new form of planning practice; an interactive, people-centred planning that works through listening, talking, being there, learning to read symbolic and non-verbal evidence such as music and stories, appreciating the contemplative knowledge of certain communities, and so on. The new urban planner is posed as the crucial intermediary, helping to mobilize the 'voices from the borderlands', arbitrating between stakeholders and ensuring that the powerful play no tricks; never losing sight of urban social justice as the binding goal. Foucauldian dissenters, however, argue that even the most deliberative settings are all about interest maintenance. An example is the elegant study by Bent Flyvberg (1998) of the power dynamics of inclusive decision-making in the city of Aalborg in Denmark. Open deliberation often conceals self-interest and institutionalized inequality. Rightly, Flyvberg suggests that the normative discussion should shift from deliberation planning to politics, from issues of good planning practice to actions to democratize existing institutions and practices.

Radical democracy

Democracy requires the democratization of institutions and the empowerment of subaltern voices in a politics of vigorous but fair contest between diverse interests. Democracy is about spirited adversarial confrontation. This is the argument of theorists of radical democracy, the third position we wish to explore (Laclau and Mouffe 1985; Laclau 1996; Mouffe 1993; Trend 1996; Benhabib 1996; Fraser 1996). These theorists reject the proposition of rational consensus, as well as universals which sublimate gender, ethnic and other differences. Chantal Mouffe (2000) explains that a constitutive paradox of liberal democracies is that individual freedom (liberalism) and equality (democracy) are neither reconcilable (for instance, via rational consensus), nor structurally irreconcilable (as argued by anti-capitalists). Instead, negotiating this tension has to be the very substance of political praxis. Mouffe proposes an 'agonistic pluralism' (contra antagonistic pluralism) as a constructive way of channelling adversarial politics. Here the public sphere is conceived as a site of difference and disagreement, but one which offers ample opportunity to the less powerful to stake (and win) their claims. Democracy, is about accepting a 'plurality of forms of being a democratic citizen' (2000: 73), and 'shared adhesion to the ethico-political principles of liberal democracy: liberty and equality' (p. 102), such that the contest is one between friendly enemies (agonism), rather than antagonists. But there is more. Agonistic politics is also a journey of development through engagement; a project of social and political transformation (not just reconciliation of pregiven interests). Preferences can be formed through agonistic confrontation, while social interaction can generate new coalitions and understandings, new hybrid identities. If commonality is to arise, it will do so out of shared meanings developed in the course of agonistic politics.

What is appealing about radical democracy as a model for urban democracy is its resonance with the contested and fluid nature of urban life, and its intense juxtaposition of difference and inequality (Massey 1999). What better a place than the city as a site of contested practices and aspirations, a zone of agonistic engagement, a place of experimentation with democracy as practice? And indeed, in the urban planning literature, the radical democratic model too is also invoked in the name of a new politics of the margins. For Leonie Sandercock, in the city as borderland in which most people live with uncertainty, 'insurgent planners' should seize the 'potential space of radical openness which nourishes the vision of a more experimental culture, a more tolerant and multifocal one' (1998: 120).

We agree in large measure with the open and participatory ideals advocated, but wonder if the social justice desired is achievable on the terms set out. Why should the politics of resistance and empowerment deliver the just city? What is to stop the politics of difference from degenerating into tribalism? What if 'chains of equivalence' (Laclau 1996) do not emerge from agonistic engagement? The radical democrat's preference for a politics of contest over the deliberative democrat's preference for a politics of consensus still does not deal with embedded power and inequality. There remains an eerie silence on the normative principles and projects which might help to bind difference. For example, Nancy Fraser accepts that radical democracy must recognize that '*cultural differences can only be freely elaborated and democratically mediated on the basis of social equality*' (1996: 207, original emphasis). And so she proposes, first, the need to 'construct a new equality/difference debate, one oriented to multiple intersecting differences'; second, to 'develop an alternative version of anti-essentialism, one that permits us to link a cultural politics of identity and difference with a social politics of justice and equality'; and third, to 'develop an alternative version that permits us to make normative judgements about the value of different differences by interrogating their relation to inequality' (p. 207). Similarly, Seyla Benhabib, echoing a desire for feminist theory and practice to move beyond celebrating difference, argues for a 'unity of the self':

> This is the vision of a social feminism that accepts that the furthering of one's capacity for autonomous agency is only possible within the confines of a solidaristic community that sustains one identity through mutual recognition. Opposed to the postmodernist vision of the fragmented subject is the assumption that the human subject is a fragile, needy, and dependent creature whose capacity to develop a coherent life-story out of the competing claims upon its identity must be cherished and protected. (1996: 38)

In both texts, however, there is no substantive discussion of the normative goals and pathways for social justice. This is not uncommon in radical democratic writing.

Rights to the City: a Politics of the Commons

In this second part of the chapter our aim is to discuss substantive goals that help to enhance active citizenship. We do so in a manner consistent with the Progressive Era, which sought social progress through a civic-minded and capable public. Our emphasis falls on institutionalized actions which can, on the one hand, enhance individual and social capabilities, and, on the other, build solidarities across the society of difference. We articulate a 'politics of the commons' centred around universal rights to citizenship. This is not as an end in itself, but as a foundation for a politics of difference based on association and allowing insurgent practices to flourish, since, as Alain Touraine notes, 'tolerance and the acceptances of differences do not in themselves make inter-cultural communication possible' (2000: 301).

We do not aspire towards a complete model, partly because we share the radical democratic model's unease over a prescribed order/telos. Nor do we outline ways of tackling structural inequality (such as disparities locked into capitalist competition or property rights), distributional inequality (concerning income and other resource allocations related to state fiscal, employment and welfare policies) or institutionalized violations of justice (state power, corporate power, patriarchy). We accept that these gaps matter. For example, Don Mitchell (2000) is right to warn that injustices committed against marginals such as the homeless are more likely to be resolved through good public housing and welfare schemes than through providing heterotopic spaces for self-expression. Our emphasis on citizenship rights is intended to complement arguments for structural and distributional equity (Harvey 2000).

The tone we wish to strike is that of universals as a right of access to participation. In his book *Le droit à la ville*, Henri Lefebvre imagines the good city as an experimental utopia based on direct democracy, aided in part through needs met through universal rights such as access to welfare and income:

> The right to the city . . . should . . . make more practical the rights of the citizen as an urban dweller . . . and user of multiple services. It would affirm, on the one hand, the right of users to make known their ideas on the space and time of their activities in the urban area; it would also cover the right to the use of the centre, a privileged place, instead of being dispersed and stuck into ghettos. (cited in Kofman and Lebas 1996: 34)

Being in the city is not about claiming abstract rights or about an essentialized ideal that transcends race, gender and sex (the abstract classical citizen). It is not about an imagined or perfect ideal state shared by all. Instead, it is all about the 'equal right to politics for all people' (Deutsche 1999: 195). It is about the right to citizenship for all, the right to shape and influence. For one, this entails the chance to live the city in a certain way. Lefebvre explains:

> The *right to the city* cannot be conceived of as a simple visiting right or as a return to traditional cities. It can only be formulated as a transformed and renewed *right to urban life*. It does not matter whether the urban fabric encloses the countryside and what survives of peasant life, as long as the 'urban', place of encounter, priority of use value . . . finds its morphological base and its practico-material realization. (1996: 138, original emphasis)

Here the city is more than a place of common access and encounter. It offers a practical and material means of meeting social needs ('use value'). And more. It is a place of becoming, and the fulfilment of social potential, of democratic experimentation through the efforts of citizens themselves, as free and socialized agents. Lefebvre again:

> The ideal city . . . would be the . . . the perpetual *oeuvre* of the inhabitants, themselves mobile and mobilized for and by this *oeuvre*. [. . .] The right to the city manifests itself as a superior form of rights: right to freedom, to individualization in socialization, to habitat and to inhabit. (1996: 173)

This is the sense of urban citizenship we wish to develop: the idea of democracy as access, mutuality, fulfilment of potential. We see the city, more specifically its institutions, providing the opportunity for citizens to become something else and for mutuality to be strengthened. This means, in contrast to the versions of urban democracy we have discussed earlier, no special role for professional mediators, no privileged status for just the visible or temporary places of social mixture (streets, squares, cafés), not action merely for those on the borderlands of exclusion, oppression and violence, and more than the credo that 'you can become what you are'. It also means the institutionalization of effort, so that the gains may be sustained. We focus next on two examples of an 'institutionalized' commons – capabilities and socialization – before returning to suggest some city-based actions.

Capabilities

Under conditions of persistent inequality – with cities revealing some of the sharpest contrasts of poverty, unemployment, exclusion and marginalization – it would be perverse for a discussion on democracy not to focus on fundamental rights and entitlements. These, as Roberto Unger puts it, 'assure people of the political, economic, and cultural equipment they need in order to stand up, go forward, and connect' (1998: 266). Some of the rights are basic human rights of the sort enshrined in international declarations of human rights, guaranteeing shelter, food, clothing, free association, personal liberty and security, protection from violence and coercion, and so on. Others – more controversial as universal rights because they relate to the internal historical negotiations within different societies – might cover rights to property, work, basic income, economic decision-making, and welfare and civil liberties. We defend these rights as well, but acknowledge their contingency on national settlements and struggles.

Unger's idea of opportunity 'to stand up, go forward, and connect' is close to Amartya Sen's (1992) proposal to tackle inequality through the development of individual and social capabilities. Like Unger, Sen is sceptical of means-based or resource-based models of equality based on the automatic redistribution of bundles of goods to vulnerable sections of society or strict rules of reward across society and generations. Such egalitarianism is considered to restrict human motivation and enterprise as well as individual and collective freedom. James Bohman sees 'the primacy of the space of capabilities' as 'the equal distribution not of resources related to the most basic human needs, but of . . . those conditions which establish the equal worth of human freedom' (1997: 328–9). While we disagree with such a sharp decoupling of resources from capabilities on the grounds that basic universals are needed for capabilities, we recognize the problems posed by a culture of resource entitlements alone.

Capabilities, of course, cover a wide range of personal and interpersonal assets – from skills, experience, creativity, judgement and reflexivity, to socialization, engagement, communication and expression. There seems to be a broad consensus, however, that education and learning are core capabilities that need to be offered as lifelong entitlements. Without education, the opportunity to 'stand up and go forward' is drastically reduced in an economy that increasingly demands knowledgeability. Similarly, continual learning is now necessitated by the erosion of stable, lifelong employment and the demand for intellectual and practical agility in the emerging economy of ever-shifting standards, technologies and preferences. The main point we wish to make, though, is that a society that values the developmental powers of education should defend learning on intrinsic grounds. This is the sign of a confident democracy. In this regard, the contemporary trend to diminish education to training, in response to labour market needs, is narrow and short-sighted. The schemes of the Progressive Era had the insight to recognize the developmental and social aspects of learning. As Unger notes: 'Education, continuing through a lifetime, rescuing people as children from the imaginative hold of their families, their class, their country, and their time, and giving them as adults access to a repertoire of generic practical and conceptual capacities, is the most important enabler of individual and collective freedom' (1998: 267).

Here the challenge posed is that of providing more than affordable education for job-related ends (although we do not wish to undervalue the importance of well-resourced organizations, of a manageable size and run by competent professionals). We could extend the line of reasoning to include the right to take leave from work or domestic duties for learning and self-improvement, perhaps through paid sabbaticals. In 1992 the Danes experimented with a voluntary Paid Leave Scheme, which gave public sector employees up to a year to pursue activities of their choice, while their jobs were offered to unemployed persons as an opportunity for work experience. We can think of other activities. 'Folk universities' (as they are called in Sweden), funded by the municipal authorities, could be opened across a city's neighbourhoods, offering all manner of vocational and non-vocational courses to people of all ages. Similarly, resources could be channelled to the multitude of voluntary and non-profit organizations that currently survive on a shoestring to provide classes of different sorts, from IT skills to wool-spinning and adult literacy.

The Sen/Unger line of thinking requires universal provision for capabilities. This raises the inevitable question of how to fund it. One innovative idea is that every individual receives an endowment – cash or cash equivalent – at birth or in adult life (not to be passed on after death). For example, controversially, Bruce Ackerman and Anne Alstott (1999) suggest that every citizen of the United States is given a one-off, non-transferable grant of 80,000 dollars on reaching early adulthood, to be used to fund basic needs. This is suggested as a low-cost option for the US, financed by an annual 2 per cent tax levy on the nation's wealth, plus repayment of the grant into a national 'stakeholder fund' by individuals at death (if their savings allow). Stakeholders would be free to spend their money as they wished, in full awareness of the consequences of their choice (such as spending the money on a yacht instead of education). For the authors, this scheme would give US citizens – all of them – the opportunity for self-betterment as well as a stake in society. The stakeholder scheme is not one without problems however. Eighty thousand dollars is not a particularly generous lifetime endowment, considering the cost of, say, technology-intensive training. Then, the libertarian emphasis on freedom of choice makes light of how to tackle the gap between those who see the value of investing in capabilities and those locked into a culture of consumer gratification. More fundamentally, it can be read as a second-best option to the universal welfare state, funded through the national tax base. But, then, this may be the closest we can get to welfare equity in a culture like the US of rooted individualism and aversion to the welfare state.

Unger suggests a more targeted and equitable solution. He too supports a lifelong endowment for all citizens (with the size of the national fund tied to national economic performance in a given time-period). But his model varies from that of Ackerman and Alstott in four important ways. First, he argues that the national fund should be tilted in favour of those at a disadvantage, by adding to a fixed sum received by everyone, a variable part that increases 'by one measure according to a principle of compensation for special need, for physical, social, or cognitive disadvantage' (1998: 267). Second, he argues that the variable part should involve competition for increments that are tied to capability-enhancing proposals. Unger is clear that the prime target should be lifetime education, not free choice over expenditure. Third, he argues that the fund should include non-cash options, so as to ease financial stress on the state. Finally, he ties a part of the fund to community-based initiatives, as a means of meeting local needs as well as mobilizing local interest in capacity building.

Unger's proposals are more explicitly egalitarian than those of Ackerman and Alstott, in targeting disadvantage and collective rights and responsibilities. They all, however, believe in capabilities as a basic democratic right. For us, cities can contribute as a key site for building capabilities. Cities bustle with learning in schools and colleges, but also universities of the third age, night schools, libraries, extramural courses, and so on. Indeed, a central aspect of cities is that they provide the infrastructure for these activities. With due recognition and appropriate investment, these spaces could help to breathe life back into the varied institutions of capability formation in a confident democracy.

Socialization

Citizenship has to be practised and valued if we want to enhance the 'ability of social actors to intervene in public life' (Touraine 2000: 292). Clearly, in circumstances of acute individual alienation, a recovery of the commons has to begin with restoring self-respect through the offer of work, education and other rights. Such entitlements, however, are not enough. We argue, through three examples below, that socialization into citizenship is also of vital necessity.

Publicity   Active citizenship continues to require a knowledgeable and discursive political community. During the Progressive Era, the obstacles included the poor circulation of information as a public good, the shortage of media to facilitate communication between spatially distant communities and the absence of a public capable of informed debate. Today there is no shortage of news and views, face-to-face contact is far from the only available means for public engagement and the culture of performance and enactment seems to have become all-pervasive (in work, recreation, public spaces, the media). But the principle of interactive and edifying political engagement is worth retaining. This is where cities could really make a difference, through their many institutions and media outlets. For example, schools have a vital role to play by re-energizing debating societies, but covering issues of everyday concern to students. This seems to us better than instructing students about civics and citizenship, as proposed by communitarians in the US and Britain. The key is to spark engagement as a means of building critical ability, voice and argument. Defined thus, there is no reason why the principle cannot spill over into afterschool centres, workplaces and other sites of gathering (evening courses, clubs, etc.). Perhaps this is where intermediaries – from deliberative planners to shop stewards and teachers – could play an important role, helping to raise awareness and mobilize voice. The options for innovation are many, including the use of legislative theatre (see box 6.1).

Face-to-face engagement in local institutions is only a start, however. There is also scope for public participation through the mass media. We know this from the spectacular success of televised chat shows, drawing as they do on the seduction of private revelation and publicity. We do not wish to defend the material and manner of chat shows – which often dramatize out of acute personal dilemmas – but their potential to challenge opinion on sensitive social and ethical matters (such as family violence, incest, sexual practices). They can be used as a way of practising citizenship in our times of increasing usage of the public sphere as a public stage (Urry 2000) on which the political is performed through personalities and spectacles, with viewers and listeners drawn into the same confident and personal space as dignitaries, politicians and the like. The mediatized stage is a vivid example of the new politics we alluded to at the start of the chapter; one that calls on the performative everyday political subject. The rise of citizens' juries is another example of the performing public. Then, in the majority of developing countries, public adjudication has always been there in meeting places, coffee-houses, verandas, streets and markets, as the daily news breaks over the radio or television. Even the scope of the electronic agora is worth considering. Alongside city internet sites for lifestyle discussions, we can find political discussion groups in cities such as Amsterdam, Berlin, Athens, and Bologna (Tsagarousianou, Tambini, and Bryan 1998). Dominated though they are by young professional males, and often frequented by sectarian or semi-illegal groups, they nonetheless register the opportunity for an 'electronic polis' based on distanciated connection and interchange.

Box 6.1   Legislative theatre

I, Augusto Boal, want the Spectator to take on the role of Actor and invade the Character and the stage. I want him to occupy his own Space and offer solutions.

By taking possession of the stage, the Spect-Actor is consciously performing a responsible act. The stage is a representation of the reality, a fiction. But the Spect-Actor is not fictional. He exists in the scene and outside of it, in a dual reality. By taking possession of the stage in the fiction of the theater, he acts: not just in the fiction, but also in his social reality. By transforming fiction, he is transformed into himself.

This invasion is a symbolic trespass. It symbolizes all the acts of trespass we have to commit in order to free ourselves from what oppresses us. If we do not trespass (not necessarily violently), if we do not go beyond our cultural norms, our state of oppression, the limits imposed upon us, even the law itself (which should be transformed) – if we do not trespass in this we can never be free. To free ourselves is to trespass, and to transform. It is through a creation of the new that that which has not yet existed begins to exist. To free yourself is to trespass. To trespass is to exist. To free ourselves is to exist. (Boal 2000: xxi)

This is the manifesto drafted in 1974 by the renowned dramatist and performance theorist Augusto Boal on the role of radical experimental theatre. It involves audience participation, through a variety of forms, around a moving script that touches on everyday experience or imagination. This might involve actors acting out short scenes proposed by local residents, spectators miming views on a theme of common interest to the spectators, or participants intervening 'decisively in the dramatic action and change it' (2000: 139). The performance might be staged, improvised on the street, use myths, photo-romances and imaginary situations. The purpose, through participation, is to listen, learn and enjoy, but also to express, connect and change; to trespass.

Boal calls this the Theater of the Oppressed, intended to politicize the less educated in developing countries. The principle can be transported to other settings: with the cities of developed countries in mind, Sennett notes that 'the most urgent requirement for democratic deliberation today is that people concentrate rather than "surf" social reality. . . . For this reason, I have come to believe that designers need to pay attention to the architecture of theaters as possible political spaces' (1999b: 280). For Sennett, innovative theatre architecture, attentive to the requirement of a 'disciplinary space for the eye and the voice' (p. 280), can be used to create 'a space of political congregation' for cities. He cites the example of Tadeo Ando's theatre in Tokyo – a portable theatre that can be re-erected in different parts of the city – deliberately designed to make speech from the audience as clear as words spoken on stage. He also cites the example of the Angel Theatre in London, with its windows designed as doors, to allow passers-by to look in and inspect. These theatrical innovations 'can attempt to develop civic connections not of the fleeting sort, as in a public square, but rather of a more sustained and focused sort' (p. 284), for the urban 'polity requires further a place for discipline, focus, and duration' (p. 285). There are many uses of the theatre for democracy.

Sociability   Part of the success of the Progressive Era lay in its ability to combine political debate with sociability. This is a link of vital significance. The idea of politicization with a light touch has prompted Sam Fleischacker to highlight pubs, public libraries and community centres as places promoting friendship and shared experience. He contrasts these 'particle' communities with 'solidaristic' communities of singular ideologies or political projects: 'A liberalism that aids insignificant communities, that supports community via the low-level activities that bring people casually together, can achieve the associational bonds it needs without so much as appearing to promote one set of ultimate human ends over another' (1998: 303).

Fleischacker is taken by the 'conversational anarchy' of these communities and proposes state funding for 'Social Houses' offering 'baseline activities' which can be shared by all citizens. He suggests locating these in every neighbourhood, open twenty-four hours and governed from below, offering recreation, leisure and meeting rooms: learning through sociability. That such sites will encourage citizenship and civic values is not guaranteed. The contemporary English pub is not a notable catalyst of civic behaviour. The point about combining political education with sociability, however, remains valid. A good example are the movements of 1968 – from worker and feminist struggles to student protests – which managed to combine theory, political action and enjoyment in quite staggering ways. They were as much about political critique and struggle as they were about alternative lifestyles and values, drawing on what might be described as a 'conviviality' or social energy (Peattie 1998) that gave life to festivals, parades, communes and many other solidaristic pleasures and experiments. The social energy breathed life back into political activity and, importantly, became a source of radical opening of new and sustainable possibilities and projects. This kind of hedonism needs to underpin a new politics of the commons.

Civic duty   Our interest in pleasure is neither gratuitous nor a prioritization of individual rights over social obligations. The problem of inculcating citizenship remains and neither of the above two socialization strategies is likely to draw in those averse to others and civic engagement (Tilly 1999). Our belief is that in order to encourage citizenship as an everyday practice, people need to experience negotiating diversity and difference. Yet this is exactly what has been put to the test in our times of associating with only those like you or whom you like. Citizenship has to develop though its *practice*, perhaps by taking individuals out of their daily communities. It must become an 'office within public community' (van Gunsteren 1998: 25) involving the practice of political equality (not social consensus) and social competence, leading to an ethical know-how based on practice (see box 6.2).

One possibility might be to encourage citizens – through the offer of tangible rewards (such as income, access to education, training certification) – to undertake social and civic duties of various sorts through state and voluntary organizations for a given period in early adulthood. There are interesting examples of civic programmes promoted by state–third sector partnerships in the US (Dahle 1999). One scheme – City Year – provided a modest living allowance and partial college scholarships to young adults from all walks of life to work on community projects such as cleaning up vacant lots, providing HIV education, tutoring other students and helping the elderly. Public Allies is another scheme that has spread to many cities, attracting a large number of participants. It has promoted citizenship by placing young people in ten-month paid apprenticeships with local non-profit organizations. Similarly, Michael Shuman (1998) writes of many youth and ethnic minority entrepreneurship schemes, as well as urban farms and food projects, which have passed on vital skills and experience to socially excluded groups at the same time as providing a grounding in active citizenship.

The politics of the commons we have outlined is shaped by two distinctive normative goals. The first is reconciliation of universal aspirations of social justice and equality with particularistic demands through solidarities built across disparate sites of contemporary society. The second

Box 6.2   Ethical know-how

In his extraordinary book *Ethical Know-How* (1999), the cognitive psychophysiologist Francisco Varela situates ethical action in the combined space of cognition rooted in sensory-motor practices and wisdom based on Confucian and Buddhist principles of non-intentional caring. His premise is that we know through 'enaction' based on perceptually guided action and recurrent sensory-motor patterns, not acts of conscious deliberation. He asks us to:

> Picture yourself walking down the street, perhaps going to meet somebody. It is the end of the day and there is nothing very special in your mind. You stop at a kiosk and buy a pack of cigarettes, then continue on your way. You are in a relaxed mood. You put your hand into your pocket and suddenly you discover that your wallet is missing. Your mood is shattered. Your thoughts are muddled. And before you know it, a new world has emerged. You see clearly that you left your wallet at the kiosk. Your mood shifts again to one of concern about losing your documents and your money. The only thing on your mind now is getting back to the store as quickly as possible. You ignore the surrounding trees and passers-by; all your attention is directed at avoiding further delays.
>
> Situations like this are the very stuff of our lives, and they involve the most ordinary situations as well as the more interesting ethical stances. We *always* operate in some kind of immediacy of a given situation. Our lived world is so ready-at-hand that we have no deliberateness about what it is and how we inhabit it. (Varela 1999: 8–9, original emphasis)

If this is how we think and act, then ethical behaviour too must work in similar ways. This has important implications for a theory of citizenship, for it suggests that it is the practice of 'being good' that really counts, rather than the religiosity of moral consciousness and/or moral sanction. From the Confucian teachings of Mencius, Varela gathers:

> Only people who act from dispositions they have at the very moment of action as a result of a long process of cultivation merit the name of *truly* virtuous. . . . Such a person does not act out ethics, but embodies it like any expert embodies his knowledge know-how; the wise man *is* ethical, or more explicitly, his actions arise from

inclinations that his disposition produces in response to specific situations. (1999: 30, original emphasis)

The 'pragmatic key to ethical expertise' is inculcation of the skills of 'spontaneous compassion' rooted in practices which allow individuals to 'personally discover and grow into their own sense of virtual self' (1999: 32, 75). For Varela, some of this training is to be found in Buddhist practices of meditation, self-discipline, living without possessions, communal existence, and community presence. But:

> Unlike mastery of an ordinary skill, mastery of the skillful means of ethical expertise results in the elimination of *all* habits so that the practitioner can realize that wisdom and compassion can arise directly and spontaneously out of wisdom. It is as if one were born already knowing how to play the violin and had to practice with great exertion in order to remove the habits that prevented one from displaying that virtuosity. Thus the true *wu-wei* of the wise is not manufactured, but uncovered. In Buddhism this is the image of the fully accomplished *boddisattva*. (1999: 72–3, original emphasis)

Now the practice of citizenship may be less dependent on spiritual conversion or revelation – consistent with Buddhist teaching – but it does require this kind of ethical action.

is establishment of a level playing field for social contestation. Power differentials and inequality run through the fabric of modern society; it would be naive to think that conflict can be resolved in favour of all citizens. However, the rights we have outlined do provide some of the equipment for social participation, helping to lift some causes of intolerance and to build voice.

City politics

The democratic city must offer more than universals, which in any case are not necessarily urban in character. We still need to address how urban spaces, institutions and practices might lead to 'cities for the many, not the few' (Amin, Massey and Thrift 2000). We want to suggest urban sites as settings for the *practice* of democracy through a confident citizenship, rather than as formative of a particular *form* of democracy, as most writing on urban politics would have it. This is not to reject the potential of the urban sites and settings traditionally emphasized (such as parks and street festivals), but simply the political aspirations attached to them. They can be reimagined in the kind of democracy we seek. Take the 'democracy' of public spaces as an example. Policies for urban design could explore not only the joys and dangers associated with intermingling in the city's open spaces, but also how they might be designed as breathing spaces – places where people can remove themselves from the rush and noise, and slow down (Amin, Massey and Thrift 2000). These places can be open spaces – parks and street benches – but also closed spaces (such as libraries or galleries).

Similarly, urban activists might tackle head-on the asymmetry of power built into co-presence in public spaces (on the tactics of aggressive panhandlers see Duneier 1999), including the possibility of setting aside spaces for vulnerable groups (gays, ethnic minorities). More fundamentally, a democracy of the city's physical spaces would consider the implications of cities as stopping places for an ever-expanding mobile population. If cities are increasingly places of passing through or arrival, not only for tourists and professionals but also for itinerants, migrants and refugees (now routinely demonized), a confident democracy should be able to offer imaginative schemes to shelter, feed, and reorient these segments of the mobile population (why covet only the transnational business elite?).

The city as a practising democracy might also support the vast network of everyday associations of sociability that is to be found in all parts of the city. This would nudge action beyond the current obsession of urban leaders with riverside cafés and bijou restaurants servicing the needs of the professional and monied classes. A very substantial volume of urban sociality involves meeting friends, attending recreation or education clubs of one sort or another, renewing community links. Cities are replete with associations – from pottery groups and amateur theatre groups, to scout clubs and swimming clubs – which are the very essence of learning, organizational capability and civic participation. Such participation needs explicit recognition, not only through state provision for associations (as is the custom in Scandinavian countries) but also by facilitating visibility through festivals, floats, street events, parades, craft fairs and so on. This too can be part of a confident urban democracy.

Finally, cities are sites of dense and varied institutional activity, situated in firms, business and public sector organizations, interest groups, voluntary and religious organizations, lobbying groups and protest campaigns, and so on. A concern with urban democracy cannot disregard the practices and policies of these institutions; to do so is to ignore the prime sites of habituated behaviour and social participation. Institutional reform too has to be part of the project to democratize urban life. There are many experiments around the world to draw on: public scrutiny of local government plans through public hearings and electronic town hall meetings; consultative and participatory decision-making within government, businesses and other governance institutions; stakeholder involvement in planning decisions; city finances scrutinized by local communities (as in Porto Alegre in Brazil), even if this means placing restrictions on the powerful (such as taxes on pollution or types of inward investment); promotion of grass-roots schemes such as derelict land reclamation plans drawn up by schoolchildren; sponsorship for initiatives employing the socially excluded to provide socially useful services (care for the elderly, management of housing estates, waste management); and encouragement of non-monetary networks of exchange among financially disabled communities. The city is replete with possibilities for such experimentalism.

A Mobile Politics

Lefebvre saw the democratic city in terms of the right to participate in urban society. We have argued in this chapter that this right cannot draw on the politics of urban design and public encounter alone, but also requires rights-based and other institutionalized actions at national and urban level to build capacity and capability across the social spectrum. It is only then, as Deutsche suggests, that an act as straightforward as 'the right literally to walk in the city becomes part of a more comprehensive freedom, the freedom to use the constructed spatial order in a way that not only actualizes but also transforms it' (Deutsche 1999: 200). We have stressed a politics 'making rights inseparable from democratic urbanism' (Deutsche 1999: 197). Our return to the language of universalism arises out of worry about an eroding commons. It is not used as a weapon against the right of people to be different, but as a basis for 'developing an account of recognition that can accommodate the full complexity of social identities, instead of one that promotes reification and separatism' (Fraser 2000: 109).

We have no model citizen or teleology in mind, only equitable distribution of the potential for development in a social world that offers more than just a 'life of your own' (Beck 2000). Our aspiration in this sense is no different from that of radical democrats, who see free and equal citizens engaged in a 'vibrant clash of democratic political positions' (Mouffe 2000: 104). But we do want to be more explicit about what the 'clash' is for. What makes it democratic has to be a desire for distributive and participatory justice and a respect for the principles of autonomy and solidarity. But there is more. A shared public space for open competition has the potential of conjuring out of positions challenged and unformulated potentialities what John Rajchman describes as a 'minor politics' that 'has another sense of time, of the future, of the vitality of the future' owing to 'circumstances that place people in situations, where, in relation to themselves and one another, they are no longer able to tell straight narratives about their "origins". Then they become "originals" without origins: their narratives become "out of joint", constructed through superposition or juxtaposition, rather than through development or progress' (1999b: 51). Thus, as Deutsche puts it, 'the problem of society can never be finally settled' in the *agon* full of 'conflicts over attempts to gain respect for *different* rights' (1999: 195, original emphasis). In such a frame, urban life can be seen as a site of experimentation linked to its defining aspect as a space of juxtaposed difference and marked temporal and spatial porosity (as we saw in chapter 1).

We end with two examples to illustrate the city as a site of politics in motion, testing new ground, rather than as the embodiment of a particular form of democracy, or the site of local particularisms (Harvey 2000). The first example relates to who has the right to claim citizenship in the contemporary city marked by cosmopolitan connections and a mobile population. Historically, rights of citizenship have been tied to territory, usually the nation. But, now a significant proportion of the temporary and permanent residents of cities consists of non-citizens (including stateless persons, asylum seekers), illegal migrants, citizens of other nations who carry limited rights of residence, and people with ties of loyalty and belonging to transnational communities and global movements. This mixed population too requires access to the full rights of citizenship – local and translocal – outlined in this chapter. Their condition requires new citizenship rules based on mobile and transferable rights of personhood (Soysal 1994), possibly in a form of world citizenship detached from national models of citizenship (Urry 2000). At a minimum, their transnational experiences and cultural connections can be examined as the constitutive elements of a translocal identity and citizenship (Inda and Miròn 1999).

The second example attends to the temporality of the city – its rhythm and pace. Sennett (1998, 2000) is right to warn of the dangers of a new brand of 'vigorous' capitalism, marked by the frenzy of achievement, multiple existence and ever-encroaching work demands. These pressures are acutely felt in the city and test the capacity of people as reflective and social beings. City spaces – parks and other open spaces, sites of learning and recreation, centres of socialization – possess some potential here, in helping to slow down time and providing a fixed point of orientation. In fact, 'vigorous' cities such as Modena in Italy and some Dutch cities have started to introduce innovative urban time-management schemes (such as flexible office and childcare times) to help busy working people regain their personal and social space. Some have suggested the introduction of 'slow-traffic' devices (for instance, trees planted at busy crossroads) so that citizens can recover a 'freedom to move distracted' and, through this, also a 'freedom of association' (Sorkin 1999: 7). Cities *can* be key sites in testing new ground.

AFTERWORD: TESTING
NEW GROUND

It is not in the nature of a book like this to produce a set of final conclusions. Like the city, this book should be seen as very much a work in progress. However, we cannot resist writing a few final words about some of the political directions we are attempting to open up.

Our first point is a very straightforward one. We see the city as an agitation of thought and practice. But this emphasis on potentiality, on virtuality and on new kinds of empowerment should not be read as a thoroughgoing voluntarism. As the reader will know, modern cities are still plagued by enveloping constraints like poverty, systematic forms of violence like racism and the small and mean-minded terrorisms that still frame so many encounters in the home and street. Yet we believe that it is important to put these forces in their place. The modern city is also so full of unexpected interactions and so continuously in movement that all kinds of small and large spatialities continue to provide resources for political invention as they generate new improvisations and force new forms of ingenuity.

Our second point follows on from the first. If there is one thing that is clear, it is how narrow a field urban politics has become. Yet, as we hope to have shown, the city is brimful of different kinds of political space. This does not just mean the presence of newly acknowledged and new actors, like animals and various kinds of machine. It also consists of the frames that surround everyday life, simple elements such as standards, metrics, software programmes and other technologies which are all the more powerful for being so rarely questioned (Latour 1988; Bowker and Star 1999). Andrew Barry (2001) has noted that a field of political contestation with considerable impact is now being formed around these kinds of technological moments. Then we would want to point to a politics of the microspaces of the city. Over the years feminists have been able to show the way here, in their ability, through theory and practice, to foreground spaces of the domestic and the various kinds of often quite vicious power plays that are acted out within them. Similarly, therapists and others called on to tackle bodily-cum-psychological problems now note just how important the microspaces of the domestic are in constituting them. Finally, there is a whole politics of embodiment, from the minutiae of gesture to the movement patterns of the crowd, which has still only rarely been systematically explored (see Varela 1999; Sennett 1994). In each of these cases, one of the pressing problems is how to think about these issues when the dividing line between private and public has been so comprehensively displaced by the mediatization of society. For example, the domestic sphere has become a public good through the influence of never-ending television and website coverage.

A third point follows on again. If we want to bring some of these new urban politics into play, then we will also need an expanded politics of representation. Modern cities are full of representational experiments and inventions, from the many children of Surrealism through to the recent work by numerous teenagers on the social possibilities of wireless communication, which are attempts to sense the city in different ways. In turn, this extraordinary resource shows the importance of ethico-aesthetic invention as a key moment in a revitalized urban politics (Guattari 1995). Increasingly, the exploration of modern urban life requires the routine deployment of what in the past would have been regarded as purely artistic modes of understanding, which have now spread into the underbelly of urban culture. For example, collage and other modes of aestheticization have now become a standard means of urban communication (Lash 2001).

This brings us to our final point, which concerns what rights to the city are for. Much of what goes on in the everyday spaces of the city is not about participation in politics with a conventional capital P. Rather, it is about new kinds of molecular politics which vie for public attention, sometimes succeeding in creating wider social and political effects (Thompson 2000). And it is also about forms of association, such as internet communities and clubs of various sorts, which allow these kinds of politics to subsist, possibly in a different public realm. Increasingly, such asssociation is driven by the desire to be with others, to act in public for the simple pleasure of acting, and to gain entry to specialist knowledges. There is a politics of sociality that needs to be revisited. In particular, with the decline of the nuclear family and overarching ideologies, friendship has become an even more important part of the urban social fabric, many of whose pleasures lie in simply relating to others – in part as a result of the increasing emphasis on relationship as a value in itself (Giddens 1991; Pahl 2000). Ironically, of course, this is where – back in ancient Greece – much of the thinking on the politics of cities began.

When we consider the overwhelming oligoptic nature of modern cities, it may seem as though we are raising false hopes and painting false horizons. Not surprisingly, however, we would dissent from this view. We see modern cities as still being the cradle of invention and creativity, and hence our hope for their future. Indeed, we would argue that the very act of claiming that such a cradle exists opens up the possibility of change. Events do not all fall back into the morass. Some set up new refrains – and new challenges, challenges which can be named and built upon.

REFERENCES

Abercrombie, N. and Longhurst, B. (1998) *Audiences*, Sage, London.

Abram, D. (1996) *The Spell of the Sensuous*, Vintage, New York.

Ackerman, B. and Alstott, A. (1999) *The Stakeholder Society*, Yale University Press, New Haven.

Agamben, G. (1993) *The Coming Community*, University of Minnesota Press, Minneapolis.

Agamben, G. (1999) *Potentialities*, Stanford University Press, Stanford.

Akbur, R. (2000) 'Imagining London in two Caribbean novels'. In G. Bridge and S. Watson (eds), *A Companion to the City*, Blackwell, Oxford.

Allen, J. (1999) 'Worlds within cities'. In D. Massey, J. Allen and S. Pile (eds), *City Worlds*, Routledge, London.

Allen, J., Massey, D. and Pryke, M. (eds) (1999) *Unsettling Cities*, Routledge, London.

Amin, A. (1997) 'Beyond associative democracy', *New Political Economy*, 1, 3: 309–33.

Amin, A. (2000) 'The European Union as more than a triad market for national economic spaces'. In G. Clark, M. Feldman and M. Gertler (eds), *The Oxford Handbook of Economic Geography*, Oxford University Press, Oxford.

Amin, A. (2001) 'Spatialities of globalisation', *Environment and Planning A*, forthcoming.

Amin, A. and Cohendet, P. (1999) 'Learning and adaptation in decentralised business networks', *Society and Space*, 17: 87–104.

Amin, A. and Cohendet, P. (2000) 'Organisational learning and governance through embedded practices', *Journal of Management and Governance*, 4: 93–116.

Amin, A. and Thrift, N. (1992) 'Neo-Marshallian nodes in global networks', *International Journal of Urban and Regional Research*, 16, 4: 571–87.

Amin, A., Massey, D. and Thrift, N. J. (2000) *Cities for the Many Not the Few*, Policy Press, Bristol.

Ansell-Pearson, K. (1997) *Viroid Life*, Routledge, London.

Ansell-Pearson, K. (1999) *Germinal Life*, Routledge, London.

Appadurai, A. (1996) *Modernity at Large*, University of Minnesota Press, Minneapolis.

Audretsch, D. (1998) 'Agglomeration and the location of economic activity', *Oxford Review of Economic Policy*, 14, 2: 18–29.

Baker, P., Funk, S. M., Harris, S. and White, P. (2000) 'Flexible spatial organisation of urban boxes, Vulpes vulpes before and during an outbreak of sarcoptic mange', *Animal Behaviour*, 59, 1: 127–46.

Barley, N. (2000) 'People'. In N. Barley (ed.), *Breathing Cities*, Birkhäuser, Basel.

Barry, A. (2001) *Technological Politics*, Continuum, London.

Barthes, R. (1976) *Sade/Fourier/Loyola*, Johns Hopkins University Press, Baltimore.

Bateson, G. (1973) *Steps to an Ecology of Mind*, Paladin, London.

Baxandall, R. and Ewen, E. (1999) *Picture Windows: How the Suburbs Happened*, Columbia University Press, New York.

Beaverstock, J. and Bostock, R. (2001) 'Expatriate communities in Asia-Pacific financial service centres: the case of Singapore', *Research Bulletin 27*, Globalization and World Cities Study Group and Network, Department of Geography, Loughborough University.

Beck, U. (2000) 'Living your own life in a runaway world: individualisation, globalisation and politics'. In W. Hutton and A. Giddens (eds), *On the Edge*, Jonathan Cape, London.

Begg, I. (1999) 'Cities and competitiveness', *Urban Studies*, 36, 5–6: 795–809.

Bell, D. (1976) *The Cultural Contradictions of Capitalism*, Basic Books, New York.

Bell, D. (1998) 'Civil society versus civic virtue'. In A. Gutmann (ed.), *Freedom of Association*, Princeton University Press, Princeton.

Bellamy, E. (1996) *Looking Backward* (1888), Dover, New York.

Bence, V. (1997) 'Internationalizing a distribution brand'. In D. Taylor (ed.), *Global Cases in Logistics and Supply Chain Management*, International Thomson Business Press, London.

Benhabib, S. (1996) 'From identity politics to social feminism: a plea for the nineties'. In D. Trend (ed.), *Radical Democracy*, Routledge, London.

Benjamin, W. (1983) *Reflections*, Schocken, New York.

Benjamin, W. (1997) *One-Way Street*, Verso, London.

Bennett, A. (1999) *Culture*, Sage, London.

Billig, M. (1995) *Banal Nationalism*, Sage, London.

Blanchot, M. (1993) *Step Not Beyond*, State University of New York Press, Albany.

Boal, A. (2000) *Theater of the Oppressed*, 2nd edn, Pluto, London.

Bohman, J. (1997) 'Deliberative democracy and effective social freedom: capabilities, resources, and opportunities'. In J. Bohman and W. Rehg (eds), *Deliberative Democracy*, MIT Press, Cambridge, Mass.

Bohman, J. and Rehg, W. (eds) (1997) *Deliberative Democracy*, MIT Press, Cambridge, Mass.

Boltanski, L. (1999) *Distant Suffering: Morality, Media and Politics*, Cambridge University Press, Cambridge.

Bolter, D. and Grusin, R. (1999) *Remediation: Understanding the New Media*, MIT Press, Cambridge, Mass.

Bourdieu, P. (1999) *Pascalian Meditations*, Polity, Cambridge.

Bowker, G. and Star, L. (1999) *Sorting Things Out*, MIT Press, Cambridge, Mass.

Boyle, P. J. (1996) *Shamans, Software and Spleens: Law and the Construction of the Information Society*, Harvard University Press, Cambridge, Mass.

Boyne, R. (2001) *Subject, Society and Culture*, Sage, London.

Buck-Morss, S. (2000) *Dreamworld and Catastrophe*, MIT Press, Cambridge, Mass.

Budansky, S. (1998) *If a Lion could Talk*, Phoenix, London.

Burgin, V. (1998) *In/different Spaces: Place and Memory in Visual Culture*, University of California Press, Berkeley.

Burton-Jones, A. (1999) *Knowledge Capitalism*, Oxford University Press, Oxford.

Callon, M. (ed.) (1998) *Laws of the Markets*, Blackwell, Oxford.

Cameron, L. (2000) *Good to Talk? Living and Working in a Communication Society*, Sage, London.

Carey, J. (2000) Review of Fort, *Sunday Times Culture Magazine*, Aug. 27.

Castells, M. (1977) *The Urban Question*, Arnold, London.

Castells, M. (1989) *The Informational City*, Blackwell, Oxford.

Castells, M. (1996) *The Rise of the Network Society*, Blackwell, Oxford.

Caygill, H. (1998) *Walter Benjamin: The Colour of Experience*, Routledge, London.

Chambers, I. (1994) *Migrancy, Culture, Identity*, Routledge, London.

Charyn, J. (1987) 'The rough adventure of the street . . .', *Dissent*, Fall: 624–6.

Clanchy, M. T. (1991) *From Memory to Written Record*, Arnold, London.

Clark, T. J. (2001) 'Phenomenality and materiality in Cézanne'. In T. Cohen (ed.), *Material Events*, University of Minnesota Press, Minneapolis.

Classen, C. (1998) *The Colour of Angels*, Routledge, New York.

Clough, P. T. (2001) *Auto Affection: Unconscious Thought in the Age of Technology*, University of Minnesota Press, Minneapolis.

Collins, H. and Kusch, M. (1998) *The Shape of Actions: What Humans and Machines Can Do*, MIT Press, Cambridge, Mass.

Copjec, J. and Sorkin, M. (1999) *Giving Ground: The Politics of Propinquity*, Verso, London.

Coyle, D. (1997) *The Weightless World*, Capstone, Oxford.

Crang, M. (2000) 'Public space, urban space and electronic space', *Urban Studies*, 37, 2: 301–17.

Crary, J. (1999) *Technologies of Perception*, MIT Press, Cambridge, Mass.

Dahle, C. (1999) 'Social justice', *Fast Company*, Dec.: 284–92.

Davis, M. (1998) *Ecology of Fear*, Picador, London.

de Certeau, M. (1992) *The Practice of Everyday Life*, University of California Press, Berkeley.

De Landa, M. (1997) *A Thousand Years of Nonlinear History*, Zone Books, New York.

de Sola Pool, I. (1981) *The Social History of the Telephone*, MIT Press, Cambridge, Mass.

Dean, M. (1999) *Governmentality*, Sage, London.

Dear, M. and Flusty, S. (1999) 'The postmodern urban condition'. In M. Featherstone and S. Lash (eds), *Spaces of Culture*, Sage, London.

Delaney, S. (1999) '. . . three, two, one, contact: Times Square Red, 1998'. In J. Copjec and M. Sorkin (eds), *Giving Ground: The Politics of Propinquity*, Verso, London.

Deleuze, G. (1986) *Foucault*, Athlone, London.

Deleuze, G. (1988) *Bergsonism*, Zone Books, New York.

Deleuze, G. (1989) *Cinema 2: The Time-Image*, Athlone Press, London.

Deleuze, G. (1992) 'Postscript to the societies of control', *October*, 59, 3–7.

Deleuze, G. (1994) *Difference and Repetition*, Athlone, London.

Deleuze, G. (1995) *Negotiation*, Columbia University Press, New York.

Deleuze, G. (1997) *Essays Critical and Clinical*, University of Minnesota Press, Minneapolis.

Deleuze, G. and Guattari, F. (1988) *Thousand Plateaus: Capitalism and Schizophrenia*, Athlone, London.

DeNora, T. (2000) *Music in Everyday Life*, Cambridge University Press, Cambridge.

Deutsche, R. (1999) 'Reasonable urbanism'. In J. Copjec and M. Sorkin (eds), *Giving Ground: The Politics of Propinquity*, Verso, London.

Dodd, N. (1994) *The Sociology of Money*, Polity, Cambridge.

Donald, J. (1999) *Imagining the Modern City*, Athlone, London.

Dosse, J. F. (1998) *Empire of Meaning: The Humanization of the Social Sciences*, University of Minnesota Press, Minneapolis.

Dovey, K. (1999) *Framing Places: Mediating Power in Built Form*, Routledge, London.

du Gay, P. (2000) *In Praise of Bureaucracy: Weber, Organization, Ethics*, Sage, London.

Duneier, M. (1999) *Sidewalk*, Farrar, Straus and Giroux, New York.

Duranton, G. (1999) 'Distance, land, and proximity: economic analysis and the evolution of cities', *Environment and Planning A*, 31, 1: 2169–88.

Dziembowska-Kowalska, J. and Funck, R. H. (1999) 'Cultural activities: source of competitiveness and prosperity in urban regions', *Urban Studies*, 36, 8: 1381–98.

Ekman, P. (1992) *Telling Lies*, Norton, New York.

Ekman, P. and Rosenberg, E. (eds) (1997) *What the Face Reveals*, Oxford University Press, Oxford.

Elster, J. (1998) 'Introduction'. In J. Elster (ed.), *Deliberative Democracy*, Cambridge University Press, Cambridge.

Ettlinger, N. (2000) 'Frontiers of flexibility and the importance of place and space', paper, Department of Geography, Ohio State University.

Fairclough, N. (1992) *Discourse and Social Change*, Polity, Cambridge.

Featherstone, M. (1998) The flâneur, the city and virtual public life', *Urban Studies*, 35, 5–6: 909–25.

Finnegan, R. (1989) *The Hidden Musicians: Music Making in an English Town*, Cambridge University Press, Cambridge.

Fleischacker, S. (1998) 'Insignificant communities'. In Gutmann, A. (ed.), *Freedom of Association*, Princeton University Press, Princeton.

Fleischer, M. (1995) *Beggars and Thieves*, University of Wisconsin Press, Madison.

Flores, F. and Gray, J. (2000) *Entrepreneurship and the Wired Life*, Demos, London.

Flyvvberg, B. (1998) 'Empowering civil society: Habermas, Foucault and the question of conflict'. In M. Douglass and J. Friedmann (eds), *Cities for Citizens*, Wiley, London.

Forester, J. (1989) *Planning in the Face of Power*, University of California Press, Berkeley.

Fort, T. (2000) *The Grass is Greener: Our Love Affair with the Lawn*, HarperCollins, London.

Foucault, M. (1979) *Discipline and Punish: The Invention of the Prison*, Allen Lane, London.

Fraser, N. (1993) 'Rethinking the public sphere: a contribution to the critique of actually existing democracy'. In B. Robbins (ed.), *The Phantom Public Sphere*, University of Minnesota Press, Minneapolis.

Fraser, N. (1996) 'Equality, difference, and radical democracy: the United States feminist debates revisited'. In D. Trend (ed.), *Radical Democracy*, Routledge, London.

Fraser, N. (2000) 'Rethinking recognition', *New Left Review*, new series, 3: 107–21.

French, S. and Thrift, N. J. (2002) 'Software writing cities', *Transactions* (forthcoming).

Freud, S. (1975) *The Letters of Sigmund Freud*, ed. E. L. Freud, Basic Books, New York.

Friedmann, J. (1987) *Planning in the Public Domain*, Princeton University Press, Princeton.

Friedmann, J. (1992) *Empowerment*, Blackwell, Oxford.

Frisby, D. (1991) *Simmel and Since: Essays on Georg Simmel's Social Theory*, Routledge, London.

Furnham, A. and Argyle, M. (1998) *The Psychology of Money*, Routledge, London.

Gandy, M. (1997) 'The making of a regulatory crisis: restructuring New York City's water supply', *Transactions*, 22: 338–59.

Gardiner, M. (2000) *Critiques of Everyday Life*, Routledge, London.

Garfield, S. (2000) *Mauve*, Faber, London.

Gatens, M. and Lloyd, G. (1999) *Collective Imaginings: Spinoza Past and Present*, Routledge, London.

Gelernter, H. (1992) *Mirror Worlds*, Oxford University Press, Oxford.

Giddens, A. (1991) *Modernity and Self-Identity*, Polity, Cambridge.

Giddens, A. (1994) *Beyond Left and Right*, Polity, Cambridge.

Gil, J. (1998) *Metamorphoses of the Body*, University of Minnesota Press, Minneapolis.

Gilmour, P. (1997) 'Managing international logistics'. In D. Taylor (ed.), *Global Cases in Logistics and Supply Chain Management*, International Thomson Business Press, London.

Gilroy, P. (2000) *Between Camps*, Allen Lane, London.

Glaeser, E. (1998) 'Are cities dying?', *Journal of Economic Perspectives*, 12: 139–60.

Glaeser, E., Kolko, J. and Saiz, A. (2001) 'Consumer city', *Journal of Economic Geography*, 1, 1: 27–50.

Godard, F. (1997) 'A propos des nouvelles temporalités urbaines', *Annales de la Recherche Urbaine*, 77, Dec.: 7–14.

Goody, J. (1996) *The Interface between the Written and the Oral*, Cambridge University Press, Cambridge.

Gordon, I. (1999) 'Internationalisation and urban competition', *Urban Studies*, 36, 5–6: 1001–16.

Gordon, I. and McCann, P. (2000) 'Industrial clusters: complexes, agglomeration and/or social networks?', *Urban Studies*, 37, 3: 513–32.

Gottdiener, M. (1997) *American Dreams, Media Fantasies and Themed Environments*, Westview Press, Boulder.

Grabher, G. (2001) 'Ecologies of creativity: the Village, the Group, and the heterarchic organisation of the British advertising industry', *Environment and Planning A*, 33: 351–74.

Graham, S. (1997) 'Imagining the real-time city: telecommunications, urban paradigms and the future of cities'. In S. Westwood and J. Williams (eds), *Imagining Cities*, Routledge, London.

Guattari, F. (1995) *Chaosmosis*, Feral, Sydney.

Guattari, F. (2000) *The Three Ecologies*, Athlone, London.

Gutmann, A. (ed.) (1998) *Freedom of Association*, Princeton University Press, Princeton.

Gutmann, A. and Thompson, D. (eds) (1996) *Democracy and Disagreement*, Belknap, Cambridge, Mass.

Hannerz, U. (1996) *Transnational Connections*, Routledge, London.

Haraway, D. (1997) *Modest_Witness@Second_Millennium.FemaleMan©_Meets_Oncomouse*™, Routledge, New York.

Harries, K. (1996) *The Ethical Function of Architecture*, Yale University Press, New Haven.

Harvey, D. (1985) *The Urbanisation of Capital*, Blackwell, Oxford.

Harvey, D. (2000) *Spaces of Hope*, Edinburgh University Press, Edinburgh.

Hayden, D. (1997) *The Power of Place*, MIT Press, Cambridge, Mass.

Hayles, K. (1999) *How We Become Posthuman*, University of Chicago Press, Chicago.

Healey, P. (1997) *Collaborative Planning*, Macmillan, London.

Healey and Baker (2000) *European Cities Monitor*, Healey and Baker, London.

Hetherington, K. (1997) 'In place of geometry: the materiality of place'. In K. Hetherington and R. Munro (eds), *Ideas of Difference*, Blackwell, Oxford.

Hetherington, K. (1998) *Expressions of Identity: Space, Performance, Politics*, Sage, London.

Hirsch, W. (1973) *Urban Economic Analysis*, McGraw-Hill, New York.

Hoggett, P. (1991) *Communities in an Uncertain World*, Free Association, London.

Holl, S. (2000) *Parallax*, Princeton University Press, New York.

Holmes, R. (1996) *Dr Johnston and Mr Savage*, Faber, London.

hooks, b. (1991) *Breaking Bread*, South End Press, Boston.

Horvath, R. (1973) 'Machine space', *Geographical Review*, 66: 166–87.

Hutchinson, S. (2000) 'Waiting for the bus', *Social Text*, 18, 2: 107–20.

Imrie, R. (2000) 'Disability and discourses of mobility and movement', *Environment and Planning A*, 32, 1641–56.

Inda, J. and Miròn, L. (1999) 'Migrant voices: fashioning cultural citizenship in translocal space', *Plurimondo*, 1, 1: 203–28.

Ingold, T. (2000) *The Perception of the Environment*, Routledge, London.

Iveson, K. (1998) 'Putting the public back into public space', *Urban Policy and Research*, 16, 1: 21–33.

Jacobs, J. M. (1998) 'Staging difference: aestheticization and the politics of difference in contemporary cities'. In R. Fincher and J. M. Jacobs (eds), *Cities of Difference*, Guilford, New York.

Jones, A. (2000) 'Networks, location and innovation in business: some survey evidence from London', paper, Local Economic Policy Unit, South Bank University.

Kaika, M. and Swyngedouw, E. (2000) 'Fetishizing the modern city: the phantasmagoria of urban technological networks', *International Journal of Urban and Regional Research*, 29: 120–38.

Katz, J. (1999) *How Emotions Work*, University of Chicago Press, Chicago.

Katz, J. and Katz, M. (1998) *Connections: Studies of the Telephone in American Life*, Transactions, New York.

Kaye, N. (2000) *Site-specific Art: Performance, Place and Documentation*, Routledge, London.

Kern, S. (1983) *The Culture of Time and Space, 1880–1918*, Harvard University Press, Cambridge, Mass.

Kesteloot, C. and Meert, H. (1999) 'Informal spaces: the geography of informal economic activities in Brussels', *International Journal of Urban and Regional Research*, 23, 2: 232–51.

Kirshenblatt-Gimblett, B. (1996) 'Ordinary people/everyday life: folk culture in New York City'. In G. Gmelch and W. Zenner (eds), *Urban Life: Readings in Urban Anthropology*, Wavelend Press, Prospect Heights, Ill.

Klein, N. (1997) *The History of Forgetting*, Verso, London.

Knight, R. (1996) 'The future of the city is open: citizens made the city', paper, Copenhagen Institute for Future Studies, Copenhagen.

Knorr-Cetina, K. (1999) *Epistemic Culture: How the Sciences Make Knowledge*, Harvard University Press, Cambridge, Mass.

Knorr-Cetina, K. (2001) 'Postsocial relations: theorizing sociality in a postsocial environment'. In G. Ritzer and B. Smart (eds), *Handbook of Social Theory*, Sage, London.

Kofman, E. and Lebas, E. (1996) 'Introduction: Lost in transposition – time, space and the city'. In H. Lefebvre, *Writings on Cities*, trans. and ed. E. Kofman and E. Lebas, Blackwell, Oxford.

Kriegel, L. (1993) 'Graffiti: tunnel notes of a New Yorker', *American Scholar*, 62, 3: 431–6.

Krugman, P. (1991) *Geography and Trade*, MIT Press, Cambridge, Mass.

Krugman, P. (1995) *Development, Geography and Economic Theory*, MIT Press, Cambridge, Mass.

Krugman, P. (1997) *Pop Internationalism*, MIT Press, Cambridge, Mass.

Laclau, E. (1996) *Emancipation(s)*, Verso, London.

Laclau, E. and Mouffe, C. (1985) *Hegemony and Socialist Strategy*, Verso, London.

Lakoff, G. and Johnson, M. (1999) *Philosophy in the Flesh*, HarperCollins, London.

Lasch, C. (1995) *The Revolt of the Elites and the Betrayal of Democracy*, Norton, New York.

Lash, S. (2001) *Critique of Information*, Sage, London.

Latour, B. (1988) 'The politics of explanation: an alternative'. In S. Woolgar (ed.), *Knowledge and Reflexivity*, Sage, London.

Latour, B. (1993) *We Have Never Been Modern*, Harvester Wheatsheaf, Hassocks.

Latour, B. (1997) 'Trains of thought: Piaget, formalism and the fifth dimension', *Common Knowledge*, 6: 170–91.

Latour, B. (1999) 'On recalling ANT'. In J. Law and J. Hassard (eds), *Actor Network Theory and After*, Blackwell, Oxford.

Latour, B. and Hermant, E. (1998) *Paris Ville Invisible*, La Découverte, Paris.

Leadbeater, C. (1999) *Living on Thin Air*, Viking, London.

Lee, R. (2000) 'Shelter from the storm? Geographies of regard in the worlds of horticulture consumption and production', *Geoforum*, 31: 137–57.

Lees, L. (2001) 'Towards a critical geography of architecture: the case of an ersatz Colosseum', *Ecumene*, 8, 51–86.

Lefebvre, H. (1991) *Critique of Everyday Life*, Vol. 1, Verso, London.

Lefebvre, H. (1996) *Writings on Cities*, trans. and ed. E. Kofman and E. Lebas, Blackwell, Oxford.

Leonard, D. and Swap, T. (1999) *When Sparks Fly*, Harvard Business School Press, Boston.

Lessig, L. (1999) *Code and Other Laws of Cyberspace*, Basic Books, New York.

Lestienne, R. (1998) *The Creative Power of Chance*, University of Illinois Press, Urbana.

Leyshon, A. and Thrift, N. J. (1997) *Money/Space: Geographies of Monetary Transformation*, Routledge, London.

Lichtenstein, R. and Sinclair, I. (1999) *Rodinsky's Room*, Granta, London.

Linde-Larsson, A. (1998) 'Small differences, large issues: the making and re-making of a national border', *South Atlantic Quarterly*, 94, 1123–43.

Lingis, A. (1998) *The Imperative*, Indiana University Press, Bloomington.

Luhmann, N. (1998) *Observations on Modernity*, Stanford University Press, Stanford.

McCarthy, A. (2001) *Ambient Television*, Duke University Press, Durham, N.C.

McCullough, M. (1996) *Abstracting Craft: The Practiced Digital Hand*, MIT Press, Cambridge, Mass.

McKenzie, J. (2001) *Perform – or Else*, Routledge, New York.

McNeil, D. (1992) *The Face*, Allen Lane, London.

McRobbie, A. (1999) *British Fashion Design: Rag Trade or Image Industry?*, Routledge, London.

Malbon, B. (1999) *Clubbing*, Routledge, London.

Malmberg, A., Malmberg, B. and Lundequist, P. (2000) 'Agglomeration and firm performance: economies of scale, localisation, and urbanisation among Swedish export firms', *Environment and Planning A*, 32: 305–21.

Marback, R., Bruch, P. and Eicher, J. (1998) *Cities, Cultures, Conversations: Readings for Writers*, Allyn and Bacon, Boston.

Margulis, L. (1998) *The Symbiotic Planet*, Weidenfeld and Nicolson, London.

Marshall, A. (1890) *Principles of Economics*, Macmillan, London.

Martin, A. (2000) 'Magic roundabouts', *Observer Magazine*, 27 Aug., pp. 23–6.

Martinotti, G. (1999) 'A city for whom? Transients and public life in the second-generation metropolis'. In R. Beauregard and S. Body-Gendrot (eds), *The Urban Moment*, Sage, London.

Marx, K. (1964) *Capital, Volume 1*, Lawrence and Wishart, London.

Maskell, P., Eskelinen, H., Hannibalsson, I., Malmberg, A. and Vatne, E. (1998) *Competitiveness, Localised Learning and Regional Development*, Routledge, London.

Massey, D. (1984) *Spatial Divisions of Labour*, Macmillan, London.

Massey, D. (1999) 'Cities in the world'. In D. Massey, J. Allen and S. Pile (eds), *City Worlds*, Routledge, London.

Massey, D. (2000) 'Travelling thoughts'. In P. Gilroy, L. Grossberg and A. McRobbie (eds), *Without Guarantees: In Honour of Stuart Hall*, Verso, London.

Massey, D., Allen, J. and Pile, S. (eds) (1999) *City Worlds*, Routledge, London.

Mattelart, A. (1996) *Theories of Communication*, Sage, London.

Mattson, K. (1998) *Creating a Democratic Public*, Penn State Press, Pennsylvania.

May, J. and Thrift, N. J. (eds) (2001) *Timespace: Geographies of Temporality*, Routledge, London.

Meier, V. (1999) 'Cut-flower production in Columbia – a development success story?' *Environment and Planning A*, 31: 273–90.

Melbin, M. (1976) *Night as Frontier*, Basic Books, New York.

Melbin, M. (1978) 'Night as frontier'. In T. Carlstein, D. N. Parkes and N. J. Thrift (eds), *Timing Space and Spacing Time*, vol. 2, Arnold, London.

Melucci, A. (1996) *The Playing Self*, Cambridge University Press, Cambridge.

Miller, D. (ed.) (2000) *Car Culture*, Berg, Oxford.

Miller, D., Jackson, P., Thrift, N. J., Holbrook, B. and Rowlands, M. (1998) *Shopping, Place and Identity*, Routledge, London.

Mingione, E. (ed.) (1996) *Urban Poverty and the Underclass*, Blackwell, Oxford.

Mitchell, D. (2000) 'Postmodern geographic praxis? Postmodern impulse and the war against the homeless people in the "post-justice" city', paper, Department of Geography, Maxwell School of Syracuse University.

Mouffe, C. (1993) *The Return of the Political*, Verso, London.

Mouffe, C. (2000) *The Democratic Paradox*, Verso, London.

Mumford, L. (1938) *The Culture of Cities*, Harcourt Brace, San Diego.

Mumford, L. (1998) *Sidewalk Critic*, Princeton Architectural Press, New York.

Nachum, L. and Keeble, D. (1999) 'Neo-Marshallian nodes, global network and firm competitiveness: the cluster of media firms in Central London', Working Paper 138, ESRC Centre for Business Research, Cambridge University.

Nardi, B. and O'Day, V. (2000) *Information Ecologies: Using Technology with Heart*, MIT Press, Cambridge, Mass.

Negri, A. and Hardt, M. (2000) *Empire*, Harvard University Press, Cambridge, Mass.

Nolan, J. (1998) *The Emotional State*, New York University Press, Albany.

Nooteboom, B. (1999) 'Innovation, learning and industrial organisation', *Cambridge Journal of Economics*, 23, 3: 127–50.

Norman, D. (1998) *The Invisible Computer*, MIT Press, Cambridge, Mass.

Nörretranders, T. (1998) *The User Illusion: Cutting Consciousness Down to Size*, Allen Lane, London.

Ogborn, M. (1998) *Spaces of Modernity*, Guilford, New York.

Oldenburg, C. (1967) *Bottle of Notes*, Rizzoli, New York.

Osborne, T. and Rose, N. (1999) 'Governing cities: notes on the spatialisation of virtue', *Society and Space*, 17: 737–60.

Pahl, R. (2000) *On Friendship*, Polity, Cambridge.

Parkes, D. N. and Thrift, N. J. (1980) *Times, Spaces, Places: A Chronogeographic Perspective*, John Wiley, Chichester.

Parsons, D. (2000) *Streetwalking the Metropolis*, Oxford University Press, Oxford.

Peattie, L. (1998) 'Convivial cities'. In M. Douglass and J. Friedmann (eds), *Cities for Citizens*, Wiley, London.

Petroski, H. (1989) *The Pencil*, Knopf, New York.

Philo, C. and Wilbert, C. (eds) (2000) *Animal Spaces, Beastly Places*, Routledge, London.

Pickering, A. (1992) *The Mangle of Practice*, University of Chicago Press, Chicago.

Picon, A. (1997) 'Le temps du cyborg dans la ville territoire', *Annales de la Recherche Urbaine*, 77, Dec.: 72–7.

Pile, S. (1999) 'What is a city?' In D. Massey, J. Allen and S. Pile (eds), *City Worlds*, Routledge, London.

Pine, J. and Gilmore, J. (1999) *The Experience Economy*, Harvard Business School Press, Boston.

Piore, M. and Sabel, C. (1984) *The Second Industrial Divide*, Basic Books, New York.

Polanyi, M. (1956) *Personal Knowledge*, Routledge, London.

Porter, M. (1995) 'The competitive advantages of the inner city', *Harvard Business Review*, May–June: 53–71.

Quah, D. T. (1997) 'The weightless economy: Nintendo and heavy metal', *Centre Piece*, Centre for Economic Performance, London School of Economics.

Rajchman, J. (1999a) *Constructions*, MIT Press, Cambridge, Mass.

Rajchman, J. (1999b) 'Diagrams and diagnosis'. In E. Grosz (ed.), *Becomings: Explorations in Time, Memory, and Futures*, Cornell University Press, Ithaca.

Rajchman, J. (2000) *The Deleuze Connections*, MIT Press, Cambridge, Mass.

Rimke, H. M. (2000) 'Governing citizens through self-help literature', *Cultural Studies*, 14, 1: 61–78.

Robbins, B. (1993) 'Introduction: the public as phantom'. In B. Robbins (ed.), *The Phantom Public Sphere*, University of Minnesota Press, Minneapolis.

Rogerson, R. (1999) 'Quality of life and city competitiveness', *Urban Studies*, 36, 5–6: 969–85.

Rose, N. (1995) *Inventing Ourselves*, Cambridge University Press, Cambridge.

Rose, N. (1999) *Powers of Freedom*, Cambridge University Press, Cambridge.

Russell Hochschild, A. (2000) 'Global care chains and emotional surplus value'. In W. Hutton and A. Giddens (eds), *On the Edge*, Jonathan Cape, London.

Sadler, S. (1998) *The Situationist City*, MIT Press, Cambridge, Mass.

Sandercock, L. (1998) *Towards Cosmopolis*, Wiley, London.

Sassen, S. (1994) *Cities in a World Economy*, Pine Forge, London.

Sassen, S. (1999a) 'Globalization and the formation of claims'. In J. Copjec and M. Sorkin (eds), *Giving Ground: The Politics of Propinquity*, Verso, London.

Sassen, S. (1999b) 'Digital networks and power'. In M. Featherstone and S. Lash (eds), *Spaces of Culture*, Sage, London.

Schiller, M. (1999) *Digital Capitalism*, MIT Press, Cambridge, Mass.

Schlör, J. (1998) *Nights in the Big City*, Reaktion, London.

Schmalenbach, H. (1977) 'Communion – a sociological category'. In G. Lüschen and G. Stone (eds), *Herman Schmalenbach on Society and Experience*, University of Chicago Press, Chicago.

Schrift, A. (2000) 'Nietzsche, Foucault, Deleuze and the subject of radical democracy', *Angelaki*, 5, 2: 151–61.

Scott, A. J. (1988) *Metropolis*, University of California Press, Los Angeles.

Segel, H. B. (1998) *Body Ascendant*, PAJ Books, New York.

Seigworth, G. (2000) 'Banality for cultural studies', *Cultural Studies*, 14, 2: 227–68.

Sen, A. K. (1992) *Inequality Reexamined*, Russell Sage Foundation, New York.

Sennett, R. (1970) *The Uses of Disorder*, Knopf, New York.

Sennett, R. (1977) *The Fall of Public Man*, Knopf, New York.

Sennett, R. (1994) *Flesh and Stone: The City in Western Civilization*, Allen Lane, London.

Sennett, R. (1997) 'The new capitalism', *Social Research*, 64, 2: 161–80.

Sennett, R. (1998) *The Corrosion of Character*, Norton, New York.

Sennett, R. (1999a) 'Growth and failure: the new political economy and its culture'. In M. Featherstone and S. Lash (eds), *Spaces of Culture*, Sage, London.

Sennett, R. (1999b) 'The spaces of democracy'. In R. Beauregard and S. Body-Gendrot (eds), *The Urban Moment*, Sage, London.

Sennett, R. (2000) 'Street and office: two sources of identity'. In W. Hutton and A. Giddens (eds), *On the Edge*, Jonathan Cape, London.

Seth, A. and Randall, G. (1999) *The Grocers*, Kogan Page, London.

Shenk, D. (1998) *The End of Patience*, Indiana University Press, Bloomington.

Sheringham, M. (1996) 'City space, mental space, poetic space: Paris in Breton, Benjamin and Réda'. In M. Sheringham (ed.), *Parisian Fields*, Reaktion, London.

Sherman, S. (1997) *Telling Time*, University of Chicago Press, Chicago.

Shields, R. (1994) *Lifestyle Shopping*, Routledge, London.

Shields, R. (1997) 'Ethnography in the crowd: the body, sociality and globalization in Seoul', *Focaal*, 30–1: 23–38.

Shoard, M. (1999) 'The urban fringe', *Landscape*, 15: 1–23.

Shotter, J. (1993) *Cultural Politics of Everyday Life*, Open University Press, Milton Keynes.

Shuman, M. (1998) *Going Local: Creating Self-Reliant Communities in a Global Age*, Free Press, New York.

Silverstone, R. (ed.) (1996) *Visions of Suburbia*, Routledge, London.

Simmel, G. (1950) 'The metropolis and urban life'. In K. H. Wolff (ed.), *The Sociology of Georg Simmel*, Free Press, New York.

Simmel, G. (1990) *Philosophy of Money*, Routledge, London.

Sinclair, I. (1999) *Dark Lanthorns: Rodinsky's A–Z*, Goldmark, Uppingham.

Smith, D. (1997) 'A life of pure thought: Deleuze's "critique et clinique" project'. In G. Deleuze, *Essays Critical and Clinical*, University of Minnesota Press, Minneapolis.

Smith, M. P. (2001) *Transnational Urbanism*, Blackwell, Oxford.

Smith, S. J. (2000) 'Graffiti'. In S. Pile and N. Thrift (eds), *City A–Z*, Routledge, London.

Soja, E. (2000) *Postmetropolis*, Blackwell, Oxford.

Sorkin, M. (1999) 'Introduction: traffic in democracy'. In J. Copjec and M. Sorkin (eds), *Giving Ground: The Politics of Propinquity*, Verso, London.

Soysal, Y. (1994) *Limits of Citizenship*, Chicago University Press, Chicago.

Spicer, N. (2000) 'Carping', *The Times Magazine*, 16 Sept.

Stallybrass, P. (1998) 'Marx's coat'. In P. Spyer (ed.), *Border Fetishisms*, Routledge, London.

Stern, D. (1998) *The Interpersonal World of the Infant*, Karnac, London.

Sternberg, R. and Arndt, O. (2000) 'The firm or the region – what determines European firms' innovation behaviour?', paper, Department of Economic and Social Geography, University of Cologne.

Stetter, A. (2000) 'Goods'. In N. Barley (ed.), *Breathing Cities*, Birkhäuser, Basel.

Stokes, S. (1998) 'Pathologies of deliberation'. In J. Elster (ed.), *Deliberative Democracy*, Cambridge University Press, Cambridge.

Storper, M. (1997) *The Regional World*, Guilford Press, New York.

Sudjic, D. (1992) *The 100 Mile City*, Harcourt Brace, San Diego.

Sudnow, D. (1978) *Ways of the Hand: The Organization of Improvised Conduct*, MIT Press, Cambridge, Mass.

Sutton-Smith, B. (1998) *The Ambiguity of Play*, Harvard University Press, Cambridge, Mass.

Tajbakhsh, K. (2001) *The Promise of the City*, California University Press, Berkeley.

Tamir, Y. (1998) 'Revisiting the civic sphere'. In A. Gutmann (ed.), *Freedom of Association*, Princeton University Press, Princeton.

Taussig, M. (1992) *The Nervous System*, Routledge, New York.

Taussig, M. (2000) *De-facement*, Routledge, New York.

Taylor, C. (1991) *Sources of the Self*, Cambridge University Press, Cambridge.

Thompson, J. B. (2000) *Political Scandal*, Polity, Cambridge.

Thrift, N. J. (1990) 'Transport and Communication, 1730–1914'. In R. Dodgshon and R. Butlin (eds), *A New Historical Geography of England and Wales*, Academic Press, London.

Thrift, N. J. (1995) 'A hyperactive world?' In R. J. Johnston, P. J. Taylor and M. Watts (eds), *Geographies of Global Change*, Blackwell, Oxford.

Thrift, N. (1996a) 'New urban eras and old technological fears: reconfiguring the goodwill of electronic things', *Urban Studies*, 33, 8: 1463–93.

Thrift, N. J. (1996b) *Spatial Formations*, Sage, London.

Thrift, N. (1997) 'The rise of soft capitalism', *Cultural Values*, 1, 1: 29–57.

Thrift, N. (2000a) 'Afterwords', *Environment and Planning D. Society and Space*, 18: 213–55.

Thrift, N. (2000b) 'Performing cultures in the new economy', *Annals of the Association of American Geographers*, 90: 674–92.

Thrift, N. J. (2000c) 'Still life in nearly present time: the object of nature', *Body and Society*, 6: 34–57.

Thrift, N. J. and Leyshon, A. (1999) 'Moral geographies of money'. In E. Gilbert and E. Helleiner (eds), *Nation States and Money*, Routledge, London.

Thrift, N. J. and Olds, K. (1996) 'Refiguring the economic in economic geography', *Progress in Human Geography*, 20: 311–37.

Tilly, C. (1999) 'Conclusion: why worry about citizenship?' In M. Hanagan and C. Tilly (eds), *Extending Citizenship, Reconfiguring States*, Rowman and Littlefield, Lanham, Md.

Touraine, A. (2000) *Can We Live Together?*, Polity, Cambridge.

Townsend, A. (2000) 'Life in the real-time city: mobile telephones and urban metabolism', *Journal of Urban Technology*, 7: 85–109.

Trend, D. (ed.) (1996) *Radical Democracy*, Routledge, London.

Tsagarousianou, R., Tambini, D. and Bryan, C. (eds) (1998) *Cyberdemocracy*, Routledge, London.

Tschumi, B. (1996) *Architecture and Disjunction*, MIT Press, Cambridge, Mass.

UNCTAD (1997) *World Investment Report, 1997*, United Nations, Geneva.

Unger, R. M. (1998) *Democracy Realized*, Verso, London.

Urry, J. (1991) *The Tourist Gaze*, Sage, London.

Urry, J. (2000) *Sociology beyond Societies*, Routledge, London.

Valentine, G. (1989) 'The geography of women's fear', *Area*, 21: 385–90.

van Gunsteren, H. R. (1998) *A Theory of Citizenship*, Westview, Boulder, Col.

Varela, F. (1999) *Ethical Know-How: Action, Wisdom and Cognition*, Stanford University Press, Stanford.

Vidler, A. (2000) *Warped Space: Art, Architecture and Anxiety in Modern Cities*, MIT Press, Cambridge, Mass.

Virilio, P. (1991) *The Lost Dimension*, Semiotext(e), New York.

Virilio, P. (1997) *Open Sky*, Verso, London.

Weigel, S. (1996) *Body and Image Space*, Routledge, London.

Weiss, B. (1996) *The Making and Unmaking of the Haya Lived World*, Duke University Press, Durham, N.C.

Whatmore, S. J. (2002) *Hybrid Geographies*, Sage, London.

Whitehead, A. N. (1978) *Process and Reality*, Free Press, New York.

Wilson, F. R. (1998) *The Hand: How its Use Shapes the Brain, Language and Culture*, Pantheon, New York.

Winograd, T. (1996) *Bringing Design to Software*, Addison Wesley, San Francisco.

Wirth, L. (1938) 'Urbanism as a way of life', *American Journal of Sociology*, 44: 1–24.

Wolfreys, J. (1998) *Writing London*, Macmillan, London.

World Bank (2000) *World Development Report*, Oxford University Press, New York.

Yates, J. (2000) 'Business use of information and technology during the industrial age'. In A. D. Chandler and J. W. Cortada (eds), *A Nation Transformed by Information*, Oxford University Press, New York.

Yeung, H. (2000a) 'Embedding foreign affiliates in transnational business networks: the case of Hong Kong firms in Southeast Asia', *Environment and Planning A*, 32: 201–22.

Yeung, H. (2000b) 'Reconceptualising the "firm" in new economic geographies: an organisational perspective', paper, Department of Geography, National University of Singapore.

Young, I. M. (1997) 'Difference as a resource for democratic communication'. In J. Bohman and W. Rehg (eds), *Deliberative Democracy*, MIT Press, Cambridge, Mass.

Young, I. M. (1999) 'City life as a normative ideal', *Plurimondo*, 1, 1: 277–84.

Zelizer, V. (1994) *The Social Meaning of Money*, Basic Books, New York.

INDEX

Index compiled by Frank Pert.